BILL GATES:
HERO OR VILLAIN

MICHAEL LANCASHIRE

For Verity.

Still and always.

(Which also prompts some free advice for young men looking for a wife: find a woman who is out of your league but fails to grasp that she could do better, then hold on for dear life.)

CONTENTS

A quick note on the format of this book

This book is a work of narrative non-fiction. What does that mean? Think of it like a docudrama such as Netflix's *The Crown* only in book form. It's non-fiction told as a story, intended to inform and entertain at the same time.

So, is it true?

In the most important way, I believe you will find as much truth in here as in any other biography or history. It is based on a huge volume of published material, including more than three quarters of a million words of interviews, books, news reports, press releases, court transcripts, and days of video and audio footage. What makes it different to reading the sources themselves, is that the information has been dramatised to make it easier to read and enjoy.

That dramatisation requires imagination.

For example if a conversation takes place between Bill and Melinda in their home then it obviously shouldn't be read as verbatim (I wasn't hiding under their sofa with a notebook!), but it will be based on known historical events, public positions and statements they've made.

The other important compromise is common to all histories: selection. To make the book readable I have omitted or combined some characters and events. For example I describe the development of Microsoft Windows and Excel and don't focus on the tens of other products Microsoft has launched over the years. A straight chronological run through of every event would be lengthy, dull, and in my view not really any more informative.

In particular to summarise Bill's run-ins with antitrust suits in any way that fits into a broader narrative and holds the interest of a reader required some careful choices. I have glossed over the initial FTC and DOJ investigations and consent decrees in the US, and not touched at all on the later EU case, choosing instead to use the main US antitrust case as indicative of them all.

But I do not believe that any of these compromises get in the way of the fundamental truth underneath the story. The goal has been to relate the story of Bill's life in a way that is both accurate and memorable. To inform and entertain.

As Bill himself said in 1999, "When somebody's successful, people leap to simple explanations that might make sense. So you get these myths. People love to have any little story."

True, but there's a reason for that, stories are humanity's original mental models. They're how we learn.

C:\PROLOGUE

After years of industry rumours of bullying and strong arm tactics, and a three year long investigation by the Federal Trade Commission that had resulted in a decision not to prosecute, the US government had decided to prove that nobody was above the law and to bring Microsoft and its chairman Bill Gates to heel.

Bill, at the time the world's richest man, leant back in his chair, folded his hands behind his head and frowned at the government lawyer.

"I went through the chain of logic that explains that to you. I don't know if you misunderstood some part of it?" Bill said, looking and sounding openly frustrated.

Gates had started Microsoft only twenty three years earlier and, through a series of clever moves on his part and a dollop of luck, the technology company had rocketed to success. Just a week after David Boies, the DOJ attorney responsible for prosecuting the case, and Gates fenced in the deposition Microsoft would knock the one hundred and six year old General Electric off the top spot as the world's biggest company.

But being the biggest comes with a price.

The Department of Justice, egged on by complaints from rivals, was bringing a case against Microsoft accusing them of abusing their monopoly to crush their competitors.

Legally the case was against Microsoft as a company, but if you were bringing a case against Microsoft then you were bringing a case against Bill Gates personally. Gates hadn't built Microsoft on his own but he was the personification of the company.

He saw it that way and in truth, so did the rest of the world. Bill and Microsoft were inseparable.

The deposition was taking place on Bill's home turf. The government's attorneys had come up to Microsoft's 200 acre Redmond campus to take his deposition and were sitting in a badly lit conference room that Bill had used many times to hold product meetings, plan strategy and rally his troops of twenty seven thousand Microsoft employees.

Boies, wasn't cowed by the surroundings. Nor was he much better behaved than his opponent.

"If I begin to tell you what I think about your answers we'll be here all day," he said at one point, prompting open laughter from his colleagues.

There was a view within Microsoft, not unreasonably, that this was a witch hunt driven by other technology companies who couldn't win fairly in the marketplace.

Microsoft's lawyers had tried to get Gates' deposition limited to a day, the judge had refused saying it would take as long as necessary.

Then they had tried to ensure that it would remain sealed. The judge again refused and ruled that it be open to the public, though this time the court of appeal overturned that decision and determined that it might be possible to keep the videotape private. As Gates evaded Boies' questions he had every reason to expect that the videotape might not see the light of day.

"What were you thinking when you wrote this sentence?" Boies asked.

"I don't remember specifically writing this sentence," Gates replied.

"Does that mean you can't answer what you were thinking when you wrote this sentence?"

"That is correct."

"Okay, since you don't have an answer to that question, let me put a different quest…"

"No. I have an answer," Gates said, cutting off the attorney. "The answer is, 'I don't remember'."

In the end they would keep going like this for three days and it would show Gates at his worst: arrogant and intentionally difficult.

But still undeniably intelligent.

C:\PART> 1: BEGINNINGS

C:\PART\CHAPTER> 1.1

"Trey! Dinner is on the table. Get down here now!" Mary Gates turned to her husband, who was already seated at the table. "Honestly, that boy, he just gets worse."

Bill Sr. smiled at her in what he hoped was a calming fashion, but Mary wasn't in the mood to be calmed.

"How long has he been in his room?" she demanded of Kristi, Bill's older sister.

"Since he got home," Kristi said, with a shrug. She was only a year older than Bill, and the idea of defending her slightly weird younger brother did not occur to her.

"I'm going to go and get him." Mary turned back to the stairs and shouted up them, "If I have to come up there Bill Gates, so help me God!…"

"Give him a minute Mary," Bill Sr. said from the table. A door slammed upstairs. "Look he's coming."

Mary stamped off to the kitchen as eleven year old Bill Gates, or Trey as his family called him when he wasn't in trouble, stomped down the stairs. He was reading as he walked but, despite apparently being absorbed in the book, he still made sure that every step landed loudly for his mother to hear.

He looked up briefly as he entered the dining room and Bill Sr., acting the peacemaker as usual, gave his son a meaningful look.

The younger Bill took his place at the table and had the good sense to mutter an apology as Mary came in behind him holding the last dish.

"Sorry'm'late," he mumbled, running the words together.

"We expect everybody to be at the table on time Trey. We're not running a hotel here," Mary said.

Bill nodded and placed his open book beside his plate while everybody else started to reach for the food in the centre of the table.

Bill Sr. saw that Mary's eyes hadn't left the top of their son's head and decided to head off what would have no doubt been another argument.

"So, work was interesting," he began and described the case that he had been working on.

Bill, without looking up from his book, challenged his dad about a couple of the points, when he was satisfied that he understood his father's answer he nodded but he hadn't looked up once. Finally Mary snapped.

"Do you have to do that at the table?"

"What, eat?" Bill answered sarcastically, fully aware of what she meant. "Well, I'd be happy to do it in my room but you told me to come down."

Kristi noticed her father bristle.

She couldn't understand why Bill made life so much harder than it needed to be. Their family dynamics weren't particularly difficult to work out and yet Bill despite being obviously, sometimes even *peculiarly*, bright, totally failed to get it.

Usually the arguments were just between the hotheaded Bill and equally hotheaded Mary, but recently they'd started to spill over into the whole family.

Now their dad looked like he was getting annoyed and experience told Kristi that that wouldn't end well for anyone on the receiving end. Bill was oblivious though, too intent on scoring the point against his mother.

"I meant reading. Do you have to *read* at the table?" said Mary through gritted teeth.

"I need to catch up on stuff. I'm behind." Bill turned a page for dramatic effect.

"Kristi doesn't read at the table and she gets straight A's."

Bill raised his head slowly and looked his mother straight in the eye (while at the same time Kristi lowered her head, not wanting to get drawn in).

"Yeah, but you don't make Kristi be a greeter at your stupid parties do you? I couldn't read last night because I was too busy taking coats for your posh friends."

Mary took a deep breath and to everyone's surprise bit her tongue as she made a superhuman effort to rein in her inclination to tell the boy off.

"Reading is important Trey but there are other things that are important as well. You can't just spend your life sitting in your room reading and doing whatever else it is you do in there," she said as calmly as she could manage.

But Bill wasn't prepared to take the olive branch.

"What I'm doing in there is thinking mom. You know, thinnnnkiiiing," he drew out the word to emphasise it. "You should try it some time."

Suddenly everyone's head snapped to the other end of the table as Bill Sr. erupted.

In one smooth movement he pushed back his chair, drew himself up to his full six foot six and swept up his glass.

"That is enough, young man!" he roared, and flung the water straight into Bill's face.

Kristi's mouth dropped open and for a moment everyone was silent. The only sound at the table was the water dripping from Bill's face.

Then Bill broke the spell, shaking his head vigorously and standing up. "Thanks for the shower!" he yelled and stormed from the table.

***

William Henry Gates III, the man the world would know simply as Bill Gates, was born on 28th October 1955, the second child of Mary Maxwell Gates and another Bill.

His father was known at various points in his life as William H. Gates II, Bill Jr, and Bill Sr. For the sake of simplicity we'll refer to him here as Bill Sr. throughout.

Bill was a precocious child, but that didn't always come out as his parents might have hoped.

"It wasn't as if he was some sort of obvious super-bright kid. I think we recognise it better looking back than we did at the time. At the time we just thought he was trouble," Bill Sr. would say later.

***

Mary and Bill Sr. sat across from the counsellor they'd found. They'd told the kids that this was for the family as a whole but they all knew the truth. The issue was between Mary and young Bill, but the counsellor wanted to talk to the rest of the family first. He was starting with Bill Sr. and Mary before speaking to Kristi to get her opinion. Libby, nine years younger than Bill, was too young.

"Things have been getting worse for a little while now," Bill Sr. said.

"In what way?"

"Just generally, most interactions with his mother have — "

"When I can get him to interact," Mary interrupted.

Bill Sr. smiled patiently. "True. He does like his own company. But I was saying most interactions with his mother have become fairly fraught. They're both very strong characters."

"Well, that's not necessarily a bad thing in a boy but it can be difficult, I appreciate. Give me an example of a situation."

"He started asking questions at the dinner table."

"Questions about what?"

"Pretty much everything, business, the nature of life, the civil rights movement. You name it."

"And how do you feel about that?"

"I like it, its interesting. Not sure his mom is as keen though."

"You don't like the debate Mary?"

Bill Sr. laughed.

"Mary is used to being in charge," he said.

"It's not that…" Mary said.

***

"Everything's safe in here Kristi, anything you say here stays in here, I just need to understand how the family works if I'm going to help get things back to normal," the counsellor said.

"Okay," Kristi said hesitantly.

"Let's get right to it then shall we, what can you tell me about your mom and your brother's relationship?"

"It's… tense."

"And what's underlying that do you think?" he asked. Kristi tilted her head, astonished that he was asking her. She was only a year older than Trey. The counsellor sensed her confusion and explained, "I could tell you a bunch of textbook reasons Kristi, but I don't live with them, you do. I want to know what you think."

"Okay, well, I guess it boils down to the fact that Trey doesn't listen to her. He thinks he knows best. And she thinks, well, like most moms I suppose, she thinks he should do what he's told."

"And that leads to arguments."

Kristi nodded again.

"And what part does your dad play in these arguments?"

"My dad's great but he's not always around, he's getting a law firm up and running. He does his best to be home for dinner most nights but even when he is he's not really the touchy-feely type. He's quiet, reassuring, sensible. He's a lawyer. When Mom and Trey kick off he usually talks them both down quietly, it's him who breaks them up. They both listen to him."

"Okay Kristi, thank you. Now I'm going to ask you an unfair question. Remember there isn't a right and wrong here, I'm looking for your opinion and it won't go anywhere else." He waited for Kristi to nod and then continued, "Whose fault is it?"

Kristi's eyes widened, and the counsellor waited her out. When it was obvious he wasn't going to say anything else she answered.

"My mom is a force. She isn't really like any other mom I know. She's on the board of the Junior League, she volunteers all over the place. And she wants our family to be a force as well. It's her who drives us, makes sure we do our best all of the time. She is kind of the centre around which the family revolves. I don't mind that but Trey? He's started to resent it." She paused, deciding whether to carry on and then took the plunge. "But then, Bill's… weird."

"Weird in what way?"

"He reads. Like, all the time. If you didn't drag him out of his room he'd read forever."

"He must know a lot then."

"Yeah. Definitely. He knows loads about history, about Napoleon, he even learnt the sermon on the mount to win a contest. But he knows nothing about how to handle people who are alive today. It's not hard to manage my parents, they're good people, they give us everything we could ever need, but Trey, he just handles her badly. He needs to learn you just need to give in to her sometimes." She hesitated again. "I think they're just too similar."

***

"Tell me a bit about your family Bill."

"What, like my mom and dad or everyone?"

"As much as you want."

"Okay. Well, I guess my family's pretty lucky. My mom always says that. She's a Maxwell. They were pretty famous bankers in Seattle, have you heard of them?"

The counsellor shook his head, "I'm not from around here."

"Her grandad, my great-grandfather I mean, got the Federal Reserve to open a branch here. And then my mom's dad basically followed on behind and became a banker too. His brother did as well."

"So banking is in the family."

"Yeah."

"Are you going into banking Bill?"

"No, I'm going to be a scientist." The boy sat up slightly straighter. "I could tell you some stuff if you're interested, I remember a lot."

"I bet you do and that sounds good, but I'd like to get to know about you first. Is that okay?"

"Sure," Bill replied, visibly withdrawing again.

"So I interrupted you, you were just telling me about your grandad."

"Not much more to tell really, he died when I was five. To be honest my grandmother is a lot more talented than my grandfather was. We call her Gam. She's a big part of my life. It was her that gave me the name Trey."

"Why Trey?"

"It's what card players call a three. William Henry Gates the third," he held up three fingers. "Three. She plays a lot of bridge. She taught me, you know."

"Not a lot of lads your age play bridge."

"No. They should though, it's a good game. You have to really think."

"And thinking is good?"

Bill's face scrunched up as though he'd just tasted something unpleasant.

"Of course thinking is good," he said with barely hidden disdain.

"So you're the third William Henry Gates, that must carry a bit of expectation?"

"Actually I'm the fourth."

"Oh? So why did they call you William Henry Gates III then?"

Bill shrugged a very teenage shrug.

"I don't know, you'd have to ask my parents."

The counsellor smiled and nodded. "Fair enough. Why don't you tell me a bit about your parents then."

Bill nodded curtly as though acknowledging they'd now reached the point of the whole exercise.

"My mom's not into banking either. She met my dad at college and they got together, he was studying law as a returning GI and she was becoming a teacher. She taught class until my older sister was born and then she left."

"Your older sister, that's Kristi?"

"Correct."

Bill fell silent and his eyes drifted off to the side. After a second it was obvious that he was thinking about something else. The counsellor was surprised until it dawned on him that this was quite a literal kid, as far as he was concerned he'd answered the question. He gave him a gentle prod to get him going again.

"So after your mom left teaching she stayed at home to raise you kids?"

"Well, kind of. She's not your normal stay at home mom. She's very busy, she does a lot in the community. Junior League, that sort of thing. Gam looks after us after school."

"She sounds impressive your mom."

"Oh she's definitely impressive."

"Kristi described her as a force, would you agree with that?"

"Yes."

The counsellor resisted a smile, he'd done it again, he'd asked a question that could be answered with a single word and Bill had done exactly that.

"Okay, tell me about your dad then."

"My dad's a lawyer at Shidler and King."

"Do you look up to him?" A flash crossed Bill's eyes and the counsellor knew he was holding back the urge to make a joke about his dad's height. He winked to show he'd spotted it. "Metaphorically, I mean."

Bill smiled. A breakthrough.

"He's a great role model. He makes sure we know what's right and wrong."

"I mentioned the expectation that comes with an inherited name earlier, do you ever feel that Bill? Do you ever feel a pressure to perform?

"Not because of my name. My grandfather on my dad's side, and my great-grandfather as well, they were businessmen over in Bremerton. They did well but my dad was the first one to go to college, the first one to be professional if you see what I mean?" The counsellor nodded and Bill continued, "So no, I don't feel any pressure because of my name."

"No pressure *because of your name…*" the counsellor repeated slowly.

"Well, we know my mom and dad want us to do well."

Bill tensed and the counsellor decided to move on for now.

"Okay, so that's your folks. Tell me a little bit about your life."

"What do you want to know?"

"Well, let's start with what home is like. You said that Gam often looks after you, what do you do on a normal evening when Gam picks you up from school?"

"We play cards."

"Just you and Gam?"

"No, my sisters play as well."

"That's nice."

"They're not as good as me and Gam. I remember a lot."

"Do they ever get competitive?"

Bill snorted.

"You bet. My family are very into competition."

"Do you like competitions Bill?"

"I like to win."

"Mhm. So what do you do when you've finished playing cards?"

"I tend to go to my room and do my homework and read."

"Reading as part of your homework?"

"No. Well, yes. But that's quick, it's always easy. I tend to read other stuff, more interesting stuff."

"What like?"

"I've just started *The Catcher in the Rye.*"

"That's very grown up."

Bill shrugged again.

"Okay, what would you say if I asked what your favourite memory is?"

Bill paused as though running through his memories and assessing each in turn.

"Going to Camp Cheerio," he said after a moment. He smiled openly as he said the name.

"What's that?" the counsellor said, smiling in return.

"It's a summer camp we go to. My mom and dad and a bunch of their friends hire it out and we all go up there for the summer. It's on Hood Canal."

"And what do you do there?"

"The usual summer camp stuff. My dad's usually the mayor. We play pickleball and have races, that kind of thing."

"Ah sounds like fun, are you good at sports Bill?"

"I'm not interested in most sports. I'm good at the ones I'm interested in. I'm good at tennis, Brock Adams taught me one time at Cheerio. He's a friend of my parents and he's just been elected to congress."

"That sounds interesting."

"Maybe. Politics is a bit interesting. Not as interesting as science though. Or math."

"Why do you prefer math to politics?"

"With math you know what you're getting, there's a right answer and a wrong answer and if you concentrate hard enough… and you're smart enough… you can work out the right answer. Politics isn't like that, too many people involved. People are messy."

"I see. And are you smart enough Bill?"

"Smart enough to what?"

"Work out the right answer."

Bill hesitated again, but the counsellor got the feeling it wasn't due to any sense of modesty, rather that there was another lightening fast assessment going on in the boy's head.

"Yeah, I'm pretty smart," he said eventually. "If I find something interesting I pick it up pretty quickly."

"Can you give me an example?"

"We had these records once in grade school, where they call out math problems and you have to write the answer down real fast. You know, they'd say 13 + 8 and you'd write down 21. I remember enjoying them a lot. That was probably the first time I noticed that I was faster than the other kids." Bill paused and then looked at the counsellor appraisingly. "Did you have those records when you were in school?"

"I don't think they'd been invented when I was a boy Bill," the counsellor smiled self deprecatingly.

"Edison invented the phonograph in 1877," Bill retorted.

"I know. But I actually meant the math test records, not the phonograph."

"Oh." Bill slumped slightly, the wind taken out of his sails that his correction hadn't landed.

The counsellor took a chance.

"But if you're really trying to ask if I'm any good at math, then you might like to know I got 790 on my math SAT. Psychology was my major but I minored in math."

Bill shifted in his chair slightly and, for the first time since their discussion started, he made eye contact with the counsellor.

The counsellor was pleased with himself, he'd judged the boy correctly. He decided now was the time to push the advantage.

"Bill I want to challenge you a bit in these discussions, how do you feel about that? Would that be okay?"

Bill shrugged very slightly.

"It's a two way thing. If you don't agree with anything I'm saying I want you to tell me. From what I understand you and your parents have fallen into a bad pattern. I want you and me to try to get you all to a better place. It's a problem and I want us to fix it together, okay?"

"Mhm." Bill mumbled. It wasn't a raining endorsement but he hadn't disagreed either, so the counsellor pressed on.

"I think discussion, disagreement, even argument can be a way that intelligent people optimise their ideas. Intelligent people should challenge each other to clarify their thinking. What do you reckon?"

"Yeah," Bill said and leant forward slightly in his chair. "Yes, I definitely agree with that."

"Good. So why do you think your parents brought you to talk to me then Bill?

"They think I'm a problem."

"And are you?"

"I don't like being told what to do." The counsellor waited and this time Bill carried on, "But why should they get to be in charge?"

"They're your parents Bill, they deserve your respect."

"Respect should be earned."

"And they haven't earned it?"

That made him pause.

"Well…"

"Yes?"

"Maybe they have, but that doesn't give them the right to tell me what to do."

"Doesn't parenthood grant them some authority?"

"If it does it's completely arbitrary."

"I agree. Presumably it's also arbitrary that they should look after you then, right? Keep you fed, give you a place to live. These are all things they do because of the arbitrary chance that they ended up being your parents."

"Hm," Bill said.

He looked thoughtful but he didn't say any more. After a moment the counsellor asked another question.

"How would you characterise your current relationship with them?"

"I'm kind of at war with them."

"War? That's a strong word."

"It's fair."

"What's fair, the war or the word?"

"The word. You said it was a strong word."

"I see. And the war itself, does that strike you as fair?"

"What do you mean?"

"You told me earlier that you like to win." Bill nodded. "In a war both sides try to inflict pain on the other, right? But it seems to me like it's not a level playing field. You'll be prepared to inflict a lot more pain on them than they will on you. They're your parents, they're basically on your side. Will it feel like much of a win if you could never lose in the first place?"

***

A couple of months later the counsellor discharged the Gateses. For the final session he invited Bill Sr. and Mary without Bill.

"I don't know what you've done Doctor but I'm grateful. Things at home are a lot better," Mary opened.

"Not perfect," Bill Sr. said.

"No, not perfect but a lot better."

"That's nice to hear and just in case you've got the wrong idea, let me be clear Mr and Mrs Gates: they are never going to be perfect. He's your child, were either of your relationships with your parents perfect?"

"Hmm," Bill Sr. said thoughtfully. "Well, we both thank you anyway."

"Not a problem at all, your son is a very impressive young man and it was fun working with him. I've written up a family plan for you to read, either with Bill or without him, but I thought it would be useful if we used this final quick meeting for me to share with you some observations that I think might help."

"Of course."

"Some of it will be obvious to you, some might be more thought provoking but they're all my genuine observations as an outsider to your family."

"Go ahead," Bill Sr. said.

"First of all I don't think he's rebelling just because of his age. Plenty of teenagers rebel solely to make a point that their parents are not in control. It's meaningless and frustrating to me as a family professional because just about the only advice I can give parents is to wait it out. Of course, there's almost certainly a bit of that with Bill as well, he wouldn't be normal if there wasn't, but for the most part I think his behaviour is a symptom of something better than that."

"Better?"

"As long as it's channeled correctly, which is what Bill and I have worked on these last few months. And assuming I'm right it gives us a bit more hope of some useful techniques to improve things at home, as you've seen."

"Indeed."

"So I have a couple of suggestions for you that might help ensure that carries on but, before we get to that, my observations. As you'll know Bill doesn't relate very easily to people he doesn't already know."

"We try to involve him in social gatherings and events to help bring him out of himself."

"Yes, he told me about it."

"He doesn't like it, does he?"

"No, but you knew that already and I wouldn't worry about it. We all have to do things we don't like. He understands that. Personally I've no doubt that it will be helpful if you keep making him do it, but it's also important to accept him for who he is and the truth is social interaction might never be his strength.

"That said, he finds it much easier to get along with people when they've won his respect. Once I'd proved to him I was worth listening to our relationship became really fruitful, enjoyable even. Before that, when he wasn't sure I was worth his time, he showed some definite flashes of impatience. I suspect in more unequal gatherings he could be quite withering, even cruel with people who don't measure up to his standards."

Mary looked shocked, Bill Sr. reached out and placed his hand on top of his wife's comfortingly.

"Sounds like he's a perfectionist like his mom," he said. "And you're doing okay Hon."

"Mr Gates is right. These aren't good or bad traits as long as Bill understands them and learns to use them in the right way. They certainly won't stop him making a success of himself. In fact with a mind like his I'd be surprised if he doesn't."

"A mind like his?" Bill Sr. Said.

"Yes, if you don't mind my saying, I think you might be underestimating his intelligence." The counsellor hesitated, this was the sensitive part. "I've seldom met anyone able to grasp new concepts quite as quickly. He got interested in the psychological aspects of our conversations so I suggested some books on Freud. He came back to the next session and tore the psychoanalytic process apart. It was one of the most interesting discussions I've had in months."

"A couple of his teachers have said similar things over the years. To be honest we just figured he was a bit of a trouble-maker. He's always been a bit of a class clown," Bill Sr. said.

"And with his scouts, he messes about there too," Mary added.

"Well, that's not unusual for bright children. If they don't find something to keep them engaged they can make their own entertainment in less constructive ways."

"So we need to find something for him to concentrate on?"

"I think he's already found it: learning. The best idea now is probably to give him the space to find a topic that fully engages him, draws him in and grabs hold of his mind. If he finds the right thing he could go far.

"In terms of how you deal with him in the home, I'd simply say two things: Firstly, above all he values reason and knowledge. Give him reasons for your decisions and rules. He'll probably still challenge them but if you can show why they matter then he'll go along more often than not. Remember though, bright kids still need parents. He's still young and in most situations he isn't the most knowledgeable person in the room. In fact God help the others when he is!" the counsellor grinned and Bill and Mary both laughed.

"And the second thing?" Bill Sr. asked.

The counsellor turned to look at Mary.

"Give him as loose a leash as you can stand. The thinking he's done with me will probably reduce the arguments you'll have for a while but in the end if you don't give him space you'll lose him. You can probably win most of the fights you'll have over the next couple of years but you will keep having them and in the end you'll push him away. If you let him be his own man, on the other hand there will still be a huge space for you in the things he will never be any good at. He'll come to recognise that and appreciate you all the more."

***

Things at Laurelhurst definitely got better after the counselling.

Maybe it was the counselling that helped.

Maybe Bill started to grow up and realised the real tests weren't likely to be against his parents but instead were with the outside world.

Or maybe what really helped was the wonder that Bill found when he returned to Lakeside for the eighth grade.

C:\PART\CHAPTER> 1.2

In 1967, when he was in seventh grade, Mary and Bill Sr. sent Bill to Seattle's prestigious Lakeside prep school. They were both big supporters of state education but they felt Lakeside would suit Bill better. Mary thought that the more disciplined environment would help him settle down. Bill Sr. thought his wife knew what she was talking about.

Bill himself was less convinced.

Lakeside had stopped being a boarding school four years earlier but from the outside it still looked very starchy. The boys (and they were all boys) had to wear a uniform of jackets and ties, they carried their books in briefcases, and were expected to call the teachers 'master'.

There had been one possible way to avoid going. To get into Lakeside you had to take an entrance exam, and that gave Bill an idea.

"You can't make me go," Bill had told his parents. "I could fail the exam on purpose."

Mary and Bill Sr. knew their son well enough not to be too worried about his threat, and in the end he couldn't bring himself to do it.

Bill had spent the first year settling into his new school without anything particularly dramatic happening. His classmates thought of him as one of the 'maths and science guys' but while finding his feet in that first year he was a B student almost across the board.

The beginning of the eighth grade would change that, just as it would change Bill's life in ways he couldn't have imagined.

***

"Right boys, I have a surprise for you today," Mr. Stocklin said one day in math class. "Grab your stuff and follow me."

The boys gathered up their bags and coats, shooting each other looks and some of them talking quietly amongst themselves.

"What's going on?"

"Where are we going?"

"Math outdoors?"

But Mr. Stocklin remained tight lipped as he led them across the school to the upper school hall.

Mr. Stocklin threw open the door to a little office off the main reception and ushered the boys inside the small room.

When they were all crammed inside he threw his arm out to show them the reason for the trip.

"So, who knows what that is?" he asked, pointing at a large, murky-beige coloured contraption sitting on a stand in the corner.

"An electric typewriter?" one of the boys near the front said hesitatingly.

"No," Mr. Stocklin said, smiling kindly. "Any other ideas?"

"It's a computer," a boy in the middle of the group said.

"Ah, exactly," Mr. Stocklin replied, somewhat disappointed to have had his moment taken away from him. "Mr Dougall, the head of the science and math departments, is convinced that computers are going to be a big part of the business world soon, so he thought that you Lakeside boys should get a head start and the Mothers Club agreed to fund it from their rummage sale. Exciting isn't it?"

The boys crowded round and a palpable buzz ran through them.

Even if they had never seen one before and had no clue what they could really do, they had all heard of computers. Several of them were science fiction fans and regularly consumed the stories by writers like Isaac Asimov about a future filled with computers and robots, but even the boys who would have laughed at the idea of robot butlers knew that in some way computers were the future.

"This," he swept his arm around to encompass the whole thing. "Is an ASR-33 lads."

"I thought computers were huge, sir? According to Scientific American they take up a whole room."

"Very good Rucker that's absolutely true. As exciting as it is, the ASR-33 isn't actually a computer itself."

The boys' faces fell, thinking they'd been the victims of an elaborate trick and wondering what the punchline was, how was this going to turn into a homework assignment or some other teacher trickery. Mr. Stocklin hurried on before he lost them.

"The real computer that we'll be using is a GE-635 mainframe. As Rucker says, computers are colossal and they cost a huge amount of money, so several of the companies that own them have started time-sharing arrangements to help them with the costs. They rent out computing time on their mainframe computer to different businesses. Lakeside has come to an agreement with the university to time-share on their mainframe."

"So is it a computer or not?" one of the boys shouted up.

Bill was transfixed and the answer presented itself to him straight away.

The system as a whole acts like a computer, he thought, but kept it to himself. *You must use this bit in the room… the ASR-33, was it?… to tell the mainframe what to do and the whole thing together is a computer.*

Mr. Stocklin kept his patience.

"Okay, think of it like this: Imagine that some of you were good at math and some of you weren't. Well, one of you who had what we might call a 'math-brain' could charge someone who wasn't good at math to do their homework for them," he shot a meaningful look at a boy in the corner who suddenly found the floor fascinating. "We could think of that as renting out time on Harmon's, sorry, the first boy's brain, right? His brain can do lots of different things but in this case he's just renting out its time to solve math problems. He gets to use his brain most of the time but his customer gets to use it as well when he needs to, as long as he pays for the time he uses. Well, that's what the university has done. They've bought an expensive computer from General Electric and they're renting out time on its brain to do things that other people want. Make sense?"

The class all made positive noises and nodded, apart from Harmon who was still looking at the floor and now appeared to be trying to shrink out of sight.

"Good. So let's take a look at what we've got here. The part you use most is in fact just like an electric typewriter," Mr. Stocklin said, nodding at the boy who'd thought that's what it was, and pointing to the keyboard and the wide roll of paper that sat immediately behind it. "You type your commands in here and they print out on the paper. But the bits that make it so exciting are the things typewriters don't have."

Mr. Stocklin moved to the left of the machine and pointed to something else.

Bill craned to see above the other, taller boys. The thing that Mr. Stocklin was pointing at was a one inch wide paper tape with little square holes in it.

"This tape is a punch-tape. You can use it to store information to tell the ASR-33 what to do without typing it in again."

"Like a record?" someone asked.

"Sort of but instead of grooves on vinyl, the computer stores the information in the pattern of holes on the tape. It does that in a new language called ASCII that some of you might want to learn."

Bill found his voice. "Can you use the same tape on other machines, Sir?"

Mr. Stocklin nodded, "Yes Gates you can, that's one of the things that makes computers powerful. As long as the computer speaks the same language and you learn it then you can make any of them do what you want."

Bill breathed out slowly, captivated.

"But this is where the real action is lads," Mr. Stocklin went on, tapping a rotary telephone dial on the right of the machine. "This is what's called a call control unit. It's what lets us talk to the mainframe. Once you've input your commands into the ASR-33, you dial up the mainframe, the GE-635 remember, through the telephone line and the call control unit sends all of your instructions to it."

"Like Bishop phoning Harmon with his homework questions!" someone shouted and the whole class, with two exceptions, laughed.

"Yes, I suppose so!" Mr. Stocklin replied, suppressing a laugh of his own. "I mean in our hypothetical example, of course. Anyway, then once the mainframe has worked out the answers it sends them back over the phone line and instructs the ASR-33 to print it out." He rested his hand on the wide paper roll. "Amazing, hey?"

Judging by the excited muttering that ran around the room, Mr. Stocklin decided they were impressed.

"But what *exactly* can it do, sir?" one boy asked.

"Well, let's see shall we?"

With a big grin on his face and his eyes twinkling, Mr. Stocklin flicked a switch on the front panel and the ASR-33 burst into life with a machine gun like rat-a-tat-tat that made Bill and several others jump.

While Mr. Stocklin spoke Bill pushed his way through the other boys to the front of the group so he could get a good look.

He didn't know yet but this was the noise that would fill his life for the next four years.

***

Bill's closest friend at Lakeside was Kent Evans. The two of them had started with very similar interests and, like lots of young friends, they gradually grew to overlap more. Bill got Kent more into computers, and Kent encouraged Bill's interest in business.

One afternoon, after they had finished for the day at Lakeside, Bill and Kent were hanging out in Kent's bedroom. Kent was lying on his bed, Bill was on the floor on his stomach. Kent's briefcase was thrown open in the corner of the room and business magazines were strewn all around them.

"But you've got to have a plan Bill," Kent was saying.

"I'm probably going to be a lawyer like my dad," Bill said, and then got the distinct feeling that he should be aiming for more. "But with a bigger firm, obviously," he added.

Kent threw down his copy of *Fortune* and looked at his friend.

"That's okay, but it's not a plan is it? I mean your dad's doing okay for himself but we're the future Bill. He's not paying for you to go to Lakeside to just do the same as he did is he? You've got to think bigger."

Bigger, Bill thought. *Yeah, I can do that.*

"What about you then, what are you planning?" he asked Kent.

"I'm not sure yet, but I'm going to make an impact that's for sure." He fell silent for a minute. "Actually maybe becoming a lawyer at first isn't a bad plan. Lots of politicians start off as lawyers."

"You want to be a politician?"

"Hm, possibly. A politician or a general."

"I could be a general, I read about Napoleon, he's impressive."

"That's exactly what I mean! Everybody knows about Napoleon right, but who's ever heard of a lawyer or a minister from eighteenth century France?"

"Richelieu was a minister. Talleyrand was a lawyer."

"Okay smart-arse but you don't know about them because of that do you? You know about them because of what they did after."

Bill shrugged, conceding the point.

"Take this guy I was reading about," Kent rapped his knuckles on the cover of the magazine he'd just thrown down. There was nobody on the cover so Bill had no idea who he was talking about. It didn't matter though, when Kent did this, firing off a thousand ideas at once, Bill found it inspiring. "He's the CEO of Boeing. That's like a multi-million dollar company that he's in charge of and he gets to make decisions that affect hundreds of people."

"Power."

"Yeah, power. I want power. Is that bad? I don't want it for its own sake, but I want to be remembered. To do something worth remembering."

"To be Napoleon not his solicitor," Bill said.

"Exactly."

"Me too," Bill said, then after a brief pause added, "I think I want it to be something to do with the computer."

Kent pointed at Bill.

"Yeah, that could work," he said and tapped the magazine again thoughtfully. "Computers don't already have a Boeing."

***

Paul Allen was two years older than Bill Gates so he was in the tenth grade when Lakeside first got the computer. He and a friend, Ric Weiland, fell in love with the possibilities it opened up almost immediately.

One day he turned up to use the machine and found a group of younger kids huddled around the machine.

That wasn't particularly unusual. Ever since it had arrived the computer had drawn attention. Mr. Wright had explained to him that the school was introducing the boys one class at a time to the machine, and Paul had noticed that invariably a small number from each class would get excited by it at first before most of them gradually drifted away.

The promise of the machine was in some ways let down by the effort needed to learn a series of languages to interact with it, and then waiting what felt like forever for the mainframe to respond with an answer that you could have worked out yourself already. For most of the boys it was basically too hard to be worth the paltry result.

But Paul thought that if you were prepared to put the time in then it was worth it. He and a couple of others had caught the bug. Badly.

Now, judging by the group surrounding the ASR, another class must have had their first lesson recently. In the centre, sat in front of the keyboard, was a small boy who looked almost too young to be at Lakeside.

He must be a seventh grader, Paul thought.

The boy had scruffy blond hair, a face covered in freckles, and his feet barely touched the floor, but there was an intensity about him that Paul liked.

Paul sat quietly in the corner and watched as occasionally the others would shout at the boy.

"Hey, you're taking too much time."

"Hey, you made a typing mistake!"

"Hey, you messed that up!"

But the boy was apparently oblivious to all of the distractions, he just sat there punching away at the keyboard with a pencil clenched between his teeth. He was reading from a notepad beside him and typing with an odd sideways kind of style.

Paul waited for the boy to finish, he recognised the feeling of flow and didn't want to disturb him. Gradually the others drifted off, having failed to distract the boy. Every now and then he stopped typing and would stare hard at his notepad then look into space, or at least the stained ceiling tiles of the little room, and rock backwards and forwards in his chair. After just long enough for Paul to think he'd lost interest he would snap back into the present and his fingers would start racing across the keyboard again in that weird crab-like typing.

Eventually he stood up, and started removing the punch tape from the spool on the machine and Paul knew it was safe to approach him.

"Hey, I'm Paul Allen," he said. "Looked like you were well into it there, what were you doing?"

"Bill Gates," said the young boy avoiding eye contact but thrusting out his hand formally as though in a business meeting. "I am trying to write a program to play tic-tac-toe. It's nearly finished, I think."

"Wait, 'Gates' did you say?"

"Yeah," the boy looked up at the much taller tenth grader suspiciously.

"You're the one who aced the national math test."

"Correct."

"I've been meaning to come and talk to you, that was great."

"I like math. I'm good at it."

Paul nodded, "And the computer too I bet, am I right?"

"That I like it or that I am good at it?"

"Both. Either."

"Both," Bill said.

C:\PART\CHAPTER> 1.3

As Paul had observed most of the kids at school came to the computer room less and less but over time a hardcore group had formed: Paul Allen and Ric Weiland, Kent Evans and Bill Gates.

They even gave themselves a name, the Lakeside Programmers Group.

Paul and Ric no doubt got a bit of stick for hanging out with the younger eighth graders but they didn't seem to care. Bill and Kent were able to keep up in part because they were both obsessive and threw themselves completely into the computer with a passion usually reserved for teenage crushes.

Before long word about the little group got out and Lakeside was approached by a local start up company, Computer Center Corporation, to see if the boys would be interested in testing their new computer system.

Fred Wright, who was still loosely in charge of the computer room, asked the four of them if they'd be interested. Since it meant an opportunity to use a computer they could think of nothing better.

One Saturday Fred took them to the offices of Computer Center Corporation, to introduce them to the executives there and agree the ground rules they would have to follow for their testing.

They met in the room the boys would be using.

They were all trying their best to look professional but it was hard not to let their excitement show. The man they were there to meet was perched on a long desk which ran along wall and had three teletype machines on it. Three! And there were another three on the other wall!

Six terminals to hook up to the computer, no more waiting your turn like at Lakeside.

The ground rules that the Computer Center representative, Dick Gruen, laid out weren't particularly complicated.

"You can do anything you want on the computer, but we need you to find problems for us. Any time you find a problem write it in the bug book and don't do whatever you did again until we tell you we've got a fix. Then you can test it again. Understand?"

They understood alright. They understood that they could do anything they want.

"When can we do our testing?" Ric asked.

"Well the idea is to crash the system so we don't want that happening while the normal customers are on. Can you work outside of normal business hours, you know weekends, evenings, is that going to be a problem?"

"Absolutely not," Kent said before anyone else had chance to answer. "We can do that. And what about payment? Mr. Wright didn't mention anything about terms."

Dick looked over at Fred Wright but the teacher shrugged his shoulders.

"Don't look at me, Dick. I'm just the chauffeur here, it's the boys you're dealing with."

The executive looked back to the four boys standing in front of him but it was Kent who drew his eyes, he was clearly the business mind amongst them.

"We were thinking that we could pay you in free time," he said. "You'd get to use the computer for your own projects without being charged until we finish the acceptance testing. What do you think?"

"Can I have a moment with my colleagues?" Kent said.

The executive tried not to smile at the fourteen year old with the serious attitude.

"Of course."

Kent waved the others over to the corner, leaving Fred to make small talk with Dick Gruen.

"What do you reckon? Do you think we should hold out for a payment?"

"I think it's great. It's all we want," Bill said.

"If they pay us for the work they won't give us the free time," Ric said. "And we'd end up spending it anyway, and it would probably cost us more."

"It's a fair deal," Paul said.

"Yeah, both sides win."

"Did you think we should hold out for more, Kent?" Bill asked.

"No, not really."

Bill frowned. "Why did you bring us over here then?"

"We don't want to look desperate, they need us and it's better business to make sure they remember that. We don't want them thinking we're just kids."

"Erm, we are just kids," Ric said.

"No, he's got a good point. We need to be taken seriously if we're going to get other gigs," Paul said.

"Are we looking for other gigs?" Ric asked.

"Why not?" Bill said. "There aren't many people who understand computers like we do, we can make it into something."

"Yeah, cool. I'm in."

"So we'll agree to his suggestion then?" Kent checked and when they all agreed he turned back to the executive. "We're happy with your proposal, Mr. Gruen but we'll want it in writing." The executive's eyebrows shot up despite his best efforts. "Erm... I mean if that's okay?" Kent added in a more nervous voice.

"Of course, very sensible, we wouldn't have it any other way. We'll get something sent over to the school."

"Refer to the Lakeside Programmers Group in the contract please," said Bill, it was the first time he'd spoken in the meeting since introducing himself and his young sounding voice caught the executive by surprise. "We might want to sub-contract to other qualified boys... staff... and I don't want the contract to prevent it."

"Well, that sounds fair Mr. ... Gates, wasn't it?" Bill nodded. "But we've met you four so I'd want to be sure you are the main workers, shall we list you as key personnel with responsibility for overseeing anybody else you bring on?"

"That's acceptable," Bill said.

"Fantastic, I believe we have a deal then. Congratulations and welcome aboard."

He stood up and shook hands with each of the boys in turn.

***

As soon as they all piled back into Fred's car he turned down the radio and got the boys' attention.

"I'm really impressed with how you handled yourselves in there lads. You've got the making of a professional outfit."

"Thanks Sir," Paul said from the passenger seat but if Fred had been expecting anything more he was disappointed as Paul immediately turned to the other boys.

"You know who that was, right?"

"Wilkinson?" Evans asked.

"No, the guy who came in and spoke to him while we were in the middle."

"No."

"Nope," Ric said.

"No."

"Steve Russell. He was part of McCarthy's artificial intelligence team at MIT. He wrote *Spacewar!* He's like a programming god!"

"*Spacewar!*, you're kidding?!"

"What's *Spacewar!?*"

"Only the first computer game, moron."

"That's not quite right actually," Ric said.

"It's the first one that mattered."

Fred Wright shook his head and left them to it, this would go on for a while.

***

35

Over the next couple of months the four of them spent pretty much every waking moment, and plenty of moments when they should have been asleep, at Computer Center Corporation (or C-Cubed as they had started calling it).

The arrangement worked well for the company. They had agreed with Digital Electric Company, the provider of their computer, that they wouldn't start paying until all of the bugs were ironed out. Until then C-Cubed, and by extension Bill and his friends, got their computing time for free.

Of course it all had to end at some point and that end came when the testing period finished and C-Cubed had to start paying for its computer time. With no further work for the Lakeside Programmers Group they sent the boys home and Lakeside School became one of the company's normal customers, connecting remotely and paying for their computer time in the usual way.

The four friends, however, had used their time to good effect, learning the ins and outs of the system well enough that one day Mr. Wright got an unexpected visit from one of the C-Cubed executives.

"Your boys keep finding things they're not supposed to."

"What like?"

"The chess program."

"Sounds fun."

"Yes, but you're not supposed to leave it running so it uses a load of computer time when you're not playing it."

"Ah."

"Quite. Anyway, that's not the biggest thing."

Mr. Wright took a deep breath, he didn't like where this was heading.

***

Twenty minutes later the members of the Lakeside Programmers Group were all assembled outside Mr. Wright's office waiting to be called inside.

"Does anyone know what this is about?" Ric asked.

"Erm, I don't *know*, no," Bill said.

Ric's shoulders slumped as he recognised Bill's I'm-being-precisely-correct-and-hoping-you'll-misunderstand approach.

"Okay, but can you take a good guess?"

"Yes," Bill replied and stopped until Ric made a circular, 'go on then' motion with his finger. "It might be something to do with their accounting program."

"Jesus Bill, what have you done?"

"It wasn't just me. Paul knew."

"Why didn't you tell me?" Kent said to Bill, while Ric just shook his head.

Paul took up the baton.

"Bill and I were alone when we found it and we thought it best if we kept it as quiet as possible. That way you two wouldn't get into any trouble if we got found out."

"That doesn't seem to have worked," Ric replied in a flat voice.

***

"So boys," Mr. Wright said when they were standing in front of his desk. "We've had a visit from the people at Computer Center Corporation. Specifically their security team. Would you like to tell me what's happened?"

"It was me, Sir," Bill said. "I found the accounting file and tried to change it."

"And did you change it?"

"Not yet Sir. We couldn't find out how but I downloaded a copy."

Ric rolled his eyes but thankfully Mr. Wright was looking at Bill and didn't notice.

"This is a very serious thing Bill. It's basically theft and Computer Center aren't amused. They have a process that says if this sort of thing happens then they have to press criminal charges."

Bill looked horrified and when Fred took in the faces of the other boys they didn't look any different. He let them hang for a moment longer and then when he figured they'd suffered enough, he put them out of their misery.

"The good news is that I've talked them out of going to the police for now." The boys visibly relaxed until Fred brought down the other shoe. "Unfortunately there is bad news as well, they are kicking you off the system."

"No!" Paul said.

"How long for?" asked Kent.

"Six weeks."

Bill didn't speak, he didn't trust himself to.

***

Later, in the spring of 1970, C-Cubed went bust. The market for resellers of computer time wasn't quite as mature as they'd hoped.

Bill and Paul later told the story that they were there when the removal firm came to repossess all of the office equipment. They were still typing furiously and trying to save their work to punch tapes even as the chairs were taken away. The lesson in how quickly technology companies can disappear would stay with them both but Bill most of all.

Of course, it was also a lesson in what happens in a repossession: the repossession company put C-Cubed's assets up for auction. And, without telling Paul or Ric, Bill and Kent went along and snagged themselves some souvenirs.

***

Ric Weiland stormed into the library and stamped over to the desk Paul was sitting at with his head in a book.

"You won't believe what I've just seen!" he said in a half whisper / half shout.

The dozen or so people in the library all turned to look at the pair of them, all except the librarian who simply spoke without looking up.

"Take it outside Mr. Weiland," she said.

"Come with me!" Ric said and pulled Paul's arm.

Paul shoved his book into his satchel and followed his friend outside.

"What is it?" he asked.

"You're never going to believe what those little weasels have done," Ric said as he marched two paces ahead of Paul towards the computer room.

"Who Ric? What's going on?"

"Gates and Evans, the bastards."

"What is it Ric?"

"You need to see it."

"Okay," Paul said, giving up and deciding to follow along quietly.

Finally they reached the computer room and Ric headed straight for the pedestal that the ASR-33 sat on and threw it open.

"Look!" he said.

Paul peered inside.

"Are those PDP-10 tapes?"

"Yeah, from C-Cubed. I saw Bill and Kent hide them in here when they thought no-one was looking. They must have bought them at the bankruptcy sale without telling us."

"Maybe they're planning to surprise us?"

Ric just shook his head.

"You're too nice Paul. If they were going to surprise us it was going to be by saying, 'Surprise, we made a fortune'. You really think they're planning to spend their own money on them and then just give them to us? Does that sound like either of them?"

Paul hesitated before answering.

"No, okay it doesn't, but still, I can't believe they'd…" he petered off as he realised he could.

The next day all four boys had been in the computer room for about an hour when Paul saw Kent raise his eyebrows and nod encouragingly at Bill.

Bill, keeping his face as straight as possible, looked at Paul.

"We know something you don't know," he said in a sing-song voice.

"Hm? What's that Bill?" Paul replied nonchalantly.

"How old are you again Gates?" Ric snapped but Paul shot him a look and cut him off.

Bill hesitated but only for a fraction of a second, then he went back to taunting Paul, although now Ric had got his attention he was sucked in as well.

"Both of you," he said. "You'd both love to know it."

"You know all sorts of things we don't Bill, you're a real clever guy."

Paul turned back to his notepad and tried not to give Bill the satisfaction of rising to his taunts. Bill wasn't prepared to let it go quite so quickly though.

"It's about something in this room. There's something here that you'll *really* wish you had."

"No doubt, anyway, sorry Bill but I'm concentrating on this bit of code, mind if I have a bit of quiet?"

Bill tried to get a reaction from Ric but, taking his lead from Paul, Ric kept his cool as well. Eventually the younger boys gave up and left the room for their next class.

As soon as they'd left the room Ric ran to the door and checked the corridor to be sure they'd really gone, they had, the coast was clear.

"See, what did I tell you? Little bastards."

"I know, I still can't believe it. As if they'd lord it over us like that, well I've got an idea, two can play their horrible little game."

***

"Which of you was it?!" Bill shouted at Paul and Ric the day after.

The boys were in the habit of going to the computer room before classes started but this time Paul and Ric had turned up late, intentionally giving Bill and Kent time to suffer a bit.

Bill's shout met them as they sauntered casually into the room together ten minutes after their usual time.

Paul shrugged and looked at Ric as though he was confused.

"Which of us was what Bill? Ric have you got any idea what he's talking about?"

"Search me. Keep it down a bit though hey Bill, you'll burst a vein if you carry on like that."

Paul and Ric took a seat and got their notepads out of their bags as calmly as they could, determined to play it out for as long as possible. Bill leapt out of his seat and almost ran over to them, shouting and punctuating his points with vigorous stabs of his finger in Paul's face.

"You knew it," he shouted, his eyes only slightly above the much taller Paul's even though he was sitting. "You knew all along. I thought there was something weird about the way you reacted."

"I'm sorry Bill, knew about what?"

"Yes, what are you talking about Bill?" Ric joined in.

Bill wheeled on him and let fire a string of invective, then almost instantly turned back to Paul, the target of most of his wrath.

"The tapes! Where are they?!" His face was completely red by now.

"Tapes, Bill?" Ric said.

"You know what we're talking about, the DEC tapes from C-Cubed. We put them under the terminal and now they're gone. You took them!"

"You had tapes from C-Cubed and you didn't tell us about them?" Paul said.

"You know we did! You must have found them!"

"Oh yeah, we found them alright. I've put them somewhere safe because I figured someone was trying to rip the four of us off. You know, *the four* of us!" Paul said, jumping out of his chair. He was taller than Evans and completely towered over the smaller Bill, but Bill wasn't deterred in the slightest.

"Hand them over Paul, they're not yours. Me and Kent bought them."

"Yeah, I got that Bill, I didn't think you'd robbed them. At least not from C-Cubed. You might as well have robbed me and Ric though!"

"What do you mean? What are you going on about? We didn't rob you!"

"You might as well have done. We did all of the C-Cubed work together, all four of us, what gives you two the right to buy those tapes for yourselves?" Paul was shouting as well now.

Bill spluttered and was about to shout back an answer when Kent intervened.

"Capitalism Paul, that's how it works you know? The guy with the money wins, Bill had the money to buy those tapes so he did. The loser doesn't get to cry about it. We don't share everything out unless you're a commie."

Paul shook his head with as much disdain as he could muster.

"This isn't Political Science 101 Kent, we're supposed to be friends. Friends don't treat each other like this."

"Just give them back to us now or..." Kent said.

"Or what?"

"Bill's dad is a lawyer you know."

"So what?!"

"So I'll get him to help me sue you," Kent said.

"Oh get a grip!"

"He's right you know Paul, we could sue you," Bill said. "You said it's like me and Kent robbed you, well you really have robbed us. They're our tapes, we bought them… Now… Give… Them… Back!" he yelled, stabbing Paul in the chest with his finger with each of the last words.

Paul looked bewildered but luckily he was saved from having to come up with a reply by the arrival of Fred Wright, drawn to the room by all of the shouting.

"Boys! That's enough. I don't know what's going on but it all stops now. Evans, Gates, sit down over there and stay very quiet or I will be straight back in here and you won't like it. Allen, Weiland, come with me."

Paul and Ric grabbed their bags and followed Mr. Wright from the room, leaving Bill and Kent red faced and breathing heavily.

Ten minutes later Paul came back in to the room, having been talked down from the ledge by Mr. Wright.

"Ric's gone to class," he said calmly. "I shouldn't have shouted at you guys, but I don't know why you wouldn't have shared them with us or at least told us about them. We're supposed to be partners, I guess I was just hurt. I'm not sorry I was pissed off, but I'm sorry I shouted. Anyway, the tapes are at my house. I'll bring them back tomorrow."

"We'll split them Paul," Bill said, earning a surprised look from Kent. "It's only fair. We'll work out a split tomorrow, you, me Kent and Ric, all four of us."

***

All four of the boys were close, and remained so despite the tape incident, however Lakeside cemented a pattern that Bill would repeat.

He would often have several collaborators but in each phase of his life Bill would have a main partner, someone he could bounce things off, someone he would become close enough to that they could communicate in a verbal shorthand, leaving others behind, and often bewildered.

While the world would soon come to be changed by the intense relationship that Bill and Paul developed, in 1971 and 1972 that partner was Kent Evans. It would probably have stayed that way and the world could have been a very different place, if it hadn't been for something none of them saw coming.

C:\PART\CHAPTER> 1.4

In January 1972 Lakeside School suffered a tragedy.

Two teachers were flying a private Cessna looking to take aerial photos of the school when they crashed and were both killed instantly.

It was a traumatic experience for the school but of course there were things that the teachers had been working on that still need to be completed. One of those things was a class schedule for 1972.

Producing schedules had always been a dog of a job and a couple of years earlier someone had had the bright idea of automating it. It seemed like the perfect task for a computer to do.

The teachers had approached the Lakeside Programmers Group but in a rare display of modesty or fear (or possibly a better understanding of how hard it was than the teachers) they had turned down the opportunity. So the job fell to Bob Haig, a middle school math teacher. While Bob worked on the schedule for 1971, Gates, Evans, Allen and Weiland had taught some of his computer classes for him.

In 1971 Lakeside merged with a local girls school to become co-ed. For many of the boys this was a blessing, for Haig, working on the schedule, it was a nightmare.

He managed to get a version cranked out for 1971 through a combination of computer input and manual alterations but was working on the full 1972 schedule at the time of the plane crash.

Not knowing where else to turn, and with Allen and Weiland having left for college in fall 1971, the school came back to Gates and Evans.

This time the boys agreed to do it.

It was as difficult as they'd expected but nonetheless they threw themselves into it with their usual 100% commitment, spending hours every day in the computer room and even bringing in cots to sleep in the school so they didn't lose programming time by travelling home to bed.

***

43

Bill didn't respond at first, he simply stared at his friend, apparently noticing his slightly overweight build for the first time. Finally he shook his head.

"I don't get it, Kent."

"I've signed up to go mountaineering."

"No, I heard you. I said I didn't get it. I mean, mountain climbing? It's not really your thing is it? You've never shown any interest in sport before."

"Well, that's the point, isn't it? You and me we're like all about the brain, right? I need to balance myself out a bit. Like Benjamin Franklin said: healthy, wealthy and wise. I've got the last bit, we're going to smash the second one, I've got to work on my body a bit."

"Franklin was talking about getting enough sleep. I'm pretty sure he didn't go jogging, much less scramble up the side of mountains. Anyway, who cares about the meat machine?! It's just a way of carrying your brain around."

"You say that but you do some sports stuff."

"Only when my parents make me."

"What about waterskiing?"

"Hmph," Bill said, unwilling to concede a point.

"Or tennis?" Bill didn't answer. "And all of those family competitions in the summer you told me about?"

"Alright, alright. I do *some* sports."

"There you go then, I don't do anything physical. Nothing. We'll be going off to college soon and I want to get into better shape before we do."

"Ohhh, right," Bill said, figuring he'd worked it out. "Girls."

That wasn't the point, or not the whole point, but Kent nodded. It was easier.

"Girls," he said.

Bill changed tack.

"What about the scheduling programme? We can't afford for you to take a break," he said.

"We can't afford for me not to. I'm exhausted."

"All the better reason not to go climbing a mountain then.

Kent tossed his head back and laughed.

"Bill, I love you man, but I'm going. I wasn't actually asking you."

"Alright, whatever. When is it?"

"This weekend."

"Okay, well, I'll be here working on the programme by myself then."

"Don't be like that."

"Nah, it's cool, really. I've got a couple of ideas to try out anyway. I'll let you know how I get on when you come back all buff and ready to impress the ladies."

***

"There's a phonecall for you Trey," Mary said. "Take it in the study."

His mother looked subdued but Bill had no idea why until .

"Who is it?"

"Mr. Ayrault," she answered. "He needs to talk to you, I'll be here when you're done."

"What is it mom? You're scaring me."

Mr. Ayrault was the headmaster at Lakeside so Bill assumed that he'd done something wrong, he hoped they hadn't found anything else from the C-Cubed days. He could do without the grief.

Mary laid her hand on her son's shoulder.

"Just take the call son. I'll be outside."

Bill walked into the study and shut the door, and Mary finally let herself shed the tears she'd held in for her son. She knew that his world was about to be shattered.

***

Kent Evans died on 28th May 1972 when he fell while mountaineering on Mount Shuksan. It was the second time Lakeside had been hit with tragic news in four months and the whole school was shocked and horrified, but none more so than Bill, Kent's best friend.

Bill felt like he'd never stop crying after Dan Ayrault told him of Kent's death.

Mary held him and when Bill Sr. came back from work that night he took the unusual step of wrapping his son in a huge bear hug.

Nothing helped.

They held the funeral in the chapel at Lakeside. The school's art teacher, Robert Fulghum, was a Unitarian minister like Kent's dad and he officiated over the service. Paul and Ric came back for the funeral but Bill barely registered them through his grief.

Afterwards Bill broke down again and couldn't leave the chapel with everybody else so Fulghum did his best to console him. But nobody really has the words to handle the death of a seventeen year old. Only time could do anything about it.

C:\PART\CHAPTER> 1.5

"Paul, it's me Bill."

Paul hadn't been expecting the call that reached him at Washington University a few weeks after he had returned to college after Kent's funeral.

"Hi Bill, good to hear from you. Is everything okay?" His heart sank with the terrible thought that Bill might be ringing with more bad news.

"Yes, yes everything's fine," Bill replied, instantly grasping what Paul was afraid of.

"Good. Good. So how are you Bill, are you doing okay?"

"Yes... No, well, you know. Anyway, that's not why I'm ringing."

"Okay, go on."

"I've realised... I need... I mean, Kent's death... Oh, shit this is harder than I thought." Bill took a breath and Paul could almost hear the lid snap down on his emotions. Sure enough, when he spoke again his voice had that familiar intensity that Paul recognised from the computer room.

"Kent and I had agreed to write some software to calculate the school schedule."

"Yep, I remember from before...," Paul stumbled over his words, not wanting to mention Kent's death. "From after Mr Haig's plane crash."

"Yes. That's right. Well, I can't do it on my own. It was going to be me and Kent. But I can't pass it on to anyone else. I need to do it. You understand?"

"I understand."

"Will you help me?"

Paul was momentarily surprised but he supposed he shouldn't be, he and Bill had always made a good team even if their ages had separated the Programmers Group into two teams of two along natural fault lines.

"Of course Bill. I'll need to work out how to fit it around college but I'll be there. We'll do it together."

"Thanks Paul."

"No problem. And Bill?"

"Yeah?"

"Kent would be proud."

Bill hung up quickly before his voice broke and gave him away.

***

"The number of variables and constraints is massive," Bill said, explaining the project to Paul. "Everybody submits their preferred classes. Some are mandatory for graduation, most are electives. There's a limit to the number of classes the teachers can teach in a row."

"What's that limit?" Paul asked his pencil poised over his notebook.

"Four," Bill replied. "They've given me a list of kids who we need to keep apart. Some classes require double lab sessions. And the girls…"

Paul interrupted. The girls had arrived in the year he left so the idea of girls at Lakeside was something of a novelty to him.

"Hey I see the tombstone is still on the lawn!"

"Yeah, do you know who put it there?"

"No, funny though."

"Bad Latin."

"So I'm told."

The gravestone was made as a prank and read 'In Memory of the Passing of the Last All Male Lakeside Senior Class 1971' with a Latin epitaph that was supposed to read Long Live Manly Vigor, but had a spelling mistake cast in stone for eternity.

"Anyway, that's not why I brought up the girls. They introduce another constraint. Some of their classes are still at St. Nicholas."

"But that's fifteen minutes away by car."

"Yeah."

"Jesus, you weren't kidding about the number of variables."

"No," Bill said before continuing with his mental list as though the diversion into the novelty of girls hadn't happened at all. "We can't have drums upstairs and choir downstairs…"

***

The two friends quickly fell into their old routine and before long it was just like old times in the computer room at McAlister Hall.

There was the same ability to speak in half formed sentences and know that the other one would grasp their meaning instantly, but it was accompanied by a growing friendship that came from the more equal nature of their relationship. Now that they were slightly older the age gap didn't matter as much.

At first Bill was extremely depressed about Kent's death and on the rare occasions when he would forget himself and have fun for a moment there would be an inevitable flash of guilt immediately afterwards. This was supposed to be his and Kent's project.

But gradually over the summer, Bill and Paul grew closer than they had ever been.

***

Watching his friend, Paul was reminded of why he had found Bill so fascinating from the moment he'd met him. And why it was that his age had never seemed to matter.

Bill was a demon and if anything he seemed to have increased in intensity in the year since Paul had been away. Iit was as though everything about him had been raised to the power of ten. Whether it was a conscious lesson from Kent's death, something subconscious, or simply a function of getting slightly older, everything about him was just slightly... *more*.

"Hey you still do it," Paul said on one occasion.

Bill turned to look at him, took the pencil he was chewing from between his lips and shrugged his shoulders.

"Still do what?" he asked.

"Rock backwards and forwards."

"I do not," Bill said, but he sounded more inquisitive than challenging.

"You do. Any time you're working on something that you're concentrating on, you rock backwards and forwards."

"Hm. My family have said it before but I figured they were making it up." Paul looked puzzled.

"Why would they make it up?"

"I don't know. That hadn't occurred to me."

"So you're not aware of it?"

"I wasn't."

"You do it when you're reading or thinking. I can maybe understand the thinking bit but the reading has always messed with my head. I don't know how you can focus on the page."

***

A couple of weeks into the work they brought some cots into the computer room so that they could work through the night and only fall into bed when they couldn't keep their eyes open any longer. On at least one occasion they didn't even make it to the cot.

One night Paul woke up and became groggily aware that he was still sitting in the chair where he'd been working. He raised his head from the yellow legal pad he had fallen asleep on, a pool of drool briefly connecting him to the notes he'd been writing when he fell asleep. He looked across to the terminal and saw that Bill had also fallen asleep with his head on the desk. Paul smiled.

We must have looked like bookends! Should I get him a blanket? Paul thought, glancing at the cots in the corner.

While he was trying to muster the energy to drag himself to the cots in the corner, Bill jolted awake and, oblivious to Paul watching him, peered intently at the printout on the terminal for thirty seconds and then started typing again, picking up where he had left off whenever he fell asleep.

"I think we might need a break," Paul said.

"What do you mean?"

"Well, I don't know how long you were out, but the last time I saw the clock was about two hours ago and…" he picked up his legal pad and waved it at Bill, "…from what I can tell through my own drool nothing I did for an hour or so before that made any sense."

For a moment he thought Bill would argue but instead he looked quickly back at the code he had been writing and then nodded to Paul.

"A break sounds like a good idea, I'm too wired to sleep though. Well, obviously not quite but you get the point."

"Yeah, me too. Cinema?"

"Sounds good, but none of those foreign films, I'm sick of them. You think they make you look clever but unless you speak Japanese they really don't."

Paul grinned at his friend and grabbed his coat from the rack in the corner. While at college he had developed a taste for foreign films, usually Japanese. Bill obviously thought it was pretentious but then neither of them were above a bit of pretentiousness. And since he'd be driving he was pretty sure which cinema they'd end up in.

***

Finally, with little time to spare a version of the scheduler was finished and ready for a trial run.

Bill entered the test data they'd set up. Four hundred fake students and assignments. They were ready for the moment of truth.

"Ready?" Bill asked.

"Do it,"

Bill hit RUN on the terminal keyboard and the familiar clatter kicked off. They sat back and waited.

And waited.

Finally the machine started printing out results.

This was already better than many of the earlier attempts when the only thing the printer had spat at them was the unwelcome ERROR message.

"Nice one!" Bill said and turned to Paul for a high five.

Paul high-fived him but instantly added a note of caution.

"We don't know for sure if it's worked until we check it."

"Yeah, but look at it Paul, it's a thing of beauty!"

Paul looked down at the printer, then fake rubbed his eyes and peered harder before looking at Bill quizzically.

"We really need to get you to meet more girls," he said and laughed.

Bill joined in and before long both boys were laughing hysterically as the tension of the last few weeks of manic work melted away.

When they finally calmed down the print out was coming to an end, so they sat and watched it finish.

Bill tore the paper from the printer and handed half to Paul without speaking. Paul leant against the wall and read by pulling the paper through his hands, letting the paper pool at his feet. Bill lay the paper on the desk, fell into the chair and bent over until his face was about a foot above the paper. A minute later he was rocking, and a minute after that he started tapping his pencil against the desk.

Paul was used to it by now and didn't even look up.

They both pored over their printouts, looking for anything that broke the constraints they'd entered.

"All good so far," Paul said when he was about halfway through his section. "You?"

"Mhm," Bill replied distractedly, lost in the job.

Paul concentrated on the paper again and kept reading.

Five minutes later Bill jumped from his chair.

"Finished! It's perfect!" he said triumphantly.

Paul, knowing his friend, realised that he'd been in a competition to finish first that hadn't been announced, but he didn't care. He was about half a page away from the end of his own so he simply held up his hand.

Bill waited as patiently as he was capable, shuffling from foot to foot and jigging on the spot as though desperate for the toilet.

Finally Paul looked up and grinned.

"Absolutely perfect!" he said. "Now we just need to run it with the real student info and then you can hand it over. Do you have to go home tonight or shall we stick around and input it now?"

"Let's do it tonight, then I can give it them finished tomorrow."

"Great, why don't you order us a pizza? I'll start setting up the data."

"Tell you what, you get the pizza, I've got a couple of little tweaks I need to make to that data set," Bill said and winked.

Paul looked at him with a raised eyebrow.

"Tweaks such as?"

"Just a couple of things that struck me over the last week or so."

Three hours later, full of pizza and holding a timetable that mysteriously had Bill as the only boy in a class made up of girls he fancied, Bill shook his head in wonder at what the two of them had achieved.

"Amazing," he said. "Do you know it used to take two men all summer to do that manually? Even Haig's computerised version took weeks to iron out by hand after the computer had done all it could."

"It's a neat hack Bill, well done," Paul said, half expecting Bill to reply in kind but he was transfixed by the terminal.

"This is it Paul, this is the future. It's all going to be about computers, and we're going to be right in the middle of it."

"Allen and Gates incorporated!" Paul said and clapped Bill on the shoulder.

"Erm… Gates and Allen incorporated."

They laughed again but this time without the hysteria.

Half a minute later Bill realised the need to congratulate Paul.

"What a team!" he said and stuck out his hand.

Paul flashed back four years to the time he'd met Bill in this very room. He was much shorter then and he'd never have believed that the scruffy haired child could become such a good friend, but standing here now it felt like they could achieve anything.

He took Bill's outstretched hand and shook it. Bill was right, it did feel like the future was waiting.

Allen and Gates. Paul and Bill. No, Bill was right about that as well. Despite the age difference, Bill was the dominant member of their partnership.

Bill and Paul.

No, even that wasn't quite it.

Bill, Paul and *the computer*.

C:\PART\CHAPTER> 1.6

Although the scheduling programme proved what Bill and Paul could achieve by writing good software, it didn't make any real money. But they were both convinced that their new idea would be the one to do that.

Bill already had some agreements up and running from a previous money making effort to transcribe traffic data for the city, but the process was completely manual.

It was nowhere near as complicated as the scheduling programme. Surely it was an opportunity to turn their technical brains to the problem and bring something to it nobody else was and steal a march on the competition.

Bill described it to Paul one night in the computer room during a break between coding bouts on the scheduling programme.

"Have you ever seen those cables that run across the road with big grey boxes on the sidewalk?"

"Yeah."

"Well every time a car passes over the cable the box punches a hole through a tape."

"Eight channel tape?" Paul asked, pointing to the inch wide paper tape on the terminal he was sat in front of at the time.

"Sixteen," Bill replied. "So I agreed with the city that I'd take in the tapes, transcribe them, load the data into a computer and produce a report for them."

"They don't already have an automated reader?" Paul asked, his mind going to exactly the same place that Bill was.

"No. I farm out the basic work to a bunch of lower school kids, some of them even get their moms to help out. They read the tapes and write them up and then I upload them into the machine. I've written a programme that produces some nice graphs once the data is in. The problem is getting the data off the tapes in the first place."

"It's totally manual?"

Bill nodded. "Completely, I'm afraid the kids are going to go blind."

"Doesn't sound like a fun job."

"No, and the uploading isn't exactly a valuable use of my time either. I just basically re-key everything they've done into a PDP-10."

"So you're thinking we automate the reading and uploading process."

"Exactly. Then it's money for old rope. All we have to do is get the city to send us the tapes, we run it through our automated reader-uploader and then my existing programme spits out the reports for them."

"Cool. And you've already got a customer?"

"One yes, but that's just it Paul, think about it. Once we've built the system then we can sell it again and again. It'll just scale up and the money will roll in."

Paul's eyes lit up. Less business minded than Bill he nonetheless liked the idea of earning a living from computers.

"We could sell them to every city government in Washington."

"Every city in the US Paul. In fact why stop there? Local governments all over the world must have to process traffic data, we could sell this to all of them."

"My God, yes, why not? But what do we process it on? Even a cheap minicomputer is going to be thousands of dollars. That'll be okay once we're selling them all over the world but until then we can't afford that sort of outlay."

He briefly looked at Bill. It was no secret between the two of them, or anyone else for that matter, that Bill's family were wealthy. But Bill was having none of it. His family were comfortably well off but they'd taught their son the value of money.

"No, we need to come up with something. Something cleverer than using a minicomputer."

"Wait, why don't we build the hardware ourselves?"

"We don't want to get sucked into hardware Paul, it's not what we're good at. Did you see my tenth grade project? Mr. Maestretti said it looked like Dr. Frankenstein had had a bad day at the office and taken it out on a Meccano set."

Paul laughed.

"No, no, we wouldn't build them all ourselves. The business... we... would get someone to do it. I just mean hardware might be the answer. You've been thinking of software running on an existing platform as the solution right?"

"Of course."

"Well, what if we designed a specialised piece of kit to do it. We could base it around Intel's new 8008 microchip. It has all of the functionality we need for a tiny computer."

Bill grimaced, remembering a conversation they had had about Intel's new chip when it first came out. Paul had been very excited about it and tried to convince Bill that it was going to launch a wave of cheap home computers. The two of them had always agreed that the days of cheap, ubiquitous computers were coming but Bill had shot him down last time. The 8008 was far too underpowered to make a useful computer.

"I told you when it came out the 8008 just doesn't have enough *umph*, enough memory, to act as a computer."

"I remember, and you're not wrong, we need to wait for the next generation for a proper computer on a chip but we don't need this to be a fully fledged computer, do we? It has everything we need. Look..."

Paul jumped up from the chair and started scribbling on the blackboard, describing the key features a traffic analysis machine would need.

Bill peppered him with questions and generally agreed with the answers.

Midway through Paul's list Bill jumped up and joined him, grabbing another piece of chalk and writing. Both of them scribbled on the blackboard, jotting down problems they'd need to solve, occasionally reaching across each other and crossing out something the other had written or finishing a thought, circling two parts of the board and joining them together.

When they had finished they stood back and took in what they'd done, then grinned at each other.

Paul leant forward, grabbed a different coloured chalk and and started ticking things off.

"The 8008 can do it all," he said.

"Yeah, I see it. I like it. But how would we programme the bloody thing? There's not enough memory to write the instructions in. Oh! Hang on..." Bill went quiet and started tapping the side of his head in a staccato rhythm like he was trying to communicate with his subconscious via Morse code. "At your house, years ago... it wasn't long after we met... You showed me an article about someone called... Larry Moss, that's it!"

"A simulator!" Paul said, swept up in the excitement.

"Exactly."

Larry Moss had developed the idea of a simulator a decade earlier in order to let a new IBM machine act like an old one.

"Yeah, we could do that. We write code that tricks a mainframe into thinking it's an 8008."

Bill collapsed back into the chair.

"It'll be easy. We could have this up and running in no time, and we'll make a fortune."

He was wrong. About all of it, actually.

***

They found someone to build it quickly enough. Paul Gilbert, a University of Washington engineering student agreed to build the prototype for them and Bill put up the money so that they could buy one of Intel's new 8008 chips for $360.

It was their partnership's largest capital outlay so far.

When they first got hold of the magical little foil wrapped device, it felt like they were holding their future in their hands. After staring at it for too long, they pulled themselves away and delivered the chip to Gilbert, and left him to work out how to wire it into a machine that could do what they needed.

Paul meanwhile worked on the simulator and the development suite that would let them write software for the 8008 chip on a different machine. Bill wrote the traffic analysis software and started to drum up leads for the new business, which he had decided to call Traf-O-Data rather than 'Gates and Allen Inc.'

They had them ready for the time that Bill had to return to school in the summer but the engineering itself was a nightmare. Paul Gilbert struggled valiantly to get the machine to work but the memory chips that went with the 8008 were so flaky that the whole thing just wouldn't function a good deal of the time.

Gilbert would spend a good deal of the next year working on getting it to work.

However, that wasn't their biggest problem.

Their biggest problem was that the government, having spotted exactly the same problem as Bill and Paul, had stepped in and offered to collate all of the traffic data for cities who were interested.

And they were doing it for free.

It's hard to compete with free.

Traf-O-Data was effectively dead before it was born, although the boys didn't know it yet and continued to plough ahead. In the meantime Paul had a job to do and Bill needed to go to college.

***

"They want me to be normal," Bill told Paul on the phone one evening. Paul snorted.

"Fat chance!" he said.

"I know! I'm not convinced college is worth bothering with. I told them I want to do something with computers. Maybe make Traf-O-Data work and if not then something else, but they think college will do me good. They both loved it. It's where they met, did I ever tell you that?"

"I don't think so."

"Well, it was, so they reckon it'll be good for me."

"Do they think you're going to find a wife?"

"Ha! No, they just want me to mix with people who aren't so into computers."

"So I'm a bad influence."

"I'm pretty sure they think it's the other way around."

"Where've you applied then?" Paul asked.

"Everywhere you'd expect."

He meant Harvard, Yale and Princeton.

"Are you sure you want to go? I mean, I love Wazzu," as he called Washington University. "But the classes are dull. The things I love are the sorts of things you'd be less interested in. The frat house, jam sessions on my guitar, that kind of thing."

"The people bits," Bill said with a self-deprecating roll of the eyes.

"The people bits," Paul confirmed. "And although you're a standout at math here it'll be different at college, at least it will at the colleges you've applied to. There'll be people who are smarter than you."

"Pah! That doesn't worry me, I like being with people smarter than me."

Paul wasn't completely convinced, but didn't push it.

"Some of them will be better than you at math."

"Yeah… Yeah. Well, probably." Bill said, hesitantly. "But if it bothers me I'll just try harder."

Paul dropped it.

C:\PART> 2: ALBUQUERQUE VIA MASSACHUSETTS

C:\PART\CHAPTER> 2.1

Bill got offers from all of the colleges he'd applied to. In the end he chose to go to Harvard.

He spent his first year in a shared dorm room in Wigglesworth Hall with two other guys, Sam Znaimer and Jim Jenkins, having asked specifically to room with an international student and an African American. As well as the inevitable computer science courses, he enrolled in economics and applied math classes and for a while he followed the usual college routine (amended slightly to suit his now established pattern of working for long hours at a stretch, collapsing, grabbing pizza and going again). But it wouldn't last.

Bill had always worn his intelligence like a badge and Harvard was no different. Lots of people at Harvard were quietly intelligent. Not Bill. He liked to argue and it was important that you knew he'd won. One of the first things that his Harvard classmates would say about him when remembering him in later years was that he was one of the smartest people they'd ever met. However, the truth is, it didn't take long to discover that Paul had been right. There were plenty of people there smarter than him, and some of them were even better at math.

Bill started spending time with one of those maths geeks, Andy Braiterman, who lived upstairs in Wigglesworth and they decided to room together the next year. They were assigned to Currier House. Currier was one of the few co-ed dorms, which as Bill would say later in life, sadly made no practical difference to him whatsoever but it did improve his view.

By the time he was a sophomore, perhaps driven by the realisation that he would never be the best mathematician, or the best economist, Bill had revised his approach to college life. He refused to attend any classes he was enrolled in, instead choosing to sit in on other classes that he thought would be interesting but for which he couldn't get a grade.

And he became obsessed with poker, engaging in all night games with the Currier House crowd. Despite his math skills he never stood out and is remembered as a perfectly competent but middling player, something that would have surprised people who later sat across a negotiating table from him.

To handle the exams for the classes he was enrolled in he would engage in marathon reading sessions beforehand, cramming his memory with the information he would need to pass the exam. It was unorthodox, which of course was the point, but it worked.

On a couple of those cramming sessions he was joined by a new friend he had made, Steve Ballmer. Steve was a big guy and an even bigger presence. Full of energy, he had the same argumentative intellect as Bill. Steve was much more outgoing than Bill but the two became close friends. Steve even tapped Bill to join the Fox Club, one of the all male final clubs that Harvard had in those days.

The most important thing that happened to Bill at Harvard though had nothing to do with classes, not the ones he was enrolled in or the ones he was actually attending, it had nothing to do with Steve (yet, at least) and it had nothing to do with poker.

It started when Paul came banging on his door one day in December 1974.

***

Andy Braiterman and Bill both nearly jumped out of their skin when someone pounded on their door.

"Who the hell is that?!" Braiterman said sitting upright in his bed.

"Beats me," Bill said. "I'll find out."

He pushed his chair back from where he had been sitting at the desk reading but he hadn't got as far as standing up before they found out.

"Bill!" came Paul's voice through the door. "Bill, open up! It's Paul we've got to talk."

Bill took two long strides across the small room and flung open the door, expecting to find his friend with a terrible problem.

"Jesus Paul, are you alright?"

Paul fell into the room, panting and Bill stood aside to let him.

Braiterman looked at him oddly. The two of them knew each other slightly through Bill but weren't friends.

"Hey Allen, you want to keep it down a bit?"

"Sorry Braiterman," Paul stuttered out through rasping breaths.

Braiterman shook his head at his odd roommate and his friend, rolled over and tried to ignore the pair of them.

Paul straightened up, dug into his jacket pocket and pulled out a rolled up magazine and thrust it under Bill's face, forgetting that the other man was even there.

"Look at this. Bill, it's here. And we're going to miss it."

"What's here?"

Bill took the magazine from him and unrolled it. When he saw the cover he knew exactly what Paul was talking about.

The magazine was the new issue of *Popular Electronics* and on the cover was a picture of what would have looked to most people, Braiterman included, like nothing more than a box with switches on.

In fact it *was* nothing more than a box with switches on because the picture was a mock up but Bill and Paul didn't know that at the time.

What had caught Paul's attention ten minutes earlier when he was crossing the quad was the headline.

World's First Minicomputer Kit to Rival Commercial Models... "ALTAIR 8800"

"Is this what I think it is?" Bill said, excitement starting to mount.

"Page thirty three."

Bill flicked through the magazine until he found the page and started reading. Paul sat down on Bill's bed and waited quietly, his own excitement put on pause until he could share it.

After a minute Bill, without looking up from the magazine, sat back down at the little desk and started rocking backwards and forwards.

Paul smiled.

Bill read as fast as he could, tuning the pages of the six page article that the Altair's inventor Ed Roberts had written. Much of it was very basic, designed for electronics enthusiasts rather than people like him and Paul who were already familiar with computers, so he was done in no time.

He sat up and shook his head in wonder at Paul.

"You're right, this is it!" He jumped up and shook Allen's shoulders. "My God this is it!"

"That's what I was telling you!"

Braiterman pulled his headphones away from his head and eyed them grumpily.

"Guys? Bring me in or pipe down."

"Sorry Andy."

Braiterman nodded and when Bill didn't say anything more he guessed he'd gone for the second option. He dropped the cans back on his head and closed his eyes.

"This is so cool," Bill said, only barely quieter. He glanced down at the article again and shook his head in amazement. "I've never even heard of MITS though, have you?"

"No."

MITS were the manufacturer of the Altair. A small outfit in Albuquerque run by a man named Ed Roberts, MITS had originally made electronic calculators but had been priced out of the market by Texas Instruments and other larger companies. On the verge of bankruptcy Roberts had invented the Altair 8800 and switched his company away from making calculators and into the as yet untapped home computer market.

The Altair really was revolutionary but, despite the editorial in the magazine proudly proclaiming that 'the home computer age is here...' the homes in question would have to be occupied by electronic hobbyists. The Altair arrived in kit form and the new owner had to solder it all together themselves.

"We'll have to see what we can find out about them," Bill said. "It says it's based on the Intel 8080. You know more about chips than me, what do you know about the 8080?"

"It's got 64k of directly addressable memory, a 2 megahertz clock speed and a 40 pin form factor. Although that doesn't matter to us it should make it easier for MITS to build into a proper computer."

"Cool! So we're not talking the 4004 here?" referring to the first time Paul had tried to convince Bill they could build a home computer.

"No. Or even the 8008 we're using in the Traff-O-Data machine."

"This thing could do real work," Bill said in a tone of genuine wonder, before he instantly fell back into character and added, "Have you seen his list of possible applications though? 'Brain for a robot', Jesus! "

"Yep, the build-your-own-robot-butler project is probably in next month's issue. But Bill, we've got to do something with this. If we don't do something fast we'll have missed our shot."

"I agree, but what can we do? Looks like he's got the machine built and anyway if the Traf-O-Data thing has taught us anything it's that we're really software guys."

Paul paced up and down the small room and tried to throw out ideas.

"What about using them as the basis for a complete traffic analysis set up? We could buy the kits from MITS, get someone to put them together and install your analysis programme straight on to them."

Bill looked underwhelmed.

"We're struggling to find takers and the federal government have started to make noises that they might do it if states ask. I'm beginning to wonder if there might not be the market we'd hoped for," he said distractedly and then fell silent again.

Bill drummed his fingers on the top of the desk as though he was typing.

"What about doing something for the users?" he said a moment later. "The article says 'a computer in every home' haven't we been saying the same thing for years?"

"Yes but it's not real is it? I mean can you see your folks inputting machine language through switches?" Paul said.

"Ha! No, not even my mom."

"Exactly, it's really still for hobbyists like us."

"Maybe some electronics guys who would have used them if it didn't mean finding a timeshare," Bill said, hopefully.

"Most of them probably aren't going to bother learning machine language either," Paul said despairingly.

"No, probably not. Shame."

"Yep."

They both fell silent again, thinking.

Suddenly Bill sat up straight.

"That's it."

"What is?"

"What you just said. My mom isn't going to programme in machine language but neither are electronics fans. Basically unless you're already interested in computers the Altair isn't going to be exciting at all. Listen. Hey, Braiterman!" He stretched out and kicked Andy's foot to get his attention.

Braiterman opened his eyes with a start.

"What is it Gates?"

"If you had to learn machine language to get a computer to, I don't know, compute the pancake flipping problem, would you do it?"

Braiterman pushed himself up in his bed. The pancake flipping problem was a well known sorting problem in mathematics. It was given to the students of Math 55, the course that Andy and Bill took together. Bill had produced a solution which stood as the best one for twenty nine years and was the subject of his only published maths paper.

"Machine language. I guess that's a structured language right?" Bill and Paul both nodded. "And how long did it take you to learn it?"

"About a week," Bill said.

Paul rolled his eyes.

"More like a month," he said.

Braiterman shrugged.

"If I needed to do it as part of my dissertation then yeah I suppose I would. Doesn't sound like fun though."

"See?" Bill said to Paul. "And that's Braiterman. He's already a geek, if he's not sure then what are the chances of a computer appearing in every home."

"Okay, I get it but how does that help us?"

"It means machine language is the weak link. MITS is going to need to get BASIC. Anyone could learn BASIC. Even Andy," Braiterman flicked him off. "It would make the Altair really useful but Roberts doesn't mention it at all in the article."

"You don't think he's written one," Paul said, getting where Bill was heading.

"Exactly. That's our niche. We'll write BASIC for the Altair like I did for the PDP-8 at Lakeside and Roberts can sell it with the Altair."

C:\PART\CHAPTER> 2.2

"Any reply from Roberts?" Bill asked Paul a week later.

"No, still nothing."

The day of their first conversation in Currier House Paul had sent a letter to Roberts at MITS offering their services to produce a version of BASIC for the Altair.

"You should ring him."

"I don't want to ring him."

"Why not?" Bill asked, witheringly.

"Well, if it's no big deal then why don't you ring him?"

Bill didn't have an answer to that so he tried another angle.

"You look older than me though, and you know what it's been like dealing with some of the city representatives on the traffic stuff. Their first thought when they see me is that we're too young to take seriously. We shouldn't give ourselves another hurdle to overcome."

"True but we're not meeting him are we? We're ringing him."

"Hm."

"Okay, what about this, you ring him and use my name, then when we need to meet him in person I'll fly down."

Bill paused for a fraction of a second.

"Agreed."

He picked up the phone and dialled the number for MITS. Luckily for Bill and Paul MITS was still a small enough operation that they got hold of Roberts without any difficulty.

Bill put on his best telephone voice.

"Mr. Roberts, this is Paul Allen of Traf-O-Data," he said. "You might have got my letter of a week ago."

"Not that I'm aware of Mr. Allen, what was it about?"

"Our company was very impressed with your development of the Altair 8088. It's obviously going to make a huge impact in the computing world, but we think there's a piece missing that will help it change the wider world and deliver on your goal to have a computer, an Altair, in every home."

Bill waited, hoping Roberts would be hooked before he revealed their revolutionary idea.

"And what's that then Mr. Allen?" Roberts sounded amused if anything.

"BASIC," Bill said simply and paused to give Roberts time to drink it in before continuing. "We think if you provide a BASIC interpreter with the Altair it will open up the machine to a much wider market. And we would like to help you. We've already got an interpreter that works on Intel's 8080 that you could sell to your customers."

"That sounds like a great idea Mr. Allen," Roberts said. Bill gave Paul a thumbs up and started to smile but his face dropped when Roberts continued, "But like I told all the other fellas who said the same thing, I need to see it working on the machine. The first person who shows me that can have the contract."

"Great," Bill said. "That'll be us. When can we show it to you?"

"My guys are still working on the Altair memory boards so you've got a month. Let's speak again and we can agree a date for you to come down. Good talking to you Mr. Allen."

"You too Mr. Roberts," Bill replied but the MITS CEO had already hung up.

Paul was sitting in the chair next to Bill so he could hear both sides of the conversation and his eyes bugged out when he heard the last exchange. Let alone not having a BASIC for the 8080 they had never even seen one, in fact they'd never even seen a full set of specs for one, how the hell were they supposed to write one in a month?!

***

"Who was that?" Bill Yates, Ed's right hand man, asked his boss as he put the phone down.

"No-one I've ever heard of. Paul Allen from Traff-O-something, you heard of 'em?"

Bill Yates shook his head.

"Well, he sounds like a kid," Ed said. "But he says he's got a BASIC for the Altair."

"Do you reckon they have?"

"No! This is the hundredth call I've had since the magazine came out, none of them really have one."

"So why did you tell him to come down?"

"Maybe he'll write it." Ed shrugged carelessly.

"You reckon?"

"This kid? No. But one of the guys who phones us will come good so we have to keep them all at it."

***

When Ed Roberts had said his team were still working on the memory boards, he had inadvertently given away the fact that there wasn't really a working Altair in the world that could have run BASIC. Even the real machines, as opposed to the mockup in the magazine, didn't have enough memory to do much more than turn on. Roberts had run the advert to drum up interest while his team finished the memory boards that would be necessary to get the machine to do anything useful.

But the fact that there was no way Bill and Paul could write their BASIC using the Altair didn't put them off. With the experience they had of building a simulator for the Traf-O-Data they knew that they could programme the chip using a bigger more powerful machine.

Knew it in theory at least.

"How will we get it done in time? The end of the month is three weeks away," Paul said.

"We've got a head start on all of the competition, you've already done a simulator and I've written a BASIC. We know what we're doing."

Paul didn't share Bill's confidence, he knew they were good programmers but he figured this could be like Bill's Harvard maths experience. Sure they were good but lots of people were good, were they really the best?

And Bill had barely got anywhere with the BASIC he was claiming to have 'written' for the PDP-8. He'd planned it out and made a start but then Lakeside had to return the machine they'd borrowed so he never actually got around to finishing it.

"Maybe MITS won't be ready by the end of the month themselves," he said, more to convince himself it was possible than Bill.

But Bill wasn't interested in taking the pressure off, he thrived under pressure.

"We can't take that chance," he said. "We have to try to meet the deadline. And anyway, even if they're not ready if someone else gets to them first then they'll get the deal."

"I know that's what Roberts said but he can't be serious!"

"Doesn't matter, does it? We don't know this guy, we need to assume he meant it and we need to beat everybody else."

Paul smiled, Bill's hyper-competitive nature was fired up despite not even knowing if anybody else was really trying. The idea that someone else might beat him was enough.

"Okay, what do we do now then?" Paul said.

"We need to just plan it out and then get it done."

It was that simple as far as Bill was concerned, just plan it and get it done. Luckily for the two students they were completely unaware that the more experienced engineers at both Intel and MITS thought that fitting a BASIC onto the 8080 was impossible. And they were lucky that Paul found Bill's confidence infectious.

"We need to update the simulator and development tools from the 8008 you did for Traf-O-Data to work on the 8080," Bill said.

"And we need to write a version of BASIC that's different enough to be ours."

"Definitely, if anyone can just copy it and claim it as their own then we make no money and there's no point. But differentiating it enough is not hard, the difficult bit is going to be getting it to fit into the Altair's memory."

"I think I should do the simulator and tools again. It would be stupid to start from scratch and I know the Traf-O-Data ones better than you," Paul said.

"Agreed," Bill agreed. "I'll write the BASIC interpreter."

***

They had worked without a break for almost forty eight hours. Paul had skipped work at Honeywell, while Bill had skipped all of his classes and even ignored his poker game. Neither of them had slept.

After they had divided up the work they gathered up all of the yellow legal pads and felt-tip pens that Bill kept in his room and rushed over to the Aiken Computer Lab on Oxford Street.

Paul had spent the time since then printing off his original code and identifying all of the changes he'd need to make. Bill had been scribbling incessantly on his pads, using the different coloured pens in a rainbow code for which the key existed in his head.

He started with diagrams, the discarded pages crumpled up and dropped to the floor around him, the successful ideas were either left in the pad or more often ripped out and tacked to the wall in front of him so that he could refer to them easily. Halfway through his second pad he switched from the block diagrams to a mix of half formed sentences and machine code written in his left handed scrawl.

Paul stood up and stretched.

"I think I've got it," Paul said to the top of Bill's head where he was hunched over his pad viciously attacking it with a green pen. "I've added all of the new instructions and updated the debugger. I still need to input it and check it out. And there'll be other bits of course, but this is the core." He tapped the pad he'd been writing on.

"Cool," Bill replied.

Bill still hadn't looked up but Paul was used to it, he knew Bill would have taken it in and 'hear' it later if necessary. He also knew this was going to be a long sprint though so they needed to make sure they kept well fed.

He checked his watch. It was 11:15pm their favourite takeaway place would still be open.

"Pizza?" he said.

That got Bill's attention properly.

"Sounds like a plan," he said and straightened himself up, stretching his neck just as Paul had done a minute ago.

"House of Pizza?" he said.

"Definitely."

***

"I've been thinking," Paul said twenty minutes later through a mouthful of House of Pizza's Harvard Special grinder, a Boston term for a sub sandwich.

The two of them were walking back to the computer lab along Massachusetts Avenue.

"Hmph?" Bill asked, his own mouth stuffed with pizza.

"What about Gilbert?"

"What about him?" Bill replied once he'd swallowed his bite.

"Well, I'm going to be using the tools we invented for the Traf-O-Data work for the Altair and he's part of Traf-O-Data, isn't he?"

"So?"

"So, don't we owe him a cut?"

"No." Bill frowned slightly and shook his head, confused.

"Ha! *'No'* that's it?!" Paul laughed. "Bill you can be brutal."

"No I can't. I mean, yes I can, I suppose but I'm not being now. Why should he be cut into this?"

"We did Traf-O-Data with him, he's still working on it and I'm using all of the tools I made for it as the basis for this."

"There you said it yourself, the tools *you* made. Look, Gilbert's a good guy but he has nothing to do with this. This is software Paul, that's you and me, it isn't Gilbert. And the Traf-O-Data thing might still take off, if it does then he'll get his fair share, but just because we did that one thing with him doesn't mean we're married to him."

"Hm, I guess you're right."

"I am. I tell you what I'll write up a contract for Traf-O-Data and we'll all sign it. Split the proceeds of that nice and legal, and make it clear that none of us have an ongoing claim on the others for any other work we might do. Sound fair?"

"Yep."

"Good."

They walked in silence for a minute, enjoying their food. When they got to Everett they turned left and headed for the lab.

"How's the BASIC interpreter coming?"

"Hm, alright," Bill replied, scrunching up his face in a way that said it wasn't as easy as he'd expected. "I'm not worried about which functions to choose. There's a pretty obvious start point in DEC's top of the range RSTS-11, and then it's just about picking the most essential functions and stripping out anything we can do without. The issue is exactly what I said at the beginning, pulling it back far enough so it fits into 4K of memory."

"Have you trie…" Paul began but was cut off by the approach of a campus policeman.

"Good evening gentlemen."

"Hi officer," Bill said, coming to a stop.

"Where are you headed?"

"The Aiken Lab," Bill said and pointed in the general direction with his pizza.

"Can I see some ID, please?"

"Sure," Bill said and produced his student ID.

The policeman took it and gave it a quick once over.

"And yours?" he said, turning to Paul.

"I'm not a student here."

"But you're going to the computer lab?"

"He's with me," Bill said.

"It's a bit late at night to be bringing a friend in, isn't it, sir?"

Paul looked worried but the exhaustion and frustration made Bill bite.

"What difference does it make to you? I'm a student here. I have access privileges to Aiken and I'm vouching for him. Do you think if we were going to rob the place we'd have started off by grabbing pizza?" he said sarcastically, waving his pizza at the man.

"It doesn't matter Bill, leave it," Paul said.

"No, this is ridiculous. You know there are real crimes you could be doing something about, right?"

"I'm just doing my job, sir."

"Yeah, well, do it on someone else. Come on Paul, we're going."

***

About four weeks after they'd first spoken to Roberts Bill and Paul were in the dining room at Currier House.

"I could do it but that would mean slowing down work on the simulator," Paul said and then eyed Bill and flicked his head towards the freshman with a mop of curly hair on the other side of the table. He looked like he was listening in.

Bill glanced his way but just shrugged, even in the math savvy crowd at Currier House most people wouldn't have a clue about computers and he was confident no-one could work out the detail anyway.

"Well, I'm the same, it's not like it's too difficult. It's just not as important as finishing the interpreter script. If I don't sort that then we've got nothing."

"Maybe we don't include floating points? Not every BASIC can handle it."

The freshman's hair bobbed and he cleared his throat but Bill carried on seemingly oblivious.

"I'd rather avoid that if we can. We want it to be as rich as possible."

"Maybe we should both drop everything else for a week and just crank this out."

"I think we may have to, even if it means a delay," Bill said, sighing and turning away from Paul. Seeing that the lad opposite had carried on following every word he finally snapped, "Can I help you?"

The boy's eyes bulged but he held his ground.

"No, but I think I might be able to help you," he stammered out.

"What do you mean?"

"Well, I couldn't help but overhear," he said, and Paul snorted. "That you're trying to write a floating point routine in BASIC?"

"Yeah. You know anything about them?" Bill asked, it was unlikely but this was a Harvard dining room after all.

"I wrote one for a PDP-8 a couple of years back. I could give you a hand with your project."

"Oh yeah?" Paul said. "How many bits did you use for the exponent?"

"Eight," Monte replied, getting the feeling he was being tested. "And twenty-three for the mantissa."

"Are thirty two bit numbers enough?"

Bill pointed his fork at Monte aggressively but Monte wasn't fazed.

"It's a trade-off," he said calmly. "I think thirty two bits is more than enough for most uses but can be implemented in most systems."

The questioning carried on through lunchtime, all three of them forgetting their food. Bill and Paul exchanged looks throughout and occasionally nodded. Eventually Paul speared another forkful of fries and realised they were cold.

Midway through the grilling Monte twigged that these guys weren't doing a college assignment.

"What's it all about? There's more to this than a college project, isn't there?" Monte asked.

"Yep, a lot more," Paul said. He looked questioningly at Bill and Bill waved his finger in a 'carry-on' motion. "Have you heard of the Altair?"

"No, should I have?"

"Not yet but if everything goes to plan then pretty soon most people will have. It's a new computer designed for the home."

"Wow."

"I know. And we," he pointed to himself and Bill. "Are selling a BASIC to the manufacturers."

"But first we have to finish writing it," Bill chimed in.

"And you haven't done the floating point routines," Monte said.

"Exactly. Either of us could do it…"

"Obviously, based on your questions," Monte said.

"Yeah, but we can't afford to stop what we're doing."

"Well, you can count me in if you want," Monte said excitedly, then immediately looked troubled. "Are you planning to use the college's PDP-10?"

Bill shrugged.

"Why not?"

"Are you allowed? It's not for university work."

"Who cares? The computers in the lab are for students. We're students."

Paul rubbed his beard thoughtfully, remembering his earlier interaction with campus police. "Well, I'm not am I?"

"Oh yeah," Bill said and hesitated for a fraction of a second. "I still don't see how it matters, I'm a student and I'm inviting you to work with me."

"On a non-university commercial project," Monte said.

Bill frowned. "Yeah," he said.

"And you think the college will be okay with that?"

"Look, if you don't want to join us, you don't have to."

"No, no, that's not what I'm saying. I just wanted to know if you had permission, that was all."

"Well, we don't."

"Might be worth asking," Paul said thoughtfully.

Bill drummed his fingers on the table, obviously thinking about it properly for the first time.

"Nah," he said after a brief pause. "I don't see how anyone will even notice and if they do then they still wouldn't object. And if they do object then screw 'em. Professors use the university's library to research the books that they publish and they're commercial projects. It's just the same."

Paul thought that it was possible the college bursars might see a small difference between the basically free library and the time sharing computer that the college used but he wasn't going to pass up the chance for free computer time, especially if it was their best shot at joining the infant computer industry.

"Cool, let's get to it. Are you in Monte?" he asked and when the other boy nodded he stood up. "Shall we take this back to your room then Bill?"

C:\PART\CHAPTER> 2.3

Bill and Paul agreed to pay Monte for his work on the math, though there was no question of him having an ownership stake in anything that came of it. They reserved that for themselves, just as they had with Gilbert.

Before long Monte had joined them in the Aiken Lab working around the clock to finish the job. He fitted in perfectly.

Once they'd explained to him that the goal wasn't just to write a BASIC but to squeeze it into a tiny amount of memory he threw himself completely into the challenge.

One afternoon early on into their partnership he got a lesson in the dynamic between the two men.

"What do you think of this?" he said.

"Not bad at all," Paul said. "I can see what you've done here." He pointed at a bit of code.

"I like how you've handled the guard digits, but it's a bit bloated don't you think?" Bill said.

"Bloated?" Monte parroted back.

"It needs to be tighter," Paul said.

"We can't afford any wasted bytes," Bill said. "We need to leave as much space for the customer to write programmes in as possible and memory is expensive."

"Yeah, I get that but it's not possible to get this into less than twenty lines."

"Don't be stupid, you can always find a way to reduce it. I could do it in less," Bill insisted.

Monte frowned and looked at Paul for back up but he didn't get any.

"He's right, it could be smaller."

"Alright, prove it," Monte said. "You've seen mine now anyway so we'll all take a copy and see if we can do the same thing in less space."

Bill and Paul started to speak at the same time.

"I don't know, I'm working on…" Paul began.

"You're on," Bill said. Then, when he heard what Paul was saying he switched gears, "Come on Paul, it's the only way the youngster will learn, we're in a place of education."

The whole thing was good natured but there was an edge under it that was obvious to all three of them.

"Okay," Paul said. "But we're only spending an hour on this okay? Then I have to get back to work and you've both got stuff you should be concentrating on. We can't all spend all night writing the same thing."

"Agreed," Bill said, instructing the machine to print out two more copies of Monte's code.

"Works for me," said Monte. "I'll look at it again but if I can't make it any smaller after fifteen minutes, I'll get on with my next thing."

Bill collected the printouts, reading as he walked back from the printer and then handed one to Paul.

"Everybody ready?"

"Yep."

"Yeah."

"Okay, go!"

They all took a corner of the room and silence descended while they concentrated.

The first sound was Monte groaning with frustration, when he saw that he could combine two of his statements into a single line.

While he worked he could see the other two out of the corner of his eye, darting glances towards each other when they thought they weren't being watched. He knew they had a history that went back to high school, and they were obviously great friends but it was equally obvious that they both wanted to win. Neither of them looked in his direction even once. He was collateral damage here.

After his original fifteen minute deadline passed Monte had shaved another line off his original twenty but was reluctant to show his hand. The other two were still bent over their paper, scribbling furiously.

Finally, seventeen minutes after they started, Paul finished.

"I can do it in thirteen lines," he almost shouted, waving his paper in the air.

"No way," Monte said, pushing himself up from his chair and wandering over to check how Paul had done it.

Bill continued rocking but otherwise didn't move or acknowledge his friend's comment. Monte read through Paul's incredibly tight code and was astonished to find out he was right. He had produced the same outputs in almost half the code.

"This is brilliant," he said.

"Thanks, it's fun when you start to…"

From across the room Bill interrupted.

"I've got it in seven!" he said, as he hurried over to show them what he'd done.

Paul rolled his eyes.

"He can't have done," Monte said.

"Don't be too sure," Paul replied under his breath.

"What do you think of that then?!" Bill said as he slapped his paper down on Paul's desk.

"Where's my code?" Monte said, looking at the blank printer paper that Bill had written on.

"It's on the back. In the end I thought it was better to start again."

Monte started to say something then thought better of it and concentrated on reading first, but Paul had already finished.

"Neat job. You're missing a command though. You need a couple of additional lines." He reached across and drew an arrow out of the middle of Bill's listing then wrote in two new lines of code.

"No I haven't, let me see that." Bill pushed past Monte and picked up his paper again. His eyes narrowed and his lips moved silently while he read Paul's additions and tried to do without them. Finally he handed the paper back to Paul. "Oh. Oh okay, so I did it in nine. I still win."

Paul nodded. "Yep, you win."

Bill grinned and then the smile dropped from his face, all business again.

"Right, back on with it then. Monte, use the new code for your subroutine. I've got to speak to MITS about those input/output commands."

And with that Bill stalked off back to the far corner of the room to make his phone call.

"How the hell did he do that? It took me all morning to write the original.

"He's like an idiot savant," Paul said to lighten the mood. "He has these flashes, he really is an amazing programmer particularly when it comes to paring things back. It's kind of like his speciality."

But Monte wasn't placated.

"What's the point of me doing any of this if you guys can do the same thing but tighter?"

"We've spent ages doing this sort of thing, you haven't. You were on the right lines, you just need to keep your mind on the cleanest implementation possible."

"If I was on the right lines then why didn't he start with my code like you did?"

"It wouldn't have looked as dramatic would it? Look again at what he did, he used the thinking you'd done and just did it better."

"That's not fair. He took credit for my work."

Paul frowned.

"Hey, hang on that's not what I'm saying." He tapped Bill's code. "This is better than the version you did. Much better, it uses less than half the space yours does. All I'm saying is that he didn't do it alone. And when the bluster of a competition is over he wouldn't pretend he did. He wouldn't have got to his version anywhere near as quickly without your work, and you didn't get to an implementation as tight as his. Who cares who did which bit? The best stuff comes when you can't pick apart your ideas from someone else's. That's what working as a team is about."

Monte looked hangdog for a moment but it didn't last long as Bill was coming back, shouting to them as he crossed the room.

"Guys, listen this is great! I spoke to Yates at MITS."

"Did he give us the instructions for the teletype?" Paul asked.

"He said he'll give us a bell back with them," he continued in a normal voice as he arrived back at Paul's desk. "But that's not the point. When I asked him he was surprised. He let slip that no-one else had asked for them."

"But you need the specs to interact with any sort of teleprinter," Monte said. "If no-one's asked for them then it means no-one else is anywhere near where we are."

"Exactly."

"So that means..." Monte started.

"That means we get to work fast. We've got to get this thing finished as soon as possible and capitalise on our lead."

"I'll get back on it. Thanks for the talk Paul,"

"No worries."

"And the coding lesson Bill," he added with a wry smile.

Bill's brow wrinkled in surprise, finally noticing that Monte was bothered by the rewrite.

"Hey Monte, you know what John Norton told me at RODS?" Norton was a programming legend Bill and Paul had briefly worked with over the summer on control room software for Bonneville Power. "The most important work is in the architecture, the conceptual framework for the programme. If you get that wrong then however tight your code you're just running faster and faster along the wrong path. Your framework was good Monte."

Monte's chest swelled slightly. "Thanks Bill, I'll get back at it."

When he'd gone Paul smiled at Bill, weirdly proud of his friend's rare moment of inspirational leadership.

"Nice one Bill, he needed that," he said, and chuckled when Bill shrugged one shoulder. He still didn't get it but at least he had done the right thing. He moved on. "This is exciting, Bill. We're going to catch it, aren't we?"

"We're going to catch it Paul."

***

One thousand, four hundred miles southeast of Seattle, Yates headed across the MITS factory floor and knocked on the door to Roberts' office.

"Y'alright Bill?" Ed asked.

"Yeah, I just got off the phone with the Traf-O-Data guys."

"Allen?"

"His pal Gates. Anyway, I reckon they might be the ones to make the BASIC."

"You're joking, those kids?"

"No joke, he rang to ask about the subroutines we use for connecting the Altair to a teleprinter."

"They must be near enough finished then."

"Yeah but more importantly it made me think, nobody else has asked me about it. Anyone spoken to you?"

"No."

"There you go then. I reckon they're going to be the first ones. You still okay with it being them if they can do it? They're obviously young."

"Well, we'd have to agree contracts and all, but I don't care how young they are if they can make it work. We need to get something we can offer with the machine. If we can sell it with BASIC then it will give it another bounce in advertising. In fact them being young might even help, the last thing I want is someone who thinks they're the boss."

"True," Yates said. He got along with Roberts but the bluff Georgian was a fiery character and he couldn't picture someone else cut from the same cloth fitting in very well.

"Tell you what Bill, next time they call set up a date for a meeting."

***

A week later Paul was sitting on a plane, waiting to take off to Albuquerque to meet Roberts at MITS and demonstrate their BASIC.

He was feeling as rested as was possible in the circumstances.

Monte had finished his math routines four days earlier and Bill's interpreter appeared to work perfectly on the simulator Paul had written, but the night before, when it was time to commit the programme to tape, Bill had had an uncharacteristic bout of self-doubt.

"If there's a single mistake then you're flying the length of the country to stand in a room and have nothing happen. That's a long way to go to be embarrassed," he'd said.

"We've done everything we can. And it isn't just down to you, the same is true if I've cocked up the simulator. You need to let it go now, just print it out."

"I have to check it one last time Paul. But listen, you go home and get a good night's sleep so you're ready."

"No, come on we're a team. If you're staying, I'm staying. Fire it up," he said pointing at the terminal.

But in another surprising flash of leadership Bill insisted.

"We are a team and it's all going to be on you tomorrow, let me do this. I'm sure you're right but I want to be one hundred percent. Go home and swing by here on your way to the airport tomorrow. I'll have the tape ready to go."

"Okay pal, if you're sure?"

"I'm sure."

When Paul had turned up at the lab this morning he'd found Bill asleep behind the PDP-10's memory banks. A massive printout of their code carpeted the floor and he was dismayed when he saw the amount of scribble in a rainbow of colours, but a wave of relief washed over him when saw that all of the routines seemed to be have a tick in green felt tip next to them. That had to be a good sign.

On the top of the printer was a roll of paper tape, the precious programme, on top of it was a note from Bill.

Paul,
The future.
Don't wake me. Call me when you're there.
Bill.

He looked at the volume of notes and realised that Bill could only have gone to 'bed' half an hour earlier.

He gathered up the code as quietly as he could and placed it all on the desk Bill usually used along with another note.

Thanks for last night, I needed it.
Call you from AQ.
Paul.

It had gone right up to the wire but now everything was ready. Paul settled back into the seat and tried to relax so he'd be at his best.

Not long before landing he started to rehearse the presentation he'd be making in his head. A second later he sat bolt upright.

"Crap!" he said. *We haven't written a loader!*

"I beg your pardon," said the old woman sitting in the aisle seat next to him.

"I'm sorry ma'am," he said automatically, he hadn't realised he'd said it out loud.

Without a loader Paul would have nothing to show at MITS.

It didn't matter how good their code was, without a proper bootup sequence the Altair would just sit there not knowing how to process the data on their tape.

The only option now would be for Paul to enter a bootup sequence by hand, flipping the switches on the Altair's front panel to enter the full code. But before he could do that he'd need to write one and he was supposed to be meeting Roberts at the airport to go straight to the factory.

He'd have to write it before they landed.

I can do this, he thought. *I can write it while we fly.*

He turned to the woman next to him again.

"Excuse me ma'am, I'm heading for a business meeting and I just realised I forgot to do something really important. Can I get to my overhead bag?"

The woman took a sharp intake of breath but started unbuckling her belt. Excruciatingly slowly.

Unfortunately before she could stand up the seatbelt light came on and the steward announced that they were preparing to make their descent into Albuquerque. To Paul's horror the woman started buckling back up.

"You'll have to wait now son," she said.

"Please, I'll be very quick. I just need the notebook and pen from my bag."

"Well, it won't be long. We'll be on the ground in ten minutes or so and you can get them then."

Paul squirmed in his seat. He knew she was wrong, it would take twenty to thirty minutes to touchdown, but he needed something to write on. He scrambled in the seat pocket and came up with the sick bag.

That'll do.

"Excuse me again ma'am, do you have a pen that I could borrow? It's really important that I get this done before we land."

The woman sighed dramatically but reached to her handbag under the seat in front.

"I'm sure I've got one in here somewhere you can borrow. I'll need it back, mind."

"Of course, no problem."

Paul resisted the urge to hurry her as she sorted through her tiny bag in search of a pen which shouldn't have been so difficult to find.

What felt like an age later but was probably only a minute, she held it up triumphantly.

"Ah here we are, I knew I had it," she said, still not handing it over.

"Thank you ma'am, I really appreciate this." He reached for it and for one horrible moment he thought she was going to hold onto it but mercifully she handed it over.

He smiled at her, and checked his watch. He probably had about twenty minutes now. Twenty minutes to write the machine language boot up code.

In base 8.

From memory.

C:\PART\CHAPTER> 2.4

Paul got off the plane and looked around the arrivals hall for anyone who could be Ed Roberts.

He had finished the boot sequence just in time. He wrote manically, and managed to upset the old woman again when she tried to engage him in conversation. He'd tried to be polite but it was fairly obvious he was trying to shut her up.

He had finally got what he was fairly confident would work just as the plane touched down. He returned the old woman's pen and disembarked as quickly as possible to meet Roberts but he couldn't see anyone in the arrivals hall who could be the CEO of one of the most important computer companies in the world.

He waited ten minutes but finally it was fairly obvious that Roberts wasn't there so he wandered outside.

The first thing to hit him was the heat. Albuquerque was slightly cooler than normal in February 1975 but for a Seattle boy a 'slightly cooler' New Mexico winter was almost like summer. The wide doors of the arrival hall opened onto temperatures in the sixties, something he wouldn't expect to get until June back home.

And dry, my God how is it so dry? he thought.

Again he waited and still there was no sign of Ed.

Finally a tall, heavyset southerner with a cigarette hanging from his mouth, swaggered up to him. The man was dressed in jeans, short sleeves and an honest-to-God string tie and Paul figured he was going to ask for directions. He was taken aback when the man addressed him by name.

"Are you Paul Allen?" he said, towering over Paul.

"Yes, did Mr. Roberts send you?" Paul said, realising this must be his ride.

"I *am* Mr. Roberts. And you can call me Ed."

Ed escorted Paul to his pick up truck and drove them both over to the MITS building for Paul's first sight of the computer they had spent last two months writing software for.

***

"Oh my God Bill you're not going to believe it, it's so embarrassing."

"Oh no, it didn't work?" Bill asked, assuming the worst.

"Huh? No, don't worry. I haven't even got to try it yet."

"What's embarrassing then?"

"Ed picked me up at the airport like we planned but I didn't know who he was, I thought he was just a driver."

"Ha! Nice one, well done!"

"He was wearing a string tie Bill. A string tie! Like cowboys wear!"

Bill laughed uproariously. Then, all of a sudden, the amusement he felt at his friend's discomfort disappeared.

"You pulled it back though, right?" he said.

"There was nothing to pull back, he wasn't bothered. But wait, it gets worse. We went over to MITS and I saw the Altair."

"It's cool?"

"Very cool. Yates had it open and was running tests on the memory boards, they'd got 7k in it Bill!"

"So how come you haven't tried the BASIC?"

"Ed said we should try it tomorrow as it was getting late." He heard his friend's snort and had to agree. "I guess they knock off early in Albuquerque, but I couldn't argue so I said yes. Anyway, we're getting to the worst bit. He gave me a lift to the hotel he'd booked for me."

"That was decent of him."

"Yeah, he's got me staying at the Sheraton."

"Fancy."

"It is. Which brings us to the embarrassing bit… I hadn't got enough money to pay for it."

"You're joking!"

"Why would I bring enough money to stay at the Sheraton, Bill?! Do you know how many times I've stayed in a Sheraton? Zero. I was expecting to be at a motel. I had to borrow money from him."

"Oh my God Paul!"

"See? That's what I said at the beginning."

***

The next morning Paul sat in front of the Altair laboriously entering the programme he'd written on the plane by flicking one switch after another. Roberts and Yates stood behind him looking over his shoulders.

At least having to wait until today means I don't have to read it from a sick bag. He'd copied it up onto a legal pad the night before, after he'd finished on the phone to Bill.

He'd checked his code again last night but until he actually tried it on the machine there was no way of knowing whether the loader would work. And that was before they even got to the main point of the show.

Five minutes of switch flicking later and the Altair rewarded him by flashing its lights at him. His airplane code worked, the machine was ready to receive their BASIC.

Here goes everything, Paul thought.

"I'll just load the code now. The Altair will take about ten minutes to read the tape, I should watch it to make sure it works but if you guys want to grab a coffee it isn't going to do anything you haven't seen before yet."

"We'll wait," Roberts said, and then lapsed back into silence.

Great!

All three men watched as the teletype pulled the paper tape slowly through the reader.

It took seven minutes to process the whole tape.

Seven minutes of silence in which all Paul could do was run through the myriad possible ways that their code might fail to work.

Finally the whole tape had passed through and all three men held their breath. After a second Paul pressed the terminal's RUN button and the printer instantly sprang into action with its familiar machine gun rattle.

"Hey, it's printing something!" Yates said.

"What? What's it printing?" Roberts asked, craning across Paul to see.

"It wants to know how much memory is on board," Paul said hoping he sounded more confident than he felt.

"It's 7k," Yates said redundantly as all three of them knew perfectly well. Paul typed in 7168 and hit RUN.

The machine stuttered again and printed a single word: OK

"Wow! It really works!" Roberts said.

"So far, so good," Paul replied, but he knew that hadn't been the real test. It proved that the BASIC didn't fall at the first hurdle but most of the internal functions weren't used simply to address the memory. He also knew that as much as he wanted to he couldn't put off the real test.

He flexed his fingers like a pianist preparing to give a concert and typed the surprisingly short:

PRINT 2+2

"This seems simple but to give us the right answer it has to run through most of the code, so it's a really good test."

He pressed RUN again and tried not to close his eyes.

After the longest second of his life the printer spat out a single digit.

4

It had worked.

Paul blinked repeatedly and fought to keep himself from punching the air, he wanted to scream or something but he was supposed to be a professional.

Roberts and Yates had no such constraint.

"Hey look at that! So it works right? That's it, everything works?" Roberts said.

"That's amazing," said Yates. "Absolutely amazing Paul. Ed, what you've got here is something else. Everyone is going to want an Altair now."

"It hasn't tested everything," Paul answered Roberts' earlier question. "We'll need to run some more tests but since that's worked it means it's basically going to all be okay. I expect we'll find some bugs but we can work them out."

"Hang on, we should try something more interesting," Yates said. "Back in a minute."

He ran across the factory floor, nearly knocking over one of the tired looking workers who'd been assembling kits to send out to Altair customers.

"What's he after?" Roberts wondered aloud.

Paul obviously had no idea so he kept quiet.

Yates was back two minutes later with a book Paul knew. *101 BASIC Computer Games.*

"Try one of these," he said, excitedly.

Paul flicked through and found *Lunar Lander.* It was a short programme that would test another couple of functions of the BASIC but just as importantly it would look good if it worked. The aim of the game was to land a spaceship on the moon by typing in commands. Paul's aim was just to get something that looked more impressive than a maths problem you'd learn in kindergarten. He knew Roberts was impressed but he also knew as soon as he described it to anyone '2+2' wouldn't sound very cutting edge.

He entered the thirty odd lines of BASIC into the teletype and then invited Yates to try to land the spaceship.

It worked first time.

"Now *that* is amazing," Yates said. "Paul, what you guys have done here is... well, I don't know what to say..."

"I know what to say," Roberts said. "How would you like a contract to provide BASIC for the Altair, Mr. Allen?"

Paul grinned and stuck out his hand.

***

Paul was finally able to let his professional mask slip when he was back at the hotel and could ring Bill.

"Bill, it's Paul."

"Paul, how did it go? I was expecting a call an hour ago. Tell me it went well," Bill rattled out.

Paul could hear the nervous energy boiling off him and he imagined him rocking backwards and forwards manically while he spoke.

Paul had toyed with the idea of messing him about earlier but in the end he couldn't contain his excitement.

"It was amazing Bill, it worked perfectly first time."

"First time, Paul that's fantastic. I wish I'd been there. Their faces must have been a picture."

"They were, and so was mine I bet. I've been trying to play it cool and not to let on how surprised I was all day."

"So what did Roberts say?"

"He wants it Bill. He wants us. We didn't do any contract work or anything but he offered it to us on the spot."

"Holy shit, this is golden!"

"Absolutely golden!" Paul parroted. "And they've given me an Altair to bring back so we can work on it directly. They can't believe we wrote the BASIC without seeing one, the idea of the simulator blew them away. Bill it worked like a dream, and it was so fast. I hadn't realised what an overhead the simulator puts onto your interpreter code, on the 8080 itself it ran like greased lightning."

"This is brilliant, we need to plan our next steps. When are you coming back up?"

"My flight is tonight. I just stopped off at the hotel to grab my stuff and let you know how it went."

"Great. Come to my dorm after you land and we can talk some more. Great job down there."

"Thanks," Paul choked up slightly, the emotion of the day catching up with him. Everything they had been doing for the last seven years had led to this. "Bill?"

"Yeah?"

"It's here. And we're going to be part of it."

"It is Paul. It is. And if I have my way we're not just going to be *part* of it, we're going to be right slap bang in the centre."

***

Mary was in the lounge of their Laurelhurst home when Bill called.

"Oh hi Trey, this is a nice surprise. I wasn't expecting you to call today."

"Hey Mom. Yeah everything's good, but can you get Dad on the other extension? There's something I want to talk to you both about together."

"Is everything okay?"

"Yeah, better than okay. I just want to tell you both together."

87

"Okay son, hold on."

He waited for a couple of minutes and then his Mom came back on.

"Hello Trey?"

"Hey Mom."

"Dad is on his way."

"I'm here," Bill Sr.'s voice joined them.

Bill got straight to the point.

"I've got great news. You remember the deal I told you about with MITS to write a programming language? Well, we got it."

"Oh well done son," Mary said.

"Yes, that's fantastic news we're really proud of you. Did you go with the royalty model we discussed?"

"Oh Bill, give him a moment to enjoy it."

At the other end of the phone Bill smiled at his parents' good natured bickering.

"Well, I'm ringing for two reasons, one is to ask if your firm would represent us Dad? I've written the contract as well as I can. I think it's in pretty good shape but I'd appreciate a proper legal review."

"I'm sure we can work out something reasonable son."

"Bill!"

"What? This is business Mary, he won't learn anything if he gets things for free."

"No, that's fine Dad. I'd appreciate the help but I'm prepared to pay for it… At family rates of course," he added hurriedly.

"Of course!"

"What was the other thing Trey?"

"I need to concentrate on the business now. They've offered Paul a full time job down there but that means he'll be working directly for MITS and we'll need someone to run our side of things. So I'm going to take a break from college for a bit while I get the company up and running."

There was an awkward silence which Mary finally broke.

"You can't drop out of college."

"You don't have to drop out of Harvard Mom, in fact you couldn't if you tried, they just put you on an extended leave of absence."

"Are you sure this is wise, son?" Bill Sr. asked.

"There's almost no risk. Sure the business might not work out but we all know I didn't grow up dreaming of becoming a lawyer. This is what I want to do and if it fails then I can just go back to Harvard and finish my studies. I won't be any older than you were when you qualified."

"Hm, I suppose but that was a different time remember. Lots of us were older because of the war. Where is MITS anyway? I remember Paul had to fly there so it's not in Boston."

"Albuquerque."

"Albuquerque!" Mary said as though he'd said the moon. "Oh Trey, I don't know about this."

"I know it's difficult Mom but it's my decision."

"Right. Well, if that's how you feel then there's nothing more to say is there."

"Don't be upset Mom."

"I'm not," she said but Bill knew his Mom well enough to know how little truth was in that statement, and that he almost certainly hadn't heard the last of it. "Anyway, I'm going to have to go now, I've got work to do for the university." Mary had recently added the University of Washington Board of Regents to her growing list of volunteering. "Bill are you coming?"

"Let me just talk contracts with Trey. I'll be down shortly."

"Okay, well, good luck Trey. Will I speak to you as normal tomorrow?"

"Of course Mom. Love you."

"Mhm," she said, then caught herself. "Thank you. I love you too, speak tomorrow."

When Bill Sr. was sure she had gone he spoke more quietly.

"Send me the contract you've written and I'll take a look at it myself. Can you fax it to the office? I assume speed is important here."

"That would be great Dad, thank you." Then hesitated before saying, "I didn't mean to upset Mom."

"Oh don't worry, you know what's she's like. She has very set ideas of what's right and this doesn't fit the script, but you know we'll all support you, don't you?"

"Of course."

"And your mom most of all, she'll be in your corner, she always has been. She just needs time so that she doesn't see it as failure. I'll speak to her."

"Thanks Dad. I'll get this contract over to you."

Bill hung up and Bill Sr. took a deep breath before going downstairs. He met Mary on her way up.

"He's never listened to us," she said.

"Not often, no. But then we were trying to raise adults weren't we? We can't complain when it turns out to have worked."

"Hmm. He thinks he knows more than we do."

"When it comes to computers he's right. He does know more about it than we do. A lot more. In fact he and that friend of his know more than most people. And you know what he's like when he sets his mind to something."

"Yes, stubborn."

"I was thinking more 'driven' but stubborn works. I wonder where he gets that from?"

She shot him a look but she couldn't argue, so she tried another approach.

"Maybe we can get someone else to talk to him. I had lunch the other day with Samuel Stroum, he's got a good idea about how all of this computer stuff works."

"Yes, it might be helpful for him to speak to someone who's done similar things."

"I'll set something up."

"That sounds like a good idea but I wouldn't expect it to change his mind."

C:\PART\CHAPTER> 2.5

"I'm going to pick up the car," Paul said one afternoon in Albuquerque. "You wanna come?"

Paul had ordered a brand new, metallic blue Chevy Monza. The Monza was new on the market that year and it would be Paul's first new car. He was excited.

"Yeah, sure," Bill replied.

It would give him a chance to speak to Paul about a couple of things they needed to get sorted. One thing in particular, he wanted to get out of the way before they went much further with the business. And definitely before anything got written up into a contract.

***

"Was there a reason you bought a stick shift when you'd never driven one before?" Bill said, as Paul stalled the car for the seventh time.

"I like the car."

"You mean you think the colour is pretty."

"Shut up, at least I ... Oh crap!" Paul said, as he slowed the car for a junction and forgot the clutch again. The car juddered and lurched to a stop. Seconds later the driver of the truck behind them was sitting on his horn.

"Pull into that carpark over there and we'll work out how to drive the thing properly," Bill said.

Paul did as his friend suggested, jolting the car forwards but managing to park it without stalling this time.

"Hey, it's still going!"

"Yeah, well done genius. Shove over, let me have a go."

The two of them took it in turns to bounce the car around the Range Cafe carpark narrowly avoiding other parked cars and, once or twice, pedestrians who didn't have the good sense to give them a wide berth.

While they juddered and shuddered around the carpark Bill took his chance.

"We need to talk about a couple of things," Bill said, as he forced the Monza the length of the carpark in first gear. He had to speak loudly above the growling of the suffering engine.

"You splitting up with me?" Paul joked.

"Not now you've got this baby," Bill said, patting the steering wheel. "No, I've been over the contract with my Dad."

"Did he have any thoughts?

"He said it was alright. He tightened up a couple of clauses but the main thing was that when I told him we really want to sell wider than MITS, he said we need to make sure that there's something in there about them making their best efforts to sell it to others."

"Why can't we just do that ourselves?"

"We can, and we should, but Roberts is positioning himself really well… Why is this thing so loud and slow?"

"You need to change gear."

"Oh… Anyway, MITS is going to be at the centre of the personal computer revolution so we should make sure they're pushing our software at the same time as selling the Altair. That way we get the best of both worlds."

"That makes sense," Paul said. "Swap seats."

Bill stopped the car, and smiled at Paul triumphantly before popping the clutch and stalling.

"Bugger!"

"Swap," Paul repeated and both men got out of the car and switched seats.

Paul slipped behind the wheel and studied the gear stick.

"I got him to draft an additional clause and I'll give it to Ed this afternoon."

"Okay sounds good. Any other changes I need to know about?"

"Not to the contract but we need a name."

Paul peered under the steering wheel to examine the pedals, then opened his door, got back out of the car and stuck his head into the footwell.

"What about Micro-Soft?" he said, his voice coming from the floor.

"Hmm, Micro-soft," Bill said, rolling his tongue around it.

Paul pushed the clutch down with his right hand and reached up to the stick with his left, feeling for the bite.

"It shows we're focused on software, but it doesn't include anything about BASIC so we don't wind up being a one trick pony," he said. "Is that in first gear?"

Bill glanced down at the gearstick. "Yeah. You don't think it aligns us too tightly to the small end of the market? What if we wanted to do stuff on mainframes or minicomputers?"

"We can always change it if it doesn't work out but at the moment the personal computer is the bet we're making, right?" Paul said as he clambered back up and got into the driving seat.

"Yeah… I like it. Micro-soft."

"That's it then. Right, now, hold tight. I think I've worked this out."

He started the engine and the car lurched forward from where he'd left it in gear.

"Ignore that! I've got it. I've got it."

Bill said nothing, knowing that the next topic was the most delicate and hoping that Paul would get the car going so he could raise it while he was driving.

Paul restarted the car and this time he didn't stall it. They pulled away and he shifted into second successfully. He slowed them to a stop using the clutch to keep the engine idling then shifted back into first to get them going again.

He turned to Bill, a stupid smile on his face.

"Hey? Hey? What do you think to that? Not bad, eh."

"Very smooth," Bill said and took his moment as Paul negotiated the switch from second to third gear. "So the last thing was that I've been thinking about the split of the company."

"Our company?"

"Yeah, Micro-Soft."

"Micro-Soft," Paul said. "That does sound good."

"It does. Obviously you got your job with a salary at MITS because of our BASIC, and I haven't been paid for all of the work I did on it while I was at Harvard."

"Hm, that's true."

"So we'll need to reflect that in the share split. And obviously I wrote most of the BASIC itself, most of your work was the rewrite of the stuff we'd already done for Traf-O-Data." Bill glossed over precisely who'd done that work for Traf-O-Data and then moved on to the punchline. "But even though I did most of the actual coding, and I didn't get paid, that wasn't because you didn't want to do it. It was just easier for me to do it. This is supposed to be our company together, isn't it? So I don't want my share to be any higher than sixty percent."

Paul brought the car to a stop (and stalled again, although this time he didn't notice).

"Sixty percent?" Paul said, studying Bill's face.

"Absolutely no higher Paul, I don't need that, we're in this together."

"So I would get forty percent. I'd thought…"

"No," Bill interrupted, still speaking as though Paul would try to argue up Bill's share, not his own. "Really, we're a partnership."

Pau was flummoxed. He hadn't been about to try to argue for less than forty percent! He'd never given the share split any thought at all, he'd just assumed it was a fifty-fifty thing. Still, what Bill said was right. He had got paid while Bill hadn't made a penny. And in fact all of the original outlay had been Bill's. Okay there wasn't a lot of it but Bill had paid for the manuals and Monte's payment, even back in the Traf-O-Data days Bill had paid for the 8008 chip.

"Okay, I guess that's fair," he said after a moment.

He started the car again and drove home the rest of the way without stalling at all. He didn't offer Bill another go.

***

"Ed, this is my partner, Bill Gates," Paul said.

The three of them were in Roberts's office, Ed behind the desk, Paul and Bill standing just inside the door.

Ed leant forward and stubbed out his cigarette in a large oversized orange ashtray and reached across the desk to take Bill's hand.

"Good to finally meet you Bill."

Roberts' meaty paw enveloped Bill's hand as he vigorously shook it.

"I love what you've done in bringing the Altair to market Ed," Bill said, his words tumbling out. "I mean, I know there's nothing particularly radical in there. In fact Paul and I were thinking of doing it if nobody else had, but we're really software guys. It's so much better that you've done it so we can focus on the software where the real challenge lies."

Ed was slightly taken aback.

"Erm, yeah," he said. "Although without the hardware you'd have nothing to run software on Bill."

"Oh definitely, I'm not knocking it. We all only have twenty four hours in a day, so you've got to focus your energy where you can make the most impact. For me that's software, but not everyone can do software. I guess it's like when you were in the airforce, right? Not everyone can be a fighter pilot, you need someone on the ground making sure the plane works. Without people like you, who are happy to stick to the hardware, us software guys wouldn't be able to do anything."

"I think what Bill's saying is that we're going to make a good team," Paul said, diplomatically.

"Yeah, exactly." Bill nodded enthusiastically, missing the fact that Paul was trying to moderate his message. "You keep churning out the machines and together we'll change the world."

"Great, that's great," Ed said slowly and then shook his head as though getting rid of everything he'd just heard. "Anyway, I'm about to go into a meeting. You're both welcome to join us if you want."

"Sounds great," Paul said.

***

"So how are we coming with those memory boards?" Ed asked his assembled team, a couple of minutes later.

"We're making progress but the error rate is still higher than we'd like."

Ed turned to Bill and Paul and explained. They were both already fully aware but neither of them interrupted him.

"We keep getting failures in the boards. Most we catch before they leave the floor but some get through quality control here and then fail when they get to the customers."

"That sounds worse," Paul said.

"Well, it depends," Yates answered. "Many of our customers have waited for a very long time for their Altair so if they get nothing then there's a chance they could cancel their order and go to one of the other manufactures who are starting up, IMSAI or the like."

"I've told you not to mention them in here," Roberts said.

IMSAI were a competitor who had, in Roberts' view, shamelessly copied the Altair design. Unfortunately for him they seemed to have solved the problem of memory boards.

"Are we quality checking them all or just a sample?" Paul asked.

"We started off with a sample but we've had to move to one hundred percent because of all the issues."

"Okay," Paul said and scribbled on his notepad, clearly thinking. "Not everybody wants extra memory but most people who do are going to want to run BASIC, right? And BASIC needs 4k of memory, so can you get enough working boards together to ship a machine with 4k to anyone who's ordered extra memory regardless of how much they asked for?"

"We wouldn't be giving them what they'd ordered," Roberts said.

"You're not giving them what they ordered now," Bill piped up in his high pitched voice. Everybody's head turned to the newcomer, surprised to hear him speak on his first day but Bill wasn't fazed. "At least this way you'd be giving them something useful. And you could follow up with the other memory they're owed when you have it ready."

"We could look at that, there might be something in it," Yates said when the dumbfounded Roberts didn't reply.

The discussion ranged on for another few minutes until eventually Roberts drew it to a close.

"I want this sorted people, it's embarrassing. It's like being king of the world and being afraid of cats."

Several of the men at the table shot each other funny looks, but Bill muttered into the notebook he had been scribbling in.

"Napoleon wasn't scared of cats," he said.

"What?" Roberts gave him a look that usually had the MITS staff backing carefully out of the room but Bill, either oblivious to it or too arrogant to care, just met his eyes calmly.

"You meant Napoleon, right? But he didn't have a phobia of cats, that was his nephew, Napoleon III. He wasn't king of the world either, but I guess you knew that and it was just for dramatic effect."

Roberts stared at him without speaking, but Bill just shrugged.

"It's a common misconception," he said. "I was very interested in Napoleon when I was young."

The room was silent for a beat and Paul looked like he wanted to hide under the table. Then Roberts broke the spell.

"French history to one side," he said, with disdain. "I want it fixed and fast. Now, I need the room. Yates wait with me."

Everybody else filed from the room and as soon as the door closed on the last of them Roberts exploded to Yates.

"Who the hell does he think he is? We can find someone else to do the BASIC, you know."

Yates wasn't surprised by Ed's reaction. In fact he had been more surprised that his boss had managed to keep his cool through the meeting. Ed wasn't known for tolerating disagreement easily, and he certainly didn't back down in an argument.

"Nobody else came close to how quickly they delivered it, and we've already announced it in the trade press. And remember he might be annoying but the kid actually is a software genius."

"I know. He's told me ten times already and I only met him today!"

Yates laughed.

"The bottom line is that we need them" he said. "And Paul's a good guy, he'll keep Bill in check."

But Ed wasn't listening.

"He corrected me about Napoleon, Jesus! He looks like he should still be in high school and he's correcting me in front of my staff."

Yates knew that Roberts liked to hold forth on all sorts of topics and peppered his discussion with metaphors from history and modern geopolitics. Few people challenged him on any of them.

"I think he might have been right about that though, I remember seeing something myself somewhere," he said.

"That's not the point," Roberts said and gave Yates the same look that hadn't worked on Bill. It worked on Yates.

"No, it's not, I'll have a word with him."

"Just keep him under control or this isn't going to end well."

Yates left the room and as soon as his back was turned allowed himself the smile he'd been suppressing all through the meeting. Maybe Ed had met his match. This was going to be interesting.

C:\PART\CHAPTER> 2.6

By early 1976 Microsoft, still occasionally written with a hyphen but gradually more often without, was doing well but nowhere near as well as it should have been.

Bill and Paul had retained the ownership of their code so they could license it to other computer manufacturers, and the clause that they had added to the contract meant that MITS had to help do the same thing. The agreement between them was straightforward. For any sales of Altair BASIC made to other manufacturers, Microsoft and MITS would split the profit 50:50.

At this early point there weren't many takers, but Bill could understand that. Roberts was concentrating on establishing the Altair and other manufacturers hadn't yet caught on.

The bit that didn't make quite as much sense was the retail side.

As Bill and Paul had expected, BASIC had become a key part of the attraction of an Altair for retail users. And the pricing that MITS set showed that Roberts realised it too, and perhaps he wasn't completely happy about it.

If a retail customer bought a copy of BASIC with an Altair it would cost them $60, on top of the roughly $800 the Altair and the essential peripherals cost. Bill and Paul got about $30 from the BASIC sale. However, if that same customer wanted to buy BASIC without an Altair, then under the terms of Microsoft's agreement with MITS they would have to buy it from MITS and Roberts was charging customers $500 for the programme on its own. Microsoft got half of that money but, as anyone could have guessed, a vanishingly small number of people bought it like that when they could get the computer as well for under $400 more.

So Bill expected most of his and Paul's revenue to come in the form of sales of BASIC to retail customers alongside an Altair. But in early 1976 it hadn't amounted to much money. And Bill smelt a rat.

***

Bill grumbled about the numbers to Paul for a week before finally storming into Roberts' office.

"Do you know how many Altairs you sold last month?" he demanded on his way through the door.

Roberts, sensing an argument coming, stubbed out his cigarette and stood up, dwarfing the diminutive looking Bill. Roberts' temper was notorious but then so was Bill's and everybody in the outside office turned to watch the two of them face off. Sure enough Bill squared his smaller nineteen year old frame up against the bigger, older man.

"Plenty thanks," Roberts said with a smile.

Bill shook his head, too irritated to be able to see that the man was just goading him.

"Almost a thousand. You know how many were sold with BASIC?" Bill said. Roberts just shrugged. "Less than two hundred."

"That's frustrating."

"It's not frustrating, it's weird. What the hell can anyone be doing with an Altair without BASIC? There's barely a thousand people in the whole country who could programme in machine language. What are the chances they all bought an Altair last month?!"

Roberts frowned. The young man wound him up but he had a point.

"Actually that is weird."

"I've worked it out. They're stealing it!"

"From us, how? Between your guys and my guys there's someone working here twenty four hours a day."

Bill waved his hand in obvious irritation at how slow he felt Ed was being.

"You don't steal software by breaking into an office. Someone has copied the code and they're sharing it for free."

"Yeah, okay I see but then your argument isn't with me, Bill."

"They're your customers! I want something done about it. Get Bunnell to put something in the next issue of *Computer Notes*. In fact forget it, I'll write it myself."

He stormed back out of Roberts' office, crossed the factory floor and threw himself into his chair to start writing.

***

In the February 1976 edition of *Computer Notes*, the MITS newsletter, Bill wrote a piece titled *An Open Letter to Hobbyists*. Never one to mince his words he came right out and accused his customer base of theft.

'As the majority of hobbyists must be aware, most of you steal your software… Who cares if the people who worked on it get paid?'

Bill's diatribe provoked a massive reaction from hobbyists, most of it unpleasant.

Not long after it was published Miriam Lubow received a call from someone demanding to speak to Bill.

"Hello, Mr. Gates, there's a gentleman on the line who wants to speak to you, he says he's from a west coast computer organisation."

West coast? Bill thought. *Well that doesn't really narrow it down. Maybe Intel? That could be interesting.*

"Okay, thanks Miriam. Put him through." He waited for a click to indicate Miriam had connected them and then said, "Hello, this is Bill Gates, who am I speaking to?"

"That doesn't matter, think of me as representing computer users everywhere."

Oh great, not Intel then!

"Oh yeah, how can I help you then Mr. Anonymous?"

"I wanted to speak to you about your letter, it's disgusting.

"I'm not sure there's going to be much point in us talking I'm afraid. And just ringing to rant at me isn't going to get what you want, whatever that may be."

"You're just too afraid to discuss it in person because you know you're wrong."

A small part of Bill knew that he shouldn't rise to it, that there was nothing to be gained by speaking to someone who wouldn't even identify himself. But it was a much smaller part than the part of him that wanted to win.

"Wrong in exactly what way?"

"In every way. You say you used computer time worth forty thousand dollars to write BASIC, well maybe it was worth forty grand but you didn't pay it did you? It's not like you're forty grand out of pocket."

"I didn't say I was."

"You implied it. But do you know who is out of pocket? The taxpayer, because you wrote it on a machine at Harvard that was paid for by the military."

"Hm, I think you might want to check Harvard's asset allocation there," Bill said but his interrogator was on a roll and didn't want to be interrupted.

"And if it is surprising that your programming time was worth less than two dollars an hour," the clear said, referring to a calculation the outraged Bill had made in his letter. "Then maybe you should have done a bit more market research. What you're seeing is the number of people who want to pay for software versus the people who don't. Have you ever heard of the free market?"

"I think you might be misunderstanding the concept of 'market' there Mr. Whoever-you-are. My whole point is that if people steal software then no-one will write any more, precisely because it means there *isn't* a market for it."

"There you go again. It's insulting. You can't call your customers thieves."

"Well, I can't call them customers if they don't buy anything can I?"

"Software wants to be free, Mr. Gates."

101

"That is the stupidest thing I've ever heard. How can it want to be free?! It's just information written by human beings, do the words in a book want to be free? Would you feel justified copying a book and giving it away, and how would you expect the author to feel?"

"That's different."

"Why? What's the difference?"

"It just is. And the biggest thing of all is that you keep moaning about pirates but if it wasn't for us you'd have nothing."

That did it, Bill lost his cool.

"You what?! How do you work that out?"

"It's true. *Your* BASIC," the man on the phone stressed the 'your' to mock Bill. "Is everywhere because of *us*. We've made it a standard. Any computer manufacturer who wants to give people what they're used to will have to come to you. That's because of us."

Bill was at a loss. He couldn't believe this man was lecturing him but he had also hit upon Bill and Paul's strategy.

"I think that's enough from you," he said. "I am going to hang up now."

He sat there for a moment, angry at this total stranger who'd rung up and ruined his morning. Then he went in search of Paul and told him about the phone call.

"Who was it?"

"I don't know, some guy with a Californian accent, anyway while he was ranting I had an idea. Two ideas, in fact. First, from now on we should license software to manufacturers for a flat fee instead of per copy royalties. That way we don't care how many they sell."

"Will they go for it?"

"I think they will, it plays into their weakness."

"Most of them overestimate what they'll sell."

"Exactly."

Paul rubbed his beard while he thought.

"What about MITS, are we going to move them to a flat fee as well?" he said, after a moment.

"Roberts won't go for it for the original BASIC, whether it's fair or not he knows perfectly well that people aren't buying them with the Altair and the truth is that isn't going to change. We'll do it for the next version."

"Okay, it could work," Paul said.

"It means we'll have to be careful though, Roberts underestimated the demand for the Altair. We'll need to be better at estimating our own projections of what we think will sell. We'll need to keep on top of the market."

"Well, that's not a problem."

"That's what I thought."

"And the second thing?"

"I still think they're thieves but there was truth in what our friendly caller said. They've helped us set a standard. From now on that's going to be our goal: we're going to set the standard."

***

Paul woke abruptly to the sound of the phone beside his bed ringing angrily. He checked the clock, 01:31, he'd only been in bed for an hour and a half.

Who the hell is ringing me at this time?

His arm flailed out and on the third try he caught hold of the phone.

"Hello," he said.

"Got arrested," the voice at the other end said.

Paul stared at the phone then again at the clock.

"Bill?"

"Yeah, who do you think it is? I'm in a holding cell and it's not a lot of fun. You're my phone call, any chance you can come and bail me out?"

"You've been arrested? What have you been arrested for?"

"Do you reckon you could stop asking stupid questions and just come get me?"

By now Paul had woken up enough to dislike Bill's tone.

"Yep, just as soon as you stop being a jerk, ask nicely and tell me what's going on,"

Bill realised he needed his friend on side so he took a breath and tried to calm down.

"I'm sorry Paul, I'm just keen to get out of here. They've got me in the drunk tank and there's a guy in here who keeps throwing up."

"Oh, nice. I assume you were speeding," Bill was infamous for never driving anywhere within the speed limit. "But how come you're in jail?"

"The cop who stopped me had no sense of humour. So how about coming and bailing me out?"

"I'm getting dressed as we speak. What do you mean he had no sense of humour?"

"He wanted to see my license."

"Obviously," Paul said, his voice muffled as he pulled on his sweater.

"Yeah, well it's obvious now but I didn't have it. It was at home so I asked why he wanted to see it."

"Oh, Bill!"

"It was a joke. I thought it was kind of funny."

"And he didn't."

"Correct. As I said, no sense of humour."

"Okay, I'll be there in about twenty minutes."

"Thanks Paul, you're a life-saver."

"Don't you forget it." Paul started to hang up, then froze. "Hang on a minute."

"Yeah?"

"Weren't you borrowing my car?!"

"Details, details Paul, just get here as fast you can," Bill said, and hung up.

***

Over the next year Bill and Paul gradually grew the Microsoft team, bringing in more programmers and a secretary, Miriam Lubow, whose official job was as Bill's secretary, although most of her time was spent helping keep the team of long haired radical programmers under a semblance of control.

They branched out into other BASIC versions, selling them mostly with their new flat-fee model but the original 8080 BASIC was still controlled by MITS.

In October 1976 Microsoft moved into their first dedicated offices, in November Paul left MITS and Bill finally decided he was leaving Harvard for good (though he hadn't told his mom that).

And Bill bought the first of many Porsches, a used, dark green 911 that let him indulge his love of late night speeding around the deserted New Mexico roads.

More importantly to the future of Microsoft, a disagreement arose between Roberts and Bill. Bill had always seen other manufacturers as customers for his languages, to Ed they were only competitors. The issue simmered for a while, but eventually a buyout deal that Roberts made brought things to a head.

In December 1976, Pertec, a disc manufacturer looking to move into computers, made an offer to buy MITS from Roberts and Roberts accepted. He hadn't told Bill anything about it, which wouldn't have been a problem except for the fact that Pertec believed that they were buying the rights to Microsoft's BASIC as part of the deal.

Unwilling to jeopardise the deal with Pertec, Roberts became even more fixed in his opposition to sales of BASIC to other manufacturers, and Bill boiled over. The resulting argument soured relations between Bill and Ed for the next thirty three years.

And prompted Bill's first legal battle.

C:\PART\CHAPTER> 2.7

In March 1977 Yates dropped by Microsoft's offices to grab lunch with Bill and Paul.

After showing him around Paul took Yates into Bill's office to collect him. Bill was behind his desk, his right hand gripping a can of coke, his left holding a pen that hovered above the contract he was reading.

Bill nodded hello to Yates but otherwise kept reading. Paul and Yates stood for a minute, waiting for an acknowledgement but there was nothing. Occasionally Bill would stab at the paper with his pen as he made a note of something that needed to change.

Watching the young man engage in his familiar rocking, Yates just smiled at Paul.

"You alright Bill? We were going to get lunch," he said, finally.

"Mhm," Bill said without looking up. "With you in a minute. Grab a chair, will you? Your shadow is distracting."

Paul pointed to the sofa in the corner and they both flopped down onto it and began chatting while they waited for Bill.

"Have you seen the vendor list for the West Cost Computer Faire? It looks really exciting," Paul said.

"Yeah, I was looking through it the other day. They reckon it's going to be huge, they've sold thousands of tickets."

"Are you going to go?"

Yates winced.

"Ed won't have it. He says because MITS aren't going we shouldn't go as individuals.

"I still don't get why MITS aren't going," Paul shrugged.

"Ed reckons if we join in we'll just be one of the crowd, by not going we're staying above it."

"That's madness, if you don't go you become less relevant, surely."

"We still have the lion's share of the market," Yates said, a defensive tone entering his voice.

"Yep, but for how long?"

Bill put down his pen and looked Yates in the eye. It took Yates by surprise, Bill seldom made eye contact unless he was in an argument.

"Paul's right," he said, proving he'd been listening to the conversation while marking up the contract. "Just about everyone else is growing market share. MITS is going to lose out if Roberts doesn't engage more."

Yates turned his hands palms up in a gesture of resignation.

"You don't need to tell me."

"Someone should talk to him," Bill said, decisively. "I'll do it. I need to discuss why he's dragging his feet with the ADDS deal for BASIC anyway."

He stood and took a swig of coke.

"Come on, let's go, I'm ready," he said.

When they'd reached the door to the street he paused and looked around the main room, when he couldn't see what he was looking for he raised his voice and called over to a woman sitting near his office.

"Miriam, where's the coke I asked you to get?"

"It's all gone Bill," Miriam replied.

"Wow! How much did you get?"

"Three six packs," she said, sounding amazed it was all gone.

Bill laughed.

"I meant a crate," he said. "Can you do me a favour? Get onto Coca-Cola's distributor, they must have one in Albuquerque, right? And get them to deliver a crate a week. Actually, how big's a crate? Never mind, speak to them and see what the best way is to get enough to keep us in coke. I don't want people to have to go out to get it."

"How much is that going to cost?" Paul said, from the doorway.

"Who cares? However much it is, it isn't going to be more than we'll lose by people stopping what they're doing to go and get their own."

Paul nodded.

"You heard the man, Miriam!" he shouted and they left the office with Yates in tow.

***

Later that afternoon Bill went over to the MITS offices and caught up with Roberts.

"Ed, people are talking about why we're not going to the West Coast Computer Faire. It's going to be the biggest computer show ever and everyone in the industry is going to be there, except MITS."

Roberts bristled instantly. Over the year and a half they'd worked together his respect for Bill's talent and brain had grudgingly increased but he had never got over his dislike for the younger man.

"I explained this at the last meeting Bill." Despite being a separate company, Bill and Paul still attended lots of meetings at MITS since their fortunes were so intertwined. "I'm sick of going over it. We need to keep the Altair apart, make it stand out."

"Oh it stands out alright. All of the other machines have sales that are growing and customer bases that are happy." Roberts started to respond to the snide comment but Bill was on a roll and didn't give him a chance. "You've got to embrace the industry more, be in with them if you want to beat them. It's like the other manufacturer deals I've been sourcing. You're dragging your feet on all of them. The only one we've got over the line is General Electric, but I've got half a dozen lined up. All it's going to take is for you to agree to them and I can close them."

"I'm not dragging my feet. I don't think they're anywhere near as close to closing as you think."

"Well, you're wrong. Take ADDS for example, they're desperate for BASIC."

"Then we need to keep them desperate, keep our advantage."

"Advantage? You have to be kidding, that's the stupidest thing I've ever heard! You aren't listening, you lost your advantage months ago. You're shrinking and everyone else is growing. These sales of BASIC to the others are a chance for you to regroup. You've done nothing to get them, I'm doing all of the legwork, all you've got to do is sit back and rake in the money. Use it to plough into research and bring out the next version that blows the others away. You did it with the Altair, you beat them all. You could do it again."

In the middle of this speech Bill had started shouting, now Ed responded by doing the same.

"You just don't get it Bill. You think you're God's gift but I've been running MITS since before you went to high school. I'm not going to blindly give away an edge to my competitors. I wouldn't even if it was up to me but Pertec won't hear of it."

"Pertec, you mean the disk manufacturer?" Bill said, demonstrating his encyclopaedic knowledge of the players in the market. "What have they got to do with anything?"

Roberts looked like he regretted saying anything, but he knew Bill well enough to know that he couldn't gloss over it now. Bill was like a terrier, if he didn't tell him what was going on then he wouldn't drop it, he'd make noise all over the industry trying to find out. Better that he contained it.

"This stays in this room, right? I'm in talks with Pertec about them buying MITS and the license for BASIC is part of that, so now isn't the right time to make any deals with other manufacturers. But believe me, the Pertec thing isn't a threat to you. It won't change your relationship with MITS."

"What do you mean it isn't a threat, you've just said they're the reason you're blocking my sales. I don't think you realise how close to the edge we are Ed. I could go broke."

"Oh don't be so dramatic!"

"I'm not being dramatic. You owe us four months of royalties. We get bugger all for 8080 BASIC, more people still copy it than buy it. And why? Because they aren't prepared to pay for your crappy memory cards."

"Watch it Bill."

"If Microsoft is going to survive it *needs* deals with other manufacturers. You knew that when we signed the contract, that's why you're supposed to help sell it. I've given up on expecting you to do that so I've been doing it myself, but now you're preventing me from doing that as well. You're strangling Microsoft. You're strangling me and Paul. We brought you BASIC, we helped make the Altair what it is. How many would you have sold if it wasn't for our BASIC?"

"You're deluded Bill. You think you're better than everyone. The Altair was a massive success before anyone ever mentioned BASIC. Now you think I should just roll over and hand the industry to my competitors to help you?"

Bill stood up and lowered his voice for the first time since they had started arguing.

"They're not your competitors any more Ed, they've won," he said calmly, turning the knife. "MITS is dying, it's just doing it slowly like everything you do. You had the lead, you could have crushed the competition but you let them grow too big. Now it's too late. MITS's time is over. And I bet you know it too, that's why you're selling out."

"I'm not selling out! And you don't get to say when MITS's time is over Gates! I'm in charge here, not you."

"Yeah, and don't we all know it. If I was in charge I would be running it better."

"Get out of my office. Now!"

***

Paul was waiting outside.

"How did it go?" he asked.

"Not as well as you might have hoped."

"So, he's definitely not going to West Coast."

"I'd say that's the least of our problems. I don't think he has any intention of letting us sell BASIC to anyone but MITS."

"But that'll kill us."

"And he's going to sell MITS to Pertec."

"The disk manufacturer?!"

"That's what I said. He's imploding and he'll take us with him if we're not careful."

***

Before the week was out Bill stormed over to Paul's desk and waved a piece of paper in front of him.

"Have you read this?!" he demanded.

"I don't even know what it is Bill, you're still holding it."

"A letter from Roberts," Bill said as he thrust the letter at Paul.

"He sent us a letter?"

"Read it."

Paul scanned the letter. After about thirty seconds he looked up at Bill with a horrified look on his face.

"He's killed the ADDS deal."

"And Delta Data" Bill said, with barely controlled rage.

Paul shook his head and quoted from the letter, "*Let me again reiterate my desire that you not contact directly any potential third party customer without our approval and involvement.* And he's never going to give that approval is he? He can't do this."

"He thinks he can but I'll see about it."

"Is it him or Pertec, do you think?

"Maybe Pertec are making it worse but let's face it, MITS has never pushed sales of BASIC to others. He hasn't liked it from the beginning."

"So what are we going to do?"

"I think we should terminate the contract."

"Woah."

"We've demonstrated we can make Microsoft a success without them, I've made all of these sales. If we weren't doing them under MITS then we wouldn't be in any trouble. What do you think?"

Paul hesitated before replying and for once Bill gave him space to think.

"I don't like it but I think you're right," he said, finally. "Let's do it."

"Okay, I'm going to speak to my dad and see what he thinks our legal position is. You find an attorney down here in case we need local representation. There's got to be a way out of this."

***

On 20th April 1977 Bill and Paul sent Roberts a letter in reply. They accused MITS of a number of breaches of their contract, including missing royalty payments, not enforcing the secrecy agreements when they licensed BASIC to hobbyists, and most importantly not making their best efforts to promote BASIC to other manufacturers.

And as a result of those breaches they formally notified Roberts that they would terminate the agreement between Microsoft and MITS in ten days.

"This isn't right," Roberts said to his attorney who was sat opposite him in his MITS office.

Joining them on the phone on the desk between them was an attorney from Pertec. Pertec were only weeks away from completing the deal to purchase MITS and they wanted to make sure that they stood the best chance of getting the value they saw in the deal, that is the rights to Microsoft's' BASIC.

"Can't this thing protect us?" Roberts said, tapping the contract on the desk in front of him.

"The contract itself doesn't give us much to go with," his attorney replied. "Essentially they're right about the obligations it puts on you. If I had seen that contract originally I might have advised you not to accept that clause about making best efforts to sell BASIC to others."

"I barely read it. I was looking out for those guys, they were much younger than me. Look, the BASIC they brought me originally was clever, it was a 'neat hack' as they always say, but you couldn't have sold it to other companies. We took a flyer on them. They used MITS resources, my computer time, to turn that thing into a viable finished product. Hell, I even gave Allen a job!"

"Well, if you believe that then the only choice we have is to take it to arbitration ourselves and argue that the finished article is much closer to MITS intellectual property."

"Does arbitration prevent them terminating?"

"Yes, that's the point."

"What about them selling it to other people in the meantime? Can they still do that?" Ed asked, mindful of the Pertec lawyer on the other end of the phone.

"I've got an idea about how to handle that," the Pertec lawyer said. "But it'll take a week or so to set up."

C:\PART\CHAPTER> 2.8

"Dad, it's me Bill. I need your help," Bill said over the phone a week later.

"What is it, son?"

"Someone was just at my apartment door. I didn't like the look of him so I didn't answer but when he'd gone I came out and I found a summons posted on the door. I can't believe MITS has done this." Bill's voice rose as he spoke.

"Okay, Trey calm down. Just tell me what it says."

"They're asking the court for a restraining order on us."

"What are the conditions?"

"It says that we can't license it to anyone else until the arbitration is complete. Can they even go to court while it's under arbitration?"

"Yes, they can. They're separate things."

"But that means I can't sell BASIC to anyone! We developed it, it's not theirs. This just isn't fair!"

"Business isn't always fair Trey, you know that. But that's what the restraining order is for, to give space for the arbitrator to work out what the contract says without the situation getting any worse."

"Okay." Bill took a breath and tried to calm himself. "Do you think I should just accept this and wait it out? The date for arbitration is only a month from now. We can pay bills for another couple of months, I think."

"Hold on son, don't get ahead of things. First, if you need money, you come to me and your mom, we can work something out. Second, I wouldn't bank on that arbitration date, they're notorious for moving about, and I don't expect any arbitrator will be used to dealing with this sort of thing so that will probably delay it as well."

"So what do I do Dad?"

"You have other work that's totally unconnected to MITS?"

"Yes, we do. We have a big project on the go for Texas Instruments but it won't pay us for a year."

"Well, you keep your people working on that. We'll see if we can't sort this mess out before then. There's no real question in my mind that you'll win the arbitration, the contract is clear, it's just a matter of riding it out and making sure you have the cash to keep afloat until it's sorted."

***

Months later they were still waiting for a decision to come down from the arbitrator and Bill and Paul were beginning to crack.

The hearings themselves had lasted ten days, and day by day the arbitrator who, as Bill Sr. had suggested had no understanding of software, had seemed to sway from side to side. One moment he seemed to favour Pertec, the next Microsoft.

It was exhausting for everybody but above all for Bill and Paul whose control of BASIC, if not Microsoft's very existence, hung in the balance.

The strain was particularly telling on Paul, Bill at least had the advantage of having had dinner each night of his childhood with a lawyer, he knew how long the legal process could take.

One night when they were out for pizza, Paul laid out his fears completely.

"I think we should settle with Pertec."

Bill froze, a slice of pizza halfway to his mouth.

"And give up BASIC?"

"We could write something else."

"Just like that? Oh yeah, pass me a pad and I'll knock something up now, what do you think it should be? FORTRAN, APL, or shall I just invent a totally new language altogether?" Bill said sarcastically.

"I know, I know. I just don't know how long we can wait," Paul said. "We're running out of cash."

Bill sensed that his friend and partner needed bolstering and dropped the sarcasm.

"We're going to win Paul, my dad says so and Milnes agrees." Paull Milnes was the Albuquerque attorney they had chosen to represent them. "Pertec just think they can wait us out because they've got deeper pockets than we have."

"Aren't you afraid they're right, Bill? I am. The arbitrator keeps pushing back the date of the decision and we can't hang on much longer. We've spent Bob's money, now we're running almost completely on the first payment from Jobs and Wozniak for Applesoft."

"This is just a cashflow thing Paul. When the Texas Instrument deal starts paying next year we'll be in the clear."

"There's no such thing as *just* cashflow Bill, you know that better than me. If we run out of cash it won't matter that the business would be good next year. Microsoft won't be here to collect on it. If we settle then we can avoid the whole thing."

"You're just tired from the fight."

"You're damn right I am, but tired or not we still need to pay the rent. Not to mention the staff."

"We just need to find a way to hang on. Reduce costs. We can stop my salary," Bill said.

"You're already paid less than everyone else."

"Okay but all I need to do is cover my bills. Maybe we could ask the guys to take a cut in salary?"

Paul looked thoughtful. The suggestion wasn't as outlandish as it would be in many businesses. They both knew that none of the staff were there because of the money. If they were they'd probably insist on having the occasional weekend or only working twelve hour days. No, the programmers were there because they loved the challenge as much as Bill and Paul.

"Most of them would do it I think," Paul said. "We'd need to work out what everybody needs. Steve and Marla would need a bit more, they've got a proper house." He paused. "I'd much rather we didn't get to that point though."

"Me too. But I want you to trust me on this one Paul. I'm scared too. And exhausted. But we need to stay tough. We'll get the answer soon and when we win we can sell BASIC to anyone we want," he said, and then in a flash he dropped the seriousness and said with his eyes twinkling, "And best of all we won't have to split the revenue."

Paul smiled, won over by Bill's passion as much as his arguments.

"Okay, we wait. But only because I trust you Bill," Paul said reluctantly.

***

Despite the show he had put on for Paul, Bill was nowhere near as confident as he was making out. After he had finished dinner instead of going back to the office as he'd originally planned he went home and rang his mom and came as close as he had so far to breaking down.

"Mom, it could all come apart. I could lose everything. Paul wants to settle and I'm afraid he's right."

Mary Gates knew her son and his mood surprised her. She also knew that just offering him a telephonic hug wouldn't help but neither would challenging him openly, he'd just fight back. The best way to help him was to remind him he was supported, lay the facts out for him and then let him work it out for himself.

"Trey, you know I was worried about you leaving college for this computer thing," she began, her voice softer than normal. "But you're making it work, I don't see why it has to stop now. It would be a shame to let what you've achieved fall away just because there are some bullies out there in the world."

"I don't think Ed's a bully Mom, at least not in any way I can't stand up to. He gave me and Paul our break, it's just... I don't know."

"Oh, I didn't mean him. I mean this Pertec, is it? They obviously thought they were buying your programme when they bought Ed's company, and now they've found out they were wrong they're trying to make good out of a bad decision. And they figure they can just roll over the top of you boys."

"Well, I might not like it but maybe they're right. Paul's definitely right that we can't fight for ever."

"Money problems?"

Bill sighed.

"It's tight," he admitted. "That's what's making Paul so worried."

"Dad and I can help you Trey, you know that. We keep offering."

"I know, but I don't want you to bail me out. I want to do this on my own."

"Okay," she said, then with her experience of the business world, she cut right to the heart of the matter. "So let me ask you a question, if you settle then there's no way they'll let you have the rights to your program is there? From what you and Dad have said they'll probably compromise on something but not that, is that right?"

Bill hesitated as he tried out different scenarios in his head, he'd said much the same to Paul but it was worth checking he was sure.

"No," he said, when he'd thought it through. "No, I don't think they would. I wouldn't if I were them. I need to carry on, don't I?"

"It's not my decision Trey, it's completely yours. But I will say that the Gateses aren't quitters. If you tell me carrying on is a bad idea then that's fine, you should settle. I'll believe you. You might be my little boy but you're one of the few experts in the world on computers. Or if you tell me you were wrong originally and this programme you and Paul wrote should really belong to Pertec because they've come in and bought MITS, then again you should back off," she spelt out M-I-T-S as its acronym instead of pronouncing it as a word, the only indication that she wasn't totally seeped in his world. "*But if you only want to give in because you're tired and afraid of the fight...* Well, that's not the Trey Gates I recognise."

She stopped speaking and let him think. Bill smiled, even one and a half thousand miles away his mom could help. He couldn't help but marvel at how she could handle all of this, and him for that matter. It was easy to see why she was a natural fit on so many boards and how she could be so effective.

"Thanks Mom," he said, and then hesitated again before adding awkwardly, "I'm... I'm very lucky to have you."

"And don't you forget it!" Mary said with a smile audible in her voice. "Hang on in there. You're in the right and the arbitrator can't wait for ever to make a decision."

***

In November, just before Bill finally had to crack and ask his parents for money, the arbitrator released his decision in a twelve page document.

In a repeat of the scene that had started their nightmare, Bill rushed over to Paul's desk waving a letter.

"Read this! Oh my God, read this!"

Paul realised instantly what it was, snatched it from Bill's hand and started reading as quickly as he could.

Despite having his eyes fixed on the paper in front of him he could still see Bill swaying on the spot above him and knew he didn't have long to read before Bill would simply tell him what was in it.

He scanned the letter and picked out key phrases until it hit him that Bill's sprint across the office had been good news. No, great news!

'undisputed testimony' he read, and *'materially breached its best efforts obligation'*, then he got to the kicker.

"Holy crap, listen to this," he said and read aloud to Bill, who of course had already read it.

"I find this an act of corporate piracy not permitted by either the language or any rational interpretation of the Contract…"

Paul looked up to see that Bill was grinning like a lunatic at him and had graduated from swaying to jiggling on the spot with nervous energy. When he met Paul's eyes the movement calmed.

"You know what this means?" Bill said.

"We won."

"Totally and completely. Pertec have to pay our legal costs," Bill said.

"We can pay the guys," Paul said.

"And the rent."

"BASIC is ours, we can sell it to anybody we like."

"And we don't have to split the money."

Bill Sr. had been right, they had not been able to find an arbitrator who understood the technical elements, but in the end that had helped Bill and Paul. It meant that the arbitrator had focussed on the contract itself, in particular his decision highlighted the clause about MITS making their best efforts to sell BASIC to other manufacturers and concluded that they had failed to live up to their side of the deal. Roberts' insistence that he treat other manufacturers as competitors, and Pertec's later blanket refusal to engage with them at all meant the arbitrator found in favour of Microsoft and approved the termination of the contract.

The connection between Microsoft and MITS was severed. MITS remained a customer of Microsoft for BASIC but they no longer had any exclusive right to it, from now on they would just be one more customer for Microsoft. Microsoft for their part no longer had either the protection or the encumbrance of a close tie to a single manufacturer.

Microsoft had benefited from the early tie to MITS, and from the illegal software sharing habits of the hobbyists, to establish themselves as the 'go to' company for personal computer languages. Now Bill and Paul were free to go their own way and they would stand or fall on their own merits.

C:\PART\CHAPTER> 2.9

As anyone who knew Bill could have predicted, severing the contract with MITS did nothing to reduce the intensity of work at Microsoft.

The small team that Bill and Paul had built around themselves was made in their own, and in particular Bill's, image. Young, driven, and fanatically focussed on technology.

Bill's expectations were very high, Microsoft paid quite well for a technology firm, particularly for one stuck out in Albuquerque where the only competition was the disappearing MITS, but they asked a lot from their employees. The hours were long, and passions ran very high with disagreements often resolved by shouting, but for the most part they all felt part of something bigger than themselves.

Still, for Bill at least, the intense focus needed equally intense ways of letting off steam.

Most nights, when he eventually left the office, Bill would race his Porsche 911 around the New Mexico desert, where long stretches of near abandoned roads let him force the car up to its maximum speed (which, as he once complained to the garage, was not actually as fast as advertised).

He would tear around the I-40 throwing up clouds of dust behind him and burning off some of the day's stress.

Some days he'd take someone from the office along with him. On this particular night he was joined by Chris Larson, one of his friends from Lakeside who was working part time at Microsoft for the summer.

Chris had always played something of the padawan to Bill's jedi. He had been one of the kids whose eyes Bill nearly wrecked with the early traffic tape transcription, and when Bill left Lakeside it was Chris who had taken over running the scheduling programme. And now he had come to work with Bill at Microsoft for a senior year project. Providing they both lived through the night that was.

His knuckles were white from gripping the seat for dear life as Bill threw the Porsche around the Albuquerque roads.

"Come and work with us full time," Bill said as he took the shallow bend at 93 miles an hour.

"I want to finish school," Chris replied, keeping his replies short in the vain hope that Bill would concentrate on the road.

"School's not important any more Chris," Bill said, turning to look at the younger man while still barreling the car along at breakneck speed. "It's an outmoded concept, designed to shove knowledge into your head on moribund subjects and turn out mediocre employees in industries that change slowly enough for the textbooks in the colleges to keep pace. Computers aren't like that, they've changed everything. Knowledge moves too fast now for schools to keep up."

Chris didn't take his eyes off the road, figuring it was important that at least one of them was looking at it.

"I'm not sure my parents would agree with that."

"Who cares? Okay, that's not fair your parents are okay people. Look, school's alright for some people but not people like us, right? We're at the cutting edge. You can learn tons more at Microsoft than you could at school."

Chris couldn't argue with that, so he just stayed quiet.

Bill finally tuned in to how little Chris was saying. He frowned, unable to think of what he could have done to wind Chris up.

"What's up? You pissed off with me or something?"

"No, I just want you to concentrate on the road Bill."

"What?!" Bill was gobsmacked, but didn't slow down and kept looking at Chris.

"You're one of the smartest people I've ever met and I'm sure if anyone can drive at a hundred miles an hour and hold a recruitment conversation at the same time, it'll be you."

"But…?"

"But I'm pretty sure *no one* can."

Bill laughed and eased his foot off the gas. Slightly.

"Better?" he asked and Chris inclined his head a little. "So you're not pissed off with me then?"

"Not at all."

"Good. And you'll think about the position?"

Chris threw his hands up in the air.

"Bill, I don't know what to say, I really…"

But Bill suddenly bent his head forward to look past Chris.

"Hang on, what's this?" he said and slammed his foot on the brake.

Chris' body was slammed against his seatbelt as the wheels locked and the Porsche skidded along the dusty road, fishtailing as Bill turned into the skid.

When it finally came to a stop he was grinning and pointed out of the window.

"Playtime Chris!" he said and jumped from the car.

Chris followed him but all he could see was a construction site.

"What? What have you seen?"

"Look around," Bill said, spinning in a circle with his arms wide. Chris did but there was nothing but the construction site with three bulldozers. "Ever driven a bulldozer Chris?"

"Are you mad?"

But Bill was already climbing up into the cab of the nearest machine.

"Coming?" he called down. "The keys are still in here."

Chris clambered up the side of the machine and joined Bill inside just as Bill revved the powerful engine.

"Oh yes. Feel that?"

In a comical repeat of his earlier stick shift lessons with Paul, Bill threw the huge machine around the construction site in a series of jerks and jolts until eventually he got control and was able to reliably drive it around the site.

"Now, which one of these controls the digger?" he thought aloud, looking at the bank of switches and levers in front of him.

The markings on most of the levers had worn away so he just reached out and pulled the first one towards him.

The huge machine lurched backwards taking both of them by surprise.

"Argh!"

"Bill we're going backwards!"

"No shit," Bill said excitedly. Somehow he hadn't stalled the dozer this time and it began to pick up speed, so he floored the gas. "Hey this is brilliant, it goes faster in reverse!"

He twisted in his seat to try to see clearly while keeping his hands on the wheel but Chris had a much better solution. He simply hung out of the side of the cab.

"Bill, stop!" he shouted almost instantly.

"Pansy," Bill shouted above the noise of the roaring engine. "We're just getting started."

"No! Stop now!"

Sensing the urgency in his friend's voice Bill stamped on the brake.

"What is it, are you okay?"

Calmer now, Chris nodded.

"Take a look." Chris jerked his thumb backwards.

Bill stuck his head out of the cab and looked behind them.

"Holy crap!" He had stopped the bulldozer about a foot and a half from the side of his Porsche. "We'd have crushed it."

"We?! You haven't let me drive the damn thing!" Chris laughed. "I'd have happily let you roll over the top of it but how would I get home?"

Bill punched his arm and joined in laughing.

When the laughter had stopped Bill pointed to one of the other bulldozers.

"Go check if the keys are in the other one and I'll race you."

"No way!"

"Come on, don't be a chicken."

Chris shook his head. He wasn't having that.

"Right, wait here," he said.

Neither Bill nor Chris claimed victory in the race. Though Chris went back to school, he continued to work at Microsoft during his summers all through college. When he graduated in 1981 he finally joined Microsoft full time.

***

When he wasn't tearing around the desert or racing bulldozers, Bill's mind was completely consumed with Microsoft. And one of the things that was occupying the company in 1978 was something he considered a distraction, where the company should be based.

"The only reason we came to Albuquerque in the first place was MITS and now that's not a consideration there's no reason for us to stay here," Paul said.

"There's no reason for us to move either though. We should just concentrate on running the business. Who cares where we're based? We write code, we can do that from here, we can do it from anywhere, God you've done it on an airplane! And I can sell from anywhere that's got a phone."

"Yep, true. But the more you sell, the more programmers we need and it's getting harder and harder to recruit out here."

Bill figured if they had to move at all then they should go to Silicon Valley, where the majority of their customers were. Paul and Steve Wood, the general manager, were pushing for Seattle.

"But we'll have the same problem in Seattle," Bill said. "The northwest is hardly a hotbed of technological progress."

"But that's just it, it's perfect. Wazzu has a really strong computer science department that churns out a steady supply of good graduates and there isn't a lot of competition for them."

"And it isn't in the middle of bloody nowhere like here," Steve added.

Bill looked at Steve and tilted his head.

"I get why he wants it to be Seattle, but why do you?"

Steve shrugged. "I don't really care to be honest, I just want us to make a decision and get going. Like he said Albuquerque isn't good for hiring new people and staying in limbo like this isn't good for the existing people. They know a move is being discussed and it's making them nervous. We need to give them certainty."

Bill turned back to Paul, they both knew that Steve was talking at least partly about himself. His wife Marla worked with them too and they were the only married couple in the company, a move that far away would impact them more than any of the other staff.

"I want to see the sea again Bill," Paul said.

"I think they have some in California."

"Your folks would be thrilled."

"No doubt, but that's not really the best reason to make a business decision, is it?"

"No, but it wouldn't just be business. We use your dad a fair bit for legal advice."

"I'm kind of hoping we won't need as much of that now we're through the MITS Pertec nonsense." Bill took a breath, it seemed like Paul really wanted this and truth be told he didn't care enough to have a proper fight about it. Besides, Paul was right, his mom and dad would be thrilled. "Okay, you win. Seattle it is, start sorting it."

"Great, I'll get Miriam to start planning the move. We'll aim to be out of here by the end of the year, that'll give us time to sort a place in Seattle and for everybody to adjust. Steve, you can start letting people know but no announcements externally until we've got more sorted."

"Great."

Perhaps now we can get back to running the company and looking for opportunities, Bill thought, unaware that one of those opportunities was about to call him.

***

"May I speak to your president?" the Japanese voice at the end of the phone said.

Miriam was used to getting calls for the boss. Despite the grand title Microsoft was still a small outfit and Bill personally took the lead on most of the sales so there was nothing unusual in getting a call for him. What was more unusual was that it was only 8am and Bill was at his desk rather than asleep on the sofa he'd bought for when he was pulling an all nighter.

"Of course, who shall I tell him is calling?" she said.

"Ny name is Kazuhiko Nishi."

"Okay Mr. Nishi, and what company are you with?"

"Ah, ASCII," the man replied after a brief pause.

Miriam called through to Bill's office.

"Bill there's a call for you, a Japanese gentleman, says he works for ASCII and his name is Mr. Nishi. I didn't catch his first name I'm afraid."

"You're sure he said ASCII?" Bill said, confused. He had already got several deals underway with Japanese customers, but ASCII was a language standard not a manufacturer. *I suppose someone might have started a company in Japan and used the name,* he thought. But if Bill hadn't heard of them then they weren't already a player. *Still, it's never wise to pass up an opportunity.*

"I'm pretty sure, he had an accent though so I might have heard him wrong. Shall I put him through?"

121

"Sure, go ahead." After a beat the line clicked and Bill said, "Hello Mr. Nishi, this is Bill Gates. How can I help you?" Bill said, a moment later.

"Mr. Gates, I am a publisher of a computer magazine in Japan and I would like to talk to you about working together."

"You want to interview me?"

"No, no. I am looking to move into software and I believe we can do good work together, ASCII and Microsoft. I could help open up Japan for you."

"I'm always very interested in working with new companies but I should point out we already have deals with a number of Japanese companies Mr. Nishi."

"Please call me Kay. Ah, these are old men you are working with, they do not know the Japanese computer market properly."

Bill checked his watch. It didn't sound like this was going to lead anywhere but he had time to try and it must have been gone midnight in Japan. Whoever this Kay Nishi was he was interested enough to be working late.

"Alright then Kay, tell me a bit about yourself. Why should Microsoft work with you not these *old men*?"

"Yes, about myself. You and I are very alike you know. I dropped out of Waseda University to work on computer magazine like you dropped out of Harvard. You have heard of Waseda? It is like Japanese Yale or Harvard. After I dropped out I designed a games console running on a General Instrument chip but here in Japan things are very traditional, GI would not give me a prototype chip unless I ordered in bulk. So I switched to writing about computers instead, and started ASCII company. But the more I write about computers the more I know I can do better than the people I am writing about. Not with hardware this time. Not yet anyway, I have some ideas but I think software is the most important thing. You know? But to do that I need an interpreter, no? So then I thought, who has an interpreter? Who would be good to work with? Microsoft!"

Nishi spoke for fifteen minutes in rapid fire sentences punctuated with questions he didn't give Bill time to answer. He spoke about what he saw as the state of the Japanese computer industry and the opportunities it presented to Microsoft. Occasionally he would break off and pause for a fraction of a second, just long enough for Bill to murmur assent and prove he was still listening and then he would launch into his staccato speech again.

Bill's eyes gradually grew wider. Kay's verbal torrent had put him in mind of the phrase he knew some of the Microsoft team used when he went off on one himself, 'drinking from a firehose'. Now he knew how they felt. On the other hand Kay hadn't said anything that made Bill think he was stupid. And Bill found it pretty easy to think people were stupid.

Finally Nishi wound down and finished with his kicker.

"Will you come over to Tokyo so we can discuss this properly? I will pay for your ticket. First class."

Bill had got used to controlling his expressions in business meetings but he couldn't help but smile. He had definitely felt himself being won over by Kay's knowledge and enthusiasm, but there was still no way he was going to travel halfway around the world off the back of a single phonecall.

"I'm afraid I can't really fit a trip to Japan into my schedule at the moment Kay, but I tell you what, if you want to meet up then why don't we grab an hour together at the National Computer Conference in June? I assume you're going."

"Of course," Kay said, thinking, *I am now.*

***

"I think we should do a deal with him Paul," Bill said, two months later in the bar of the hotel they were staying in for the National Computer Conference.

"I thought you didn't want to waste the time meeting this guy."

Bill had said as much to Paul just that morning, in fact right up until the meeting started he had begrudged the time that he had put aside to see this Japanese publisher who didn't seem to have any concrete plans and didn't really have any prospect of becoming a customer.

But as soon as they met in person Bill had remembered why he'd taken the meeting in the first place. Nishi's enthusiasm for all things computer related was infectious and the hour long meeting that he'd planned and then resented, had turned into a marathon conversation.

"I was wrong. We spoke for eight hours."

"Eight hours?!"

"I know. But it was fascinating. He knows nearly as much about the industry as you and me, and more of the ins and outs of the Japanese market."

"So what did you talk about?"

"All sorts of things. New chips; Japanese manufacturers he thinks will stick with computers and the ones whose business model it doesn't really fit; how he thinks computers will soon be as accepted as televisions are today. How the Japanese consumers are taken with all things western and that might be a useful marketing thing."

"Sounds like you hit it off."

"Yeah, we did. For a guy from Japan, Kay's more like me than probably anybody I've ever met."

"Even more than me?" Paul joked. "So he doesn't play the guitar?"

"Actually I don't know, I didn't ask."

Which kind of summed up the difference between Bill and Paul. Bill could spend eight hours talking to someone and not leave the subject of computers. Paul would have held his own in that conversation but would have wanted to know whether they had any other interests as well.

"It doesn't matter, I was joking," Paul backed off the topic. "I still don't get how we do a deal with him though, is he looking to set up a new manufacturer?"

"I was thinking he could be our boots on the ground in Japan."

"Oh, so when you said do a deal with him you're not thinking we sell him stuff, but that we sell through him?" Paul was intrigued. Japan looked like a growing market to him and the idea of having someone who understood the territory and was on hand to drive deals was appealing.

"Exactly. He wants to branch out into software, he gets that's what's really important," Bill said glossing over Nishi's definite interest in hardware. "But why start from scratch developing his own languages when he can partner with us?"

"So he'd be like our agent."

"Yeah. Why don't you meet him, see whether you think we can work with him."

"We're heading back to Albuquerque first thing tomorrow."

"I'll tell him to come down. He came all the way from Tokyo he's not going to mind a couple of hours flight to New Mexico."

"Okay but this is more your end of things than mine. If you like him then isn't that enough?"

"Well, yeah but I want you to okay him. I don't want us getting bed with someone like this if you're not happy with them."

"Okay then, set it up."

A couple of days later Kay flew down to Albuquerque and Paul fell for his enthusiasm as well. The three of them agreed to make a new company called ASCII Microsoft which Kay would run as Microsoft's exclusive East Asia agent.

Kay became a part time executive vice president of Microsoft and Microsoft had its first international office.

C:\PART\CHAPTER> 2.10

Nishi demonstrated his worth quickly. The first major customer he brought Microsoft's way was Kazuya Watanabe, an executive at NEC.

Watanabe was leading the project to deliver the PC-8000, NEC's first personal computer that was intended to corner the Japanese market.

Nishi had sold Watanabe's right hand man, Tomio Goto, on Microsoft providing the BASIC for the system but before the deal could be struck Mr. Watanabe wanted to visit the small company himself.

A trip from Japan specifically to Albuquerque didn't have many other draws but the US put on several trade shows a year which the Japanese manufacturer found useful, so Nishi came up with an idea. Watanabe would fly in to Albuquerque ahead of one of the shows, and Bill and Paul would meet with him to show him around Microsoft before taking him to the trade show with the rest of the Microsoft team and meeting Nishi there.

***

Bill and Chris Larson had driven over to the airport to pick up Watanabe while Paul remained at the office finishing off some work, but he made sure he was on hand to meet their guest when they got back.

When Bill escorted Watanabe through the door he was in full flow, talking at a mile a minute, and the Japanese man seemed to be paying close attention, but what struck Paul most was his ashen face.

Bill spotted Paul and broke off mid monologue, gesturing to him.

"And this is Paul Allen, my partner," Bill said.

Watanabe inclined his head in Paul's direction managing to convey more of a reserved bow than a nod.

Paul copied the man and decided now was the time to roll out his extensive Japanese vocabulary.

"Konichiwa," he said.

Watanbe, relieved to have found someone he could confide in, replied in a string of Japanese that would have been too fast for Paul to understand even if he had known more than the single word he had already used. Watanabe's relief evaporated as quickly as it had arrived and he switched to English.

"Mr Gates, he always drive so fast?"

Suddenly the pale face made sense.

"Yep, I'm afraid so," Paul replied. "Can I get you a drink? Water, Coke, something stronger?!"

Watanabe smiled.

"Water will be fine thank you."

Bill pantomimed outrage behind Watanabe's back then said in his most professional voice, "Shall we give you the tour Mr. Watanabe?"

"Yes, that would be good thank you."

Bill and Paul led Watanabe around the small open plan office space. Most of the desks were empty. It was, after all, only half past ten.

Bill was describing some of the work that they had already done for Japanese firms when Watanabe interrupted.

"You are a very small team," Watanabe said with a frown.

"We have about twelve programmers," Bill said. "But it's still early."

Mr. Watanabe's eyes widened.

"Early? At NEC we start at 7am with the company song and then begin work."

"Rest assured our people eat, sleep and breathe Microsoft, Mr. Watanabe, and we only employ the smartest programmers. We let them choose the hours that suit themselves and a couple of them start early as you can see, but we tend to be more night owls here. Most of us work late into the night and then stop work around two or three in the morning, go home to get a few hours sleep and then come back in. Most of the team spend no less than fifteen hours in the office." Watanabe nodded an acknowledgement but he didn't look any more impressed, prompting Bill to add quickly, "It's unusual but we've never been late on a delivery yet."

At that Paul had to look away quickly to stop Watanabe seeing the look on his face.

As they spoke they arrived at a table in the centre of the office which was covered with test machines from a variety of manufacturers.

"You have BASIC for all of these machines?" he asked.

"We do," Bill said.

"Either launched or in development," Paul corrected, earning himself a withering look from Bill.

"I don't recognise some of these machines."

"They're not all out yet," Bill said. "Lots of manufacturers find that the best thing to do is to give us a prototype machine before anyone else so we can work on the code on the machine itself. It speeds up delivery."

"And this?" Watanabe asked pointing to the crates of coke under the table. "You are also working with Coca-Cola?" It was an attempt at a joke but his dry delivery and the tension the boys were starting to feel meant they didn't notice.

"Oh we give all of our workers free coke," Paul said.

"One less reason to leave the office," Bill said with a nervous smile.

Miriam Lubow came over and spoke quietly into Bill's ear.

"Miriam is running across the street for hamburgers for the guys, do you want anything Mr. Watanabe?"

"A hamburger? At this time?" He frowned.

"No, well obviously if you don't want one that's fine. But for some of them this is almost lunchtime."

"I will try one."

"Okay, what would you like?"

"Whatever you suggest Mr. Gates."

Bill swallowed and turned back to Miriam, "Would you get Mr. Watanabe one of my usual cheeseburgers, please Miriam?"

"No problem, and you Bill? Paul? Do either of you want anything?"

"No. Yes," Bill had a rare moment of uncertainty, as his mind failed to process the correct social behaviour. Was it rude to eat in front of his guest or rude not to share a meal with him? "Yes please, the same," he said in the end.

"No thanks," Paul said with just slightly more composure.

Bill exchanged a look with Paul. He had no clue how this had gone.

***

After an uncomfortable ride to the conference, Bill and Paul said goodbye to Mr. Watanabe and threw themselves into the conference.

The Microsoft guys weren't actually running their own stall this time so they had time to look around at what other people had to offer.

It was fun, a chance to catch up with like minded people.

Paul went from stall to stall talking about the technology underpinning each one, while Bill networked and tried to get more sales leads. A couple of other Microsoft people were there too and it was a rare opportunity to take a break from the nose-to-the-grindstone programming.

Kay Nishi was nowhere to be seen but Bill saw Watanabe in the distance a couple of times.

Each time Bill managed to avoid eye contact and lose himself in the crowd. It wasn't like he was scared of him, he told himself. He was used to dealing with tough customers, Jesus, just a couple of months earlier John Roach, the head of Tandy, had told him the price he was asking for was 'horseshit'! Bill hadn't flinched. He didn't find negotiating with big customers particularly difficult despite his age. But Watanabe's emotionless review of Microsoft left him unaccountably nervous.

As night fell the conference gradually slowed down and people started congregating in the bar. Before long the young Microsoft team, Bill, Paul, Chris Larson and Steve Wood invited the dozen or so manufacturers' reps they were drinking with upstairs to the adjoining suites that Bill and Paul had booked.

They broke out the booze and Paul blasted Hendrix from a ghetto blaster that somebody had produced. They left the door to the suite open so people could come and go, there were rarely fewer than twenty of them in the room.

Midway through the night Bill started ransacking the drawers until he found what he was looking for beside the Gideon bible. A deck of cards.

"Spoons!" Bill cried out.

Half of the Microsoft guys groaned while the others laughed.

"We haven't got any spoons Bill."

"Send down for them," Chris said.

"What is it?" one of the DEC guys asked.

"It's a game he made up."

"He never loses."

"Does he change the rules?"

"Oi!" Bill said. "I made it up but I don't cheat, I'm just better than you guys."

"Paul, are you playing?" Steve asked.

"Do I have to?"

Paul had the longest experience of any of them of playing games against Bill, their chess matches had become legendary until they had stopped playing them a few months earlier. The way Paul told it, it was because Bill couldn't stand to lose. Bill remembered it slightly differently but the end result was the same. No more chess.

"You have to Paul, come on let's show these hardware folk what real smart guys do," Bill said.

"That's fighting talk," said someone else from DEC. "Yeah, you can't back down now Paul."

"We can use coins instead of spoons," Steve said pulling out his wallet.

"Great," Bill said excitedly, and threw himself onto the floor, crossing his legs and sitting like a child. "Who's playing?"

He sat down and before long almost everyone had joined him, including Paul.

Steve put a coin down in front of each of them while Bill explained the rules to the non-Microsoft folk.

"Okay, it's like poker but at the beginning of every round we call out a hand and whoever gets that hand has to grab their spoon."

"Coin," Steve interrupted.

"Coin," Bill nodded. "As soon as you see someone reaching for a coin you try to grab your's first. The winner is the first person to hold their coin."

"So it's like poker but with reaction speed thrown in."

"Sounds easy enough."

"Yeah," Bill went on. "But you're allowed to bluff and if someone touches a coin on a bluff then they're out. It'll make sense after a few practice rounds. Look…"

He dealt out the cards and they played a couple of practice hands slowly. Steve won one, Paul another.

Then Bill spoke up, "Everybody got it?"

"Yeah."

"Sounds simple enough."

"Sure."

Chorused the grown men sitting cross legged on the floor staring hard at a couple of coins, determined to show this cocky young man that he wasn't the cleverest one in the room.

"Okay, let's start properly."

The small group played for an hour, but there was a steady stream of newcomers to the party some of whom would hover on the edge of the game for a few minutes before joining in.

Bill didn't lose a round.

As the night progressed the drink started flowing more freely, which helped no-one but Bill who stuck to a Shirley Temple, but it did make it funnier. By the end people were sitting behind Bill watching his hand to see if there was some secret way he was cheating. He wasn't. He was probably smarter than many of them, he was good at bluffing and he had fast reactions, but in the end the answer was simple: he just cared more about winning than anyone else.

Eventually the game broke up when they couldn't find anyone Bill hadn't already beaten but everyone had had fun. The suite was filled with laughter that only became louder when Kay Nishi showed up at the door at a little past eleven o'clock with a party of drunk Japanese prospects in tow.

"Bill!" he shouted. "My friend!"

"Kay! Come in, come in. Have we ever played spoons?"

"What?"

This time everybody groaned.

"Enough, enough!"

"Bill," Kay said. "My colleagues here are looking for somewhere to sleep and I told them Microsoft can help them."

"Of course, we can get some rollaway beds and they can sleep in here. Chris!" Bill shouted to Larson who was on the other side of the room. "Can you help Kay sort some beds for his guests?"

"Sure Bill, how many?" Chris shouted back.

Bill looked at Nishi and Nishi, somehow managing to keep a straight face despite a skinful of drink said, "Seven."

He gestured off beyond the door and sure enough, seven Japanese businessmen looking slightly the worse for wear paraded into the room in single file, one of them clutching a briefcase.

Bill didn't blink.

"D'you hear that, Chris? Seven."

Chris got on the phone to housekeeping and struggled to make himself heard above the noise of the party. At some point somebody had brought an electric guitar and amp, and Paul had switched off the ghetto blaster and started playing himself. It was loud enough that, if the hotel hadn't been hosting the conference, Chris would probably have been asked to leave when he rang the front desk. As it was, he got his message across and a few minutes later seven bellboys appeared at the door with as many rollaway beds. They looked non-plussed but were happy enough when Chris gave them the tip Bill had passed him.

Once they had gone and Chris had safely shut the door he turned back to the room.

"Right, what say we celebrate?"

"What are we celebrating?"

"Living in the future!" Chris said and threw the clothes he'd brought out of his bag then held it up for everyone to see that the bottom was full of bottle rockets.

The party stumbled out onto the balcony and started launching the rockets towards Central Park.

As the first rocket shot up someone in the crowd called out a toast, and pretty soon they were taking it in turns to fire a rocket and shout a toast.

"To the good people of Intel who gave us the 8080!" *Whoosh! Boom!*

To a bunch of young geeks, drunk on a combination of alcohol, fun and the feeling of power that comes from knowing they were cresting a wave, it was amazing.

When Bill's turn came he bent over the rocket and lit it and shouted as loud as he could, "To the Altair!" *Whoosh! Boom!*

He straightened up and looked into the face of Mr. Watanabe standing in the background. Watanabe was standing above Paul who was sitting on one of the rollaway beds with the guitar propped on his knees and a joint in his hand.

"Ah, Mr. Watanabe," he said, becoming serious in a moment. He pushed his way through the crowd so that he could hear the other man. "How can I help you?"

Watanabe looked around the room and took it all in without any visible reaction.

"I was hoping that we would be able to meet before I leave in the morning Mr. Gates."

"Of course, unless you would like to talk now? I can clear everybody out of here. Or we could go somewhere else?"

"No, that is alright you enjoy your... evening... and we will speak in the morning. Seven thirty in the lobby?"

"That will be fine."

Watanabe turned and left without another word.

Bill nudged Paul with his foot.

"I don't think he likes us very much."

Paul looked around the room then down at himself.

"Not really his cup of tea," he said.

Both of them burst out laughing.

***

Bill finally became aware of the alarm at 07:25 and dragged his head off the pillow where he had been lying face down, dead to the world.

He shook his head to clear it, hit the button to turn off the alarm with a little more venom than was strictly necessary, then shook his head again in amusement when he saw the Japanese man lying comatose beside him, still fully dressed in his business suit, shoes and tie.

He pulled on the clothes he had been wearing the night before and hurried to the elevator. He hopped from foot to foot while he waited for it to arrive and considered running down the stairs but they were on the tenth floor so he knew it was pointless.

Just like the meeting, he thought. There was no way Watanabe was going to give them the contract, the meeting was obviously just a formality, a mark of etiquette from the strait-laced older Japanese man.

The elevator finally arrived and Bill dived in, pressing the button for the lobby and then repeatedly punching the 'door close' button before anyone else turned up and made him even later.

As the elevator descended quickly through the floors, mercifully not stopping at any others, Bill studied his reflection in the mirrored metal interior. He ran his fingers through his hair in a doomed attempt to make himself look vaguely respectable. It was a stretch, but then he had only gone to bed an hour and a half earlier.

Bill stepped from the elevator, pushed his glasses back up his nose and swept the lobby looking for Watanabe. He saw the other man standing rigidly to attention in the corner and Bill made his way over to him.

"Konichiwa," he said, having noticed that Watanabe had been impressed with Paul's attempt the day before.

"Ohayō gozaimasu," Mr. Watanabe replied with the first hint of a smile Bill had ever seen on the man's face. "I just wanted to speak to you before I left, Mr. Gates."

"Of course," Bill said, pushing down the rising bile he could feel at the back of his throat.

"I was slightly surprised to see your organisation for myself Mr. Gates, but it is exactly what Nishi-san told me."

Bill had a sinking feeling, he would have to work overtime on this one when the conference was over. He had to be able to win them back. Or maybe they'd be better concentrating on some of the other manufacturers? Then Watanabe blew him away.

"Microsoft is exactly what we need. Your company is nothing like NEC but that is precisely why we are coming to you. Young people are the only ones who can make computers for other young people."

"Of course," Bill repeated in the same dejected tone. Then his sleep deprived brain caught up with what Watanabe had actually said and he desperately tried to shift mental gears quickly. "I mean, yes, you're absolutely right Mr. Watanabe."

"I will return to Tokyo now Mr. Gates and I will tell my superiors that we will be buying the BASIC for our new machine from Microsoft, where the programmers drink free coca-cola, eat hamburgers for breakfast, do not wear ties," he flicked his own tie as he spoke. "And above all are young enough to understand our customers. I will be in touch shortly to agree a contract."

Bill was almost lost for words but he managed to stammer out a reply.

"That's great," he said. "For both of us, I mean. You're making the right decision Mr. Watanabe."

The Japanese man gave Bill one of his nodding bows and left.

Bill stood there for a moment astonished, he couldn't believe what had happened. But it was only the first surprise of the morning.

***

When he went back upstairs Paul and their Japanese guests were awake, Paul met him at the door and pushed him back out into the hallway, frantically widening his eyes so that Bill knew something was up.

"You're not going to beli…," Bill began, but Paul interrupted.

"Well whatever it is can wait a moment because you're not going to believe what I've got to tell you either and you need to know before you go in there." Paul flicked his head back towards the open door.

Bill's eyebrows furrowed.

"Okay then," he said. "You go first."

"This is so weird," Paul said in a whisper. "You see the guy in the corner, don't look now! You remember the one with the briefcase he wouldn't put down?"

"Yeah, what about him?"

"Well, he'd like to buy one of everything we've got."

"What do you mean 'one of everything we've got'? That is weird."

"That's not the weird bit. The weird bit is that to prove he's serious he brought cash. Ten thousand dollars of it. In that brief case. From Japan."

Bill's mouth dropped open.

"You're joking!" he laughed. "Okay that was weirder than mine, you win. So what did you say to him?"

"Well you're the salesman Bill, so I went with the straightforward 'thank you' and grabbed the briefcase full of cash!"

Bill smiled and shook his head.

"What a bizarre morning. Okay I'll speak to Miriam we need to get that money into the bank quickly so we're not carrying it around."

"So what did you have to tell me?" Paul said.

"Oh yes! I nearly forgot, I don't know if you noticed but last night Watanabe asked me to meet him in the lobby this morning."

Paul shrugged. "What for? Did he want to tell you how disappointed he was with us?"

"No that's just it, I thought I was going down there for a bit of a kicking and in fact he told me he wants us to provide the BASIC for the new NEC machine! We got the deal!"

"But he's looked annoyed with us every time he has sings," Paul said, confused.

"I know but apparently we are just the sort of thing they are looking for."

"I don't believe it!"

"I told you, you wouldn't."

C:\PART> 3: LAYING THE GROUNDWORK FOR WORLD DOMINATION

C:\PART\CHAPTER> 3.1

The official move to Seattle took place on 1st January 1979 although the team had been drifting northwards over the preceding few weeks. Bill was 23 and Paul only twenty days from his 26th birthday when they returned to their home town with their small staff.

Miriam Lubow was the only one of the team staying in Albuquerque. Bill had tried to persuade her to come with them but her husband had objected, afraid that such a young company in a young industry, led by an equally young boss, was not worth uprooting a family for and travelling across the country.

Despite the hard work that everyone was putting in at Microsoft it was hard to argue with him. Microsoft had come a long way since Bill and Paul had first sold BASIC to Ed Roberts. In 1978, their first full year outside of the MITS agreement, they had racked up their first million dollar year in revenues, but it was still perfectly possible that Microsoft would go bust before too long. By the time they left Albuquerque, Pertec wasn't far away from winding up MITS.

Miriam's parting gift had been to organise the move into the Bellevue offices at 10800 NE 8th Street. In a move that would have amused computer aficionados, the new Seattle phone number ended in 8080 in memory of the original chip used in the Altair. Some people said that Bill used his mom's connections to get the number. Mary Gates' rise through the corporate and charitable world of Seattle had continued while her son was away and she was now on Pacific Bell's board of directors. It was nonsense of course, Mary wasn't about to behave inappropriately so that her son could make a handful of geeks smile briefly when they called his office.

As befitted a gang of computer whizz kids the thing that most excited the team about the move to Seattle was that for the first time they would have their very own mainframe, a mucky orange coloured, filing cabinet sized, DECSYSTEM 2020 from Digital Equipment Corporation.

It is amazing to think that until this moment one of the most successful computer language companies in the world still used timeshare arrangements over a teletype, just as fourteen year old Bill had done when he first encountered the machine in the computer room at Lakeside.

Now, they had their very own machine, a spiritual descendant of the PDP-10 that they had worked on at C-Cubed. They just had to make sure that their fledgling company didn't go the same way as that Seattle enterprise had done.

***

"Trey you've got to take it," Mary said over the family dinner table a few months later.

Microsoft had been in Seattle for half a year now and the company was doing increasingly well. So well in fact that Bill had already received a number of offers for mergers and even outright acquisitions. None of them had been attractive enough to warrant much real interest on Bill's part, but the latest approach had been from Ross Perot and *that* had made him sit up and pay attention.

Perot was the founder and CEO of Electronic Data Systems, a company that made software for mainframes.

EDS was huge, selling software and data processing services to big corporations and government agencies. It even had the contract for the computerisation of Medicare records, just like Bill had done on a much smaller scale with the traffic data for the city authority years earlier. Perot had started the company himself with just a thousand dollars after leaving IBM and had made such a success of EDS that in 1969, a year after going public and while Bill was just learning about computers in the Lakeside computer room, his shares in the company were worth more than a billion dollars. Even more impressive to Bill, whose only interest in money was as a marker of success, Perot had remained outwardly unfazed when in 1974 his shares lost $450 million in a single day, and it was reported across the country that he had lost more money than any American ever lost on the stock market.

Basically Perot was everything Bill hoped to be if things went right for Microsoft. And now the Texan had let it be known that he was interested in buying Microsoft. It was impossible for Bill not to consider it, but he didn't like the idea of giving up his baby.

"I'm not so sure Mom," he said, putting down his knife and fork.

"Tell him Bill," she said to her husband.

"We don't even know how much he's offering yet Mary, it would be foolish to decide before he's met the man and had a discussion."

"See Mom, that's what I said."

"But it's even more stupid to rule it out before you've heard what he has to say," Bill Sr. said to his son.

Mary smirked at Bill and Bill stuck his tongue out cheekily. Their relationship had long since matured from his troubled childhood. He now found that he relied on his parents for advice in a way that proved Paul had been right to push for the move to Seattle. Mary and Bill Sr. were just about the only people he spoke to outside of the computer industry. If Bill wasn't at the office or asleep at the house that his mom had helped pick out for him, he was almost always at their house talking over business.

None more so than since Perot had started courting them. Of course it was important that Paul agreed but this was largely a business decision and Paul was considerably less interested in that side of things than Bill. Providing he was able to ensure that they would have a role at the company he was sure Paul would be happy to sell out. No, this decision would come down to him and that's why he needed the counsel of his parents.

***

A day later Bill landed at Dallas and stopped off to get his haircut at a barber he found in the airport. He hadn't had time before he left and even though he was pretty sure he didn't want to sell, he wanted to make a good impression.

A couple of Perot's people met Bill at the airport and he spent the day with them, exploring their plans for Microsoft if they bought it. As he'd expected they wanted him and Paul to stay with the company for a couple of years, but beyond that, or perhaps because of it, he was disappointed at how little they'd got planned.

In the afternoon they escorted him to the seventh floor to meet Perot but when they got there they were greeted by an assistant who told them Perot wasn't ready.

"Mr. Perot asked me to meet you here, I'm afraid he is running a bit behind," he said. "If you don't mind waiting here then he should be along shortly."

"No problem."

"I'll leave you to it then if you don't mind, I have to get back to a project I'm working on."

"I totally understand."

The well dressed young man left and Bill was on his own. He looked around and took in his surroundings. From what he could tell the whole floor was given over to Perot's office apart from this anteroom, and if this was just the anteroom he couldn't imagine what Perot's office must be like.

He'd been in plenty of museums, country clubs and even stately homes over the years due to the circles in which his parents moved, and this room could have stood next to any of them. His dad could have held a Bar Association dinner here.

Since there was nothing else to do, Bill worked his way around the room slowly examining the art. He'd reached a brass statue of an American eagle when he heard a faint ping over his shoulder and then a voice called across the room in a strong Texan accent.

"You must be the famous Bill Gates I've heard so much about."

Bill turned and saw an elevator door closing behind a short man who was striding across the room to meet him with his hand extended.

"Bill, you don't mind if I call you Bill? I'm Ross." He'd reached Bill now and pumped his hand energetically.

"Bill's fine. It's nice to meet you Mr. Perot."

"Ross."

"Ross."

Perot gestured through the office door and strode in front of Bill, still talking as he went.

"You like the eagle then?"

"Yes, very impressive. Your collection seems to be based on patriotism?"

"Much of it is yes, but that eagle is a coincidence. I keep it around to remind me of a quote I use when I'm looking talent, 'Eagles don't flock. You have to find them one at a time.' "

Bill tried to place the quote but couldn't.

"Who said that?" he asked.

Perot smiled, happy that the kid was more interested in finding things out than looking like he already knew the answers.

"I did," he said.

"Cool."

Bill liked the quote but he thought it was wrong, he found his best work happened when he bounced off someone like Paul. For once though he kept his thoughts to himself, he couldn't imagine going home and explaining to his mom that there'd be no buyout because he'd corrected Perot. She'd disown him!

Perot clapped his hands.

"So let's get to it, shall we?"

***

Bill made his decision on the plane. Despite how much he liked the idea of working with Perot, it wasn't that difficult.

Back in Seattle, Bill went straight to Paul's office and explained his thinking.

"They were good people, I think we'd get on fine as part of EDS. They're more established now but they're obviously cut from the same sort of cloth as us."

"So what's the problem? It's obviously a 'no', I can tell by the look on your face."

"Two things. The first is money, their offer doesn't really reflect the value I think we have in Microsoft."

"What is he offering?"

"There wasn't a concrete one, but he was talking mid seven figures."

"Okay. And what's our projected end of year revenue this year?"

"Easily a couple of million. And we're on track to double the number of staff which probably means the next few years grow again, although to be fair I haven't done a proper forecast on that yet."

Paul did a bit of mental maths. He and Bill were still the sole shareholders, so Perot's offer, concrete or not, would make them both multi-millionaires overnight. But if they did hit Bill's projection, and he had been right each year so far, then it probably was undervaluing the company. Particularly if the market continued to grow as they both believed it would.

"I'm with you, it would need to be higher to be worth cashing out this early. What was the second reason?"

"I was surprised that the people I spoke to didn't have a real plan for what they'd do with Microsoft."

"What about Perot himself, did he not have a plan?"

"No, he's not a technology guy."

"Smart though?"

"Super smart. He knows when to get people in who know more about a particular field than him and he's got a sharp brain."

'Super smart' was Bill's highest compliment, unless you were a programmer of course, then he would be assume you were super-smart and the compliments, or more likely the opposite, would revolve around how tight and neat your code was.

"It's just odd that they didn't have any well thought through ideas for the personal computer. If I was them I'd have majored on the synergies between our two markets. They'd open up the corporate world to our languages while Microsoft could open up the personal computer market to them."

"But they didn't go there?"

"No, nothing. No vision. I just don't think they'd thought it through."

"Oh well, right decision then, we can't step off this now Bill."

"I agree. I'll send them a letter and let them know."

"Nicely though, right? If he's a bright guy and you got along then we might want to work with him in the future."

"Definitely, on the right project. I'd even sell to him if the timing, or the price, was right… And I'm always nice."

Paul didn't bother replying to that.

***

Once Bill had finished talking to Paul he went next door to his own office and called his parents. He knew his mom in particular would want to know what he'd decided as soon as possible.

"I'm not going to go for it Mom," he told her as soon as she came on the phone.

"Well, it's your decision son, but why ever not?"

"The price wasn't right."

"You don't have to tell me but do you want to give me a rough idea?"

"Of course, he was talking about a mid seven figure range."

"Bill! Do you know the flexibility that would give you? To get that much at your age, you could choose to do anything you wanted."

"This is what I want Mom, I'd want to do the same thing again but if they've got any sense then they'd put in a non-compete clause and after a handover period when I was locked in to work for Perot, I'd end up having to do something different because I couldn't set up a similar company."

"Well, you don't know that for sure," Mary said although her own knowledge of the business world was good enough that she knew her son was right.

"It'd be surprising if he'd got where he is and didn't put something like that in, wouldn't it?"

"Well, yes, it would," she admitted. "So does this mean you've definitely made up your mind?"

"Yes, I think it's best that we stick with it ourselves and look to grow the business. It's still a growing market and there's room fo us to take much more of it. We can achieve more if we keep our independence Mom."

He's never going back to Harvard, Mary thought with a sigh, but she believed in her son.

"Well, it's your call Trey but don't burn your bridges with him okay? There might be a time when you'll want to sell and he might be the right person."

"I'm not going to burn my bridges, why does everyone keep saying that?!"

***

By the end of 1979 Bill and Paul could justifiably feel that they had made the right decision both to turn down Perot and to focus on the Japanese market.

Microsoft revenue for the year was $2.4 million, slightly higher than Bill had told Perot in his 'thank you but no' letter. And half of that revenue was coming from Japan.

NEC launched the PC-8001 in September and it became a huge success, ultimately gaining NEC 45% of the Japanese personal computer marketplace. And Microsoft were right there with them.

Every time a Japanese consumer or business loaded BASIC at the top of the screen they would see the words "Copyright 1979 (C) by Microsoft" (followed, of course, by the now ubiquitous "OK" prompt that Bill had first chosen to save memory space for the Altair).

Orders poured into Microsoft from other Japanese manufacturers and before long it was almost impossible to use a computer in Japan that didn't have Microsoft software.

C:\PART\CHAPTER> 3.2

Paul looked up at the knock on his door and was surprised to see Bill walking in. Bill never knocked. Nobody ever really knocked. But if Bill wanted to discuss something he usually just shouted from next door and they met in the corridor outside.

He was even more surprised when Bill closed the door behind him.

"You alright Bill?"

"Yeah, I've just got something I want us to talk about in private," Bill said walking around Paul's desk, ignoring the chair opposite and perching instead on the edge next to Paul's chair.

"Okay, go on."

"You and I don't know anything about running a big company, not really. We've been figuring it out and doing well enough but wouldn't it be easier if we got someone who actually knew what they we're doing?"

"I guess," Paul said.

"I mean, you and I can look at technical stuff together but the business aspects just don't interest you as much." Paul started to object but Bill raised his hand to calm him. "It's not a criticism, you've always been more into the technology than the business side of things. And that's cool but I need to focus on sales as well and there's only so much bandwidth that any of us have. I think we need to bring someone in to help me with the business side."

"So are you thinking of going to somewhere like Intel or DEC? If we have to have someone new then we need them to understand the industry as well as management."

"I'm not sure we do, Microsoft isn't like those other technology companies. And we want to stay different. Besides it's like I said, you and I can cover the technology side. We don't need anybody else to bring more of the same. It could even bring problems if they had a strong technology view and they disagreed with us," Bill said glossing over the gargantuan disagreements he and Paul already occasionally had.

"Okay Bill, you've obviously already got someone in mind, so who are you thinking of?"

"Steve Ballmer." He paused briefly in the hope that Paul would show some sign of recognition but in the moment the name obviously escaped him. "You remember Steve, you met him a couple of times when I was at Harvard."

"Oh yes," said Paul. "I remember him now, the guy who looks like he works for the secret police?"

Bill chuckled remembering Paul had said as much years ago. He'd said it was the piercing eyes but when Bill had run and told Steve about it, he'd focused on Steve's huge frame and prematurely balding dome.

"Yes, that's him. After he left Harvard he worked at Procter & Gamble doing some of their marketing stuff and now he's at business school at Stanford."

"He was doing maths with you wasn't he?"

"Yeah, applied. But he stuck around and finished it. In fact he graduated magna cum laude. He's super smart Paul and he works like an ox."

"Okay, well it sounds sensible. Sound him out."

"Right, yes, I will, great." Paul thought that was it but Bill didn't get up. He adjusted his glasses and cleared his throat. "There's one other thing."

"Yep?"

"Yeah. Obviously Steve is on a higher track than most of our guys and we'll be bringing him in to manage them."

Bill hesitated so Paul prompted him.

"Yes…"

"And he'll be giving up a lot by joining us…"

This time Paul just waited, whatever it was Bill could just spit it out. Eventually he did just that.

"I think if we want to get him on board we'll need to give him some equity."

"What?!"

Paul was already sensitive about the equity split between the two of them which, after another couple of adjustments over the years, had settled after on a 64:36 split in favour of Bill.

"It's only reasonable. We're not going to get anyone to join us at this stage without offering them an equity stake unless we offer them a salary that would be out of our price range."

Paul took a deep breath, despite his irritation he knew that Bill was basically right. Equity stakes were becoming more common in the technology industry, in fact several of the programmers had already raised that point with him. *Which will no doubt be its own headache if we give equity to Ballmer and not them,* he thought. *But we'll cross that bridge when we come to it.*

"Okay, but we need to be really careful about this getting out. I can't see the team being very happy if we give away a stake in the company to someone who hasn't done anything to build it."

"Agreed," Bill said, obviously relieved that Paul had conceded. He started to stand up as he said, "And we'll keep it a small amount. No more than ten percent."

"Ten percent!" Paul said, pushing his chair back from the desk so he could look Bill more squarely in the eye. "We're not giving him ten percent."

Bill blinked repeatedly and looked nonplussed.

"Well, what do you think is right then?" he said.

"Five. No more."

"Okay, five. I'll speak to him. I really think this is the right thing Paul, he'll bring a huge amount to the table."

"Yep, I'm sure. Is there anything else or can I get back on with this?" he said gesturing at the pad on his desk.

"No, that's cool. That's everything."

Bill got up and left, leaving the door open behind him.

***

"Do you know anybody as good as you?" Bill said.

Bill had invited Steve Ballmer up to spend some time with him in Seattle and had decided to start his recruitment drive in the Porsche on the way to a meal with his parents.

The more Bill had thought about it the more he'd realised he desperately needed a partner he could trust on the business side of things. He'd come to realise that whenever he'd been at his best it was with a strong partner, whether Kent in the early days getting fired up about starting a business, Paul on the technology itself, or Kay in the breakthrough to Japan. He worked best with someone to bounce ideas off, someone who'd challenge him even if he did ultimately make the decision.

And he'd decided it was going to be Ballmer. There was no way he was letting him go without getting him on board.

"As good as me, it's hard to imagine there'd be two of us."

"I'm serious, I need help and it has to be someone who's as good as you. Someone who can keep up with me you know? At the moment the whole place reports to me."

"What's happened to Paul, isn't he still with you?"

"Nothing's happened to him, Paul's okay and he's still absolutely at the heart of Microsoft. He's brilliant, easily as smart as us, but he's really a tech guy. I need someone who gets business. Someone like you. Do you have a twin you've never told me about?"

Ballmer turned in his seat and levelled with his friend.

"Cut the shit Bill. If you want me to do it, then come on out and ask me."

Bill smirked.

"Okay. I want you to do it. Why wouldn't you?"

"Oh I don't know, perhaps because I know absolutely nothing about computers. I've never even used one!"

"You don't need to know about computers, I've got that covered. I need someone who knows sales and, you know, general management stuff. You did that at P&G right?"

"Well, yes, I guess."

"And you're getting a grasp of the theory side of things at Stanford?"

"Sure."

"Yeah, of course you are. But who wants to just do theory right?" Ballmer rolled his eyes at the transparent push his friend was making. "You want to make an impact in the world. You're not going to do that if you finish at Stanford and then join some boring old company like General Motors, are you?"

"Boring old company or established company Bill? No offence but how do I know that if I join Microsoft it will still be here in two years time."

Bill surprised him by just shrugging.

"You don't," he said. "But you'll have had a hell of a ride in the meantime. And you get a chance to change the world instead of spending a year trying to convince people to lie a box on its side."

"Low blow."

Bill took his hand off the steering wheel and held them up to indicate surrender.

"Tell me I'm wrong."

"Hmph."

Ballmer was silent for a moment and Bill let him think.

Ballmer's big coup at Proctor and Gamble had been to reorient the packaging for one of their products so that it took up more shelf space and crowded out the competition. He'd been quite proud of it and told Bill about it. Hearing Bill sum it up like that did rather take the shine off his achievement.

After a moment he reached a decision.

"Okay, I'm interested but it still depends on what you can offer. Maybe 'established' is boring but it pays well."

"Understood."

"And I am going to need an equity stake."

"Again, understood. In fact we'd figured as much. Listen, I've got to go away for a week to the Caribbean. I can't get out of it and the flight is a redeye so I need to be at the airport for midnight. Why don't we have dinner with my folks, then you can drop me at the airport, take the Porsche back to my place and Paul will give you a lift back to the airport tomorrow to catch your flight? In the meantime read this," he leant across Ballmer and fished in the glovebox, pulling out an envelope and dropping it on his lap. "And I'll be in touch from the boat."

"Don't tell me, Paul knows he's giving me a lift already?"

"I thought it might be a good idea for you two to get to know each other better. You know, just in case you make the right decision."

Bill flicked his eyebrows cheekily and Ballmer got a sense of the trap closing around him. That sense only increased over dinner as Bill's parents, obviously part of the plan, grilled him about his plans for his future and talked up how great it was to live in Seattle.

***

"*Doo-Wah Doo-Wah* to Ballmer. Over. Are you receiving me? Over." Bill said into the CB-like microphone of the ship to shore phone.

It was a couple of days after their meeting and he was cruising around the Caribbean on a rented boat called the *Doo-Wah Doo-Wah* with his girlfriend; Blair Newman, the computer industry maverick as famous for his experimentation with drugs as his work on technology; Newman's girlfriend; and Kay Nishi and his new wife. All of them were either drunk or high depending on who you believe.

"Yeah, I got ya Bill," Ballmer's voice came back broadcast across the boat from the speaker of the tinny radio. "And I'm pretty sure you only say 'over' at the end of a transmission. Like this. Over."

Bill giggled.

"What did you think of the offer? *Doo-Wah Doo-Wah* Over."

Bill didn't even ask if Ballmer was going to join them, he'd just assumed that he would and moved the discussion instantly to the terms.

"I'm interested Bill but there are two points I need you to move on."

Steve loved the idea of working with Bill but he really did have other options open and he'd decided to hold fast. Bill was about to learn that having someone business minded to bounce off meant that he wouldn't always win these types of conversations.

"Go on," Bill said, dropping the nautical game.

"The equity needs to be higher. Even with the higher salary that you're going to agree in a minute, I'll be giving up a lot by not going to one of those boring old companies you don't think I should work for."

Unseen by the other man Bill smiled.

"What are you thinking then?"

"I want a bigger number, but you'd be right to ask what you're getting for that so I've got a suggestion. Why don't we start it at a floor of four percent, that's one percent less than you're offering, but tie an additional six points to performance. If I increase company sales by x% a year, and we can agree on what x is later, then I get a higher percentage. And we'll cap it so I never get more than ten percent however much extra revenue I bring in."

Bill thought for a moment.

"Sounds fair, go for it," Kay shouted in a stage whisper.

Bill spun round, he had forgotten that their conversation could be heard by everybody else on the boat. Lounging on the deck with the other four, Kay was giving him the thumbs up. Bill had a flash of irritation but judging by the innocent look on Kay's face he must have thought he was being discreet enough that only Bill could hear him so he let it go.

"Agreed. What about the salary then?"

"You've offered forty. I'm going to want sixty."

"Sixty is ridiculous Steve, forty is more than we pay anyone else."

"You don't have anyone else do what you're asking me to do."

"I might be able to go higher than forty but sixty is out the question."

"Hey! Give him what he wants!" shouted one of the women from the front of the boat. Bill spun around again to see Kay, struggling to put his hand over the mouth of Newman's girlfriend while his own wife looked on aghast.

"Sounds like you're having fun there," Ballmer said so that his friend knew he could hear.

"Hm," Bill said. "Ignore them this is a conversation between you and me."

"So give me another number Bill but it will need to be closer to sixty than forty."

"Just pay him what he wants!"

Bill couldn't tell which of them had shouted that so he moved to put the phone's speaker behind him to keep an eye on the jokers at the front of the boat. Kay was fighting a losing battle to keep them under control. His wife had gone below deck, obviously fed up of the whole thing.

"Okay, Steve, listen you can hear it's mental here. I'm not going to be able to hold a proper conversation and I don't want to insult you by messing around. I want you but it's going to be a hard enough sell to Paul already with a higher percentage so why don't we just call it fifty grand and seal it now? If you want to hold out for more then we'll need to talk when I'm back and I'm not sure I'll be able to, or even want to, make it fly. How does that sound?"

"That'll do me Bill."

"Great, then we've got a deal."

"Absolutely. Hey Bill, I'm really looking forward to working with you man, it's going to be like old times."

"Me too Steve, I can't wait. Now... *Doo-Wah Doo-Wah* over and out."

***

Paul stormed into Bill's office without knocking and slammed a copy of a letter onto the desk in front of him.

"Paul, what's up?"

"This is up, Bill. What the hell do you mean by this?"

"What is…" Bill started to say but then he recognised the letter. It was his offer to Steve, setting out the terms they'd agreed. "Ah, yes, I've been meaning to talk to you about it but I was away and then when I got back you were off at that meeting in California."

"And you couldn't find a phone?"

"I'm sorry Paul."

"Do you know how I found out? Somebody found it on the word processor and it's been all over the office. One of the programmers brought it into me assuming I knew what was going on and demanded to know why a non-techie is getting stock when, and I quote, 'the people who make all of your money for you' don't get anything."

Bill bristled.

"I hope you told him that we pay them well enough."

"I did as it happens. I didn't let on to him how deeply betrayed I felt."

"Betrayed?" Bill tried his best to look innocent.

"You know damn well what I mean. We agreed five percent and then you went behind my back and gave him ten."

"It isn't a straightforward ten Paul, look…" Bill tried to point to the clause setting out the performance targets but Paul wasn't interested.

"It's a breach of faith Bill, that's what it is. Well, you can forget it. I don't want us to hire him any more."

"We can't do that, we've made an offer."

"No, *you've* made an offer! And you can't give away my shares without my agreement so it's not an offer that stands legally is it?"

"Okay Paul I understand you're mad but listen, we still need him."

"Why? we've been doing fine without anyone in the role. In fact that's another thing, 'Assistant to the President', what even is that?!" he yelled, slamming his finger down on the part of the letter that listed Steve's title.

"There has to be a title and we want him to have as wide a range as possible so he can support us."

"Do we Bill? And exactly who is 'we' now? Because it doesn't feel like it's me any more. And if he's so great why is he even leaving Stanford? He can't be that good if they're letting him go."

"Alright, let's calm down a bit here," Bill said. "As it happens he was the best in his class, he won twenty thousand dollars' worth of prizes to prove it. But that isn't the point, the point is that we - *you and me* - want him here to help build the business. If he does that then we - *you and me* - will do very well out of it. It's not unreasonable that he should have his own reward tied to that performance. I get that the programmers are upset about it, we need to ride that one out for now and then maybe when Steve's on board we can get him to think about how we might reward them with stock options or something." He paused to see if his words were having any effect on Paul. "What do you think?"

"Great, that will help the programmers, but you still went behind my back and gave away part of my ownership of a company that wouldn't exist without me. I didn't argue back when you took a bigger share for yourself originally, but this is just taking the piss."

Bill was uncharacteristically silent for a beat, his brain racing to work out how to fix the mess he'd got himself in. Then a solution hit him.

"What about if I make up the extra out of my own share?"

"Explain."

"We'll each put up two and a half percent from our stakes to cover the five we agreed, but if he outperforms and earns the additional I'll take it out of my share alone. Does that sound fair?"

Paul hesitated, still angry but unable to argue with that.

"Yes," he said finally.

Bill's shoulders sank as he breathed out with relief.

"Okay good, that's settled then." He stood up and smiled, hoping they could put this behind them. "Don't blame Steve, Paul, he's a good guy and I want him to get off on the best foot he can here."

"I don't blame *him* Bill, he's just a guy going for a job, it makes sense for him to try to get as much as he can. I blame *you*. You're supposed to be my friend."

C:\PART\CHAPTER> 3.3

"Bill Gates speaking."

"Mr. Gates, this is Jack Sams from IBM. I appreciate this is a little out of the blue but I'd like to come up and see you to discuss… a possible opportunity we're exploring."

"Of course, Mr. Sams I'd be delighted." *IBM, cool!* "Can you give me an idea of what it will be about so I have the right people on hand?"

"I'd rather not. Sorry about the cloak and dagger nature."

"Not at all," Bill had been flicking through his diary as he spoke. "I'm pretty maxed this week but I can move things around next week to suit you."

"Ah, I was thinking more like tomorrow. My secretary is booking a flight for me as we speak that leaves this evening."

IBM didn't do anything quickly, so Bill guessed if they were looking for a meeting tomorrow then there was something big going on here. And he wanted to be in on it.

"Okay, come up tomorrow Mr. Sams. I will rearrange my meetings and we can talk."

"Thank you Mr. Gates, I really appreciate the flexibility."

Bill put the phone down on Sams and practically ran to Ballmer's office.

"Steve! IBM are coming."

"When?"

"Tomorrow."

"Best put on a suit then."

"Why do you think I'm inviting you? No one else here has one."

***

Sams looked at the young man standing in front of him with his hand extended and did a double take.

This is Gates?! This kid is the boss? Sams thought.

He looked like he should still be in college. Hell, he looked like it was borderline whether he should have started college. And he appeared to have borrowed a suit from a slightly larger man.

Jesus, Don is going to blow his top. This is dead before it begins. Still, I've come all this way now.

"Thank you again for seeing me on such short notice Mr. Gates."

"No problem, and it's Bill." Bill gestured to the empty seats at the small conference table and then at the much larger, balding man standing on the other side of the table. "This is Steve Ballmer, he'll be joining us today, I assume that's alright."

"Of course, nice to meet you Mr. Ballmer… Steve. This is Pat Harrington with our contracts department. Now, before we start, I will need you both to sign our non disclosure agreement."

Sams took a seat, while Pat pulled IBM's standard NDA from his briefcase and slid two copies across the table. Bill and Steve took a copy each and quickly read through it.

While he skimmed the document Bill considered his guest. If he had been asked to imagine an IBM representative he would have imagined Jack Sams.

Sams was a thin, well dressed man, turned out in a dark grey, almost black, pin stripe suit with a paisley tie and an easy smile that fitted his southern accent perfectly. He wasn't actually a salesman, but he had a natural affability and confidence that meant Bill could imagine people would happily buy encyclopaedias or vacuums from him.

"That's all fine," Bill said first and then signed it before pushing it back across the table. A moment later Steve did likewise.

"Thank you," Pat said and stowed the papers back in his briefcase.

"Now, I suppose you'd like to know what all of the secrecy is about?" Sams said.

"Yes please."

Sams glanced briefly at Harrington, who nodded and then sat back.

"IBM has initiated a piece of work called Project Chess. The aim of that project is to consider if, and how, we should make a move into the personal computer market," Sams said simply.

Steve looked surprised, since he had joined a couple of weeks ago he had been pumping everybody he could for information on the industry, cramming information into his prodigious brain and one thing that had come up was that IBM was a mainframe player.

Bill was less surprised.

"I thought you'd shelved the Datamaster project," he said.

"Not quite shelved, more delayed," Sams replied, impressed at the knowledge this outsider had of a supposedly secret IBM project. "But this isn't that."

"Oh? Well, how can we help?"

"Do you mind if I give you a bit of history first? It will help to set the context. Though I'll ask you to remember that everything I tell you here today is confidential," Sams said and rapped on Pat's briefcase to indicate the NDAs they had signed. Both men nodded, so Sams began. "We have, as you already know, got a project underway to develop a small desktop computer called the Datamaster. It is behind schedule. Very behind schedule. My boss's boss has come up with the idea that we should develop an alternative using a radically different approach. The Datamaster is applying everything IBM knows about mainframe development to the microcomputer. Bill Lowe, that's the boss's boss, he thinks that's the problem. He says if we want to compete with a market that is being led by companies started in people's garages then we need to think the same way as they do. I would assume you agree? Anyway, he persuaded the CMC..."

"I'm sorry," Bill interrupted by raising a finger. "CMC?"

"The Corporate Management Committee..."

Bill interrupted again, repeating Sams' words slowly, "Corporate. Management. Committee?"

"Yes, it's the IBM board that makes decisions like this."

"Hm. I see, carry on."

Bill shot a sidelong look at Steve and considered the reaction of his programmers if he introduced a group with a name like that. Three words could hardly have been chosen that would less suit Microsoft's style. In fact, it was hard to imagine two more different organisations than Microsoft and IBM.

"I understand what you're very discreetly not saying Bill, believe me. IBM is a fantastic company to work for, I've been there twenty years and I intend to work there for a long time to come. We can do some great things, but this is not our natural playground. And that's Lowe's whole point. So he's appointed a team to prove we can do it and to show the CMC."

"Understood," Bill acknowledged the other man's candour with a nod. "So what brings you to Microsoft, Jack?" He hoped he knew the answer but he needed to hear it from the man.

"I headed the team developing BASIC for the Datamaster project, it's a large part of why we're behind schedule on that one and I want to avoid the same thing here." Sams paused before coming out with it. "I want to buy Microsoft BASIC for the new IBM personal computer."

Bill nodded and sat slightly more upright but he resisted the urge to speak, it was always best to give people a bit of rope at these times. It wasn't a surprise really, there weren't that many reasons IBM would visit Microsoft but he was excited.

When it was obvious Bill wasn't going to say anything else Sams continued.

"And potentially other languages as well but I need to be sure that you could deliver them on schedule. We're talking an aggressive timeline here."

"How long?"

"We want to release the machine for sale in a year."

"We can do that," Bill said without hesitation.

"FORTRAN, COBOL and BASIC?" Sams asked, rattling off the most popular languages.

"Sure, we've done it plenty of times. But do you mind if I ask you some questions?"

"As long as you're not offended if I refuse to answer."

"No, I understand. If there's anything you can't tell me then just don't."

Bill proceeded to grill Sams on the details of the computer that IBM were planning, most of which Sams either couldn't or wouldn't answer and at some point the conversation turned into a demonstration of some of the other machines that Microsoft currently had on their test table.

"These are all on the market?" Sams asked.

"No, no, several are in development. It helps us build faster to have early prototypes. And it gives us a better understanding of where the market is heading. Like, have you thought about using a 16-bit chip for your machine? If IBM get into this then you have a good chance to set the standard and it would be in everybody's interest if the standard was 16-bit not 8."

"Wouldn't it slow you down if we used 16-bit? You don't currently have any 16-bit versions of your languages for sale," Sams said, sidestepping the question.

"No, it wouldn't slow us down. We have been pushing 16-bit for a couple of years now, we have base versions of most of our languages in 16-bit. Most of them aren't finished of course because almost nobody's made the leap but it's going to happen shortly and if I were you I'd want IBM as future proof as possible on this."

"Hm," Sams grunted noncommittally and then distracted Bill with a question about a Japanese Matsushita machine.

"This is all great Bill. It's possible, probable even, that the CMC will kill the project but if it doesn't I'd say we'll be having an interesting follow up conversation on the language front. Now, what about an operating system? We know that you folks use one in your Apple Softcard so we'd want to license that from you as well."

Bill winced.

"I'm afraid that's not possible. We don't do operating systems, for the Softcard I licensed CP/M from Gary Kildall at Digital Research and we don't have the rights to sub-license."

Sams looked crestfallen.

"That's a shame. I was hoping to have a single vendor on the software side."

"A single throat to choke?" Bill chuckled. "Gary's a good guy, we've worked with him a fair bit. Do you want me to make a call for you and set up a meeting?"

"If you already know him that would be helpful, thanks. It'll need to be as soon as possible, though."

"Don't worry, I'll tell him. I'm sure he'll fit you in like I did. When you can get there?"

"Tomorrow probably, where are they?"

"Pacific Grove, California."

"Yes, tell him I can be there tomorrow."

Bill picked up the phone on the desk next to them and called Digital Research there and then.

"He knows the number by heart?" Sams said quietly to Ballmer.

"He has a good memory for numbers," Steve said, long used to his friend's peculiar memory tricks.

After demanding to speak to Gary, Bill got straight to the point, or at least as much of the point as he could without breaking the NDA.

"Gary, it's Bill Gates... I've got some important customers here with me who are looking for an operating system. I'm sending them your way... No, no problem but listen, these guys are in a hurry, can you meet them tomorrow?.. Good... No. I can't tell you now. But they're real important Gary, you won't regret it. Treat them nice... Ha! Yeah, I know... Okay, gotta go. Speak soon."

He put down the phone and looked at Sams.

"He'll meet you tomorrow morning at ten," he said.

***

"So what did you think of them?" Sams asked Harrington as they walked to their rental car.

"Ballmer was quiet."

Sams smiled. "So were you! Anyway, he's only just joined. Been there a coupe of weeks. I mean the outfit as a whole though. And Gates. What did you think of him?"

"It was better than I'd been expecting, most of these software houses are little three-person affairs. Looks like they've got a serious business here."

Sams decided to lay his cards on the table.

"I think I'm going to recommend them. Gates is smart. Very smart. I like the way he's thinking ahead as well. He could sell us the 8-bit stuff with practically no effort and make a healthier short term margin but he's pushing us to do 16-bit because he thinks it will be better for the market."

"I thought Don," Harrington said, meaning Don Estridge, the project leader under Lowe. "Had already said we'd be using a 16-bit chip?"

157

"He has, but I can't tell Gates that yet."

"No, that makes sense." Harrington paused. Technology wasn't really his bag, he was a contract guy, but he had been around long enough to spot a pattern that was already emerging. "It's not just better for the market though, is it? If the industry moves to a 16-bit standard then won't all of the companies he's sold his languages to need to buy new versions?"

"Well, yeah, that's true."

"Not quite an altruistic move then?"

"Maybe not," Sams conceded. "But it's still the right call and he is running a business after all."

"Fair enough. Hey, what do you think of their security?" he asked with a grin.

"Oh my God!" Sams slapped his forehead. "Can you imagine Don being happy with an IBM machine sitting on that little table out in the open?!"

"And him demonstrating it to every competitor who wanders by the office!"

"Definitely something to work into any contract we agree with them."

"I'll make a note when we're at the airport."

***

Bill and Steve stood at the conference room window, watching Sams and Harrington across the road below them.

"Who are Digital Research?" Steve asked.

"Gary Kildall and his wife, Dorothy. I knew him back in Seattle actually. Well, our paths crossed. It was when I was a kid at C-Cubed, did I ever tell you about that?" Ballmer shrugged. "I'll tell you another time, funny story. Anyway Gary wrote CP/M. There isn't one standard operating system that all manufacturers use but CP/M is the most popular one. Like our BASIC."

"But why send them to him, can't we do it ourselves? It's all just programming, isn't it?"

"We could but we kind of have a tacit understanding that we focus on languages and they focus on operating systems." Ballmer looked unconvinced. "Besides, they need it in a year. If they do decide to go with a 16-bit chipset then we'll have to rewrite everything apart from BASIC and we have to make sure we deliver the languages on time. We aren't about to develop an operating system at the same time in under a year."

***

Sams called Bill back two days later. He wasn't happy.

"Bill, we went to Digital Research like you recommended but it didn't work out."

158

Bill frowned at the phone.

"What do you mean it didn't work out?"

"Kildall didn't show up. I met his wife, Dorothy..."

"She's his business partner as well. You could do the deal with her," Bill interrupted.

"Well, that's just it, we couldn't get far enough to talk about doing a deal. We spent the whole day arguing over the NDA."

Bill's eyebrows shot up.

"She didn't sign the NDA?"

"No, she said it was too one sided."

And she's right, Bill thought. But that was the price of doing business with someone like IBM. You felt like the junior partner because you were. If you wanted a chance of playing you sucked it up like he had.

"So where did you leave it?"

"We're still trying to get a conversation going but to be honest I don't like it, I want to deal with someone easier."

"Okay... operating systems... I assume you're still considering both 16 and 8-bit... who else can I recommend..." Bill thought aloud.

"You're missing the point Bill," Sams said patiently. "I want it to be you. We always wanted one person to deal with and this has just proved it. We've got a lot to get done if we're going to make the deadline and I need someone managing it who can just handle it for me. What was it you said? 'One throat to choke'!"

"I wasn't volunteering Jack."

Sams laughed.

"I know, but seriously Bill, is there no way you can do it?"

Bill hesitated.

"Leave it with me."

"I'm hearing that as a yes," Sams pushed. "Tell me it's a yes. If this gets the go-ahead then you'll make a pitch for the whole thing?"

"Alright... Yes."

Now I just need to work out how the hell to do it, Bill thought.

***

Forty five minutes later, following some discreet phone calls Bill met with Paul, Kay and Steve in his office.

"I'm pretty sure IBM are serious," he said, starting with the good news.

"Do they just want BASIC or more?" Paul asked.

"It still needs to be approved by their committee but if they can solve their other problems then I think they'll buy all the languages we can give them."

"That's great," Steve said.

"Wow. IBM," Paul said, reflecting on how far they'd come.

"Yeah, I know. But there's a problem."

"Problem?" Nishi parroted.

"Kildall ballsed up the operating system pitch. They don't want to buy from him. They want to it buy from us."

"That's good isn't it?" Steve said. "We just speak to Kildall and arrange to be an intermediary. We can put a markup on top and resell his thing. Money for nothing."

"Yeah, except that's the next problem. I don't think it exists. Gary's been talking about a 16-bit version for a while now, so I figured he'd got it ready and, like us with 16-bit BASIC, he was polishing it behind the scenes until he got a real customer. But I tapped up a couple of my contacts and no-one's seen it. I don't think he's actually written it."

Paul stroking his beard thoughtfully.

"He's got a hundred different 8-bit versions though, if IBM do an 8-bit machine then there's no problem. Do we know for sure what chipset they'll be using?" he asked.

"No, but I'd be gob-smacked if they wen't for 8-bit, wouldn't you?"

"Yeah," he agreed, reluctantly. "They'd have to be stupid. And they've already got that Datamaster project that's supposed to be doing exactly that, so why bother with a new one."

"Exactly," Bill said.

Everyone fell quiet for a moment, trying to think of a solution. Finally Steve spoke.

"Can we just tell IBM they should do an 8-bit thing? They seemed to be listening to you."

"No!" Nishi cried as though he was in physical pain.

"Kay's right," Bill said. "It would be embarrassing for them to bring out an 8-bit machine this late. And you heard me, I made a bit of a big deal about them using 16-bit, I'd look like an idiot."

"So what do we do then?" Steve asked.

There was another moment's silence until Nishi surprised everyone by jumping up and waving his hands in the air excitedly.

"We've gotta do it! We've gotta do it!" he said, looking around the room at the other three men. "You know we can do it. We can write one."

"How?" Paul said, shaking his head. "We don't have the programmers and we don't have the time. An operating system is no small thing."

"That's what you said to me yesterday," Steve said to Bill, who screwed up his face in response.

"I will get the ASCII people to do it," Kay said enthusiastically, referring to the couple of programmers who worked exclusively on the Japanese market versions of the existing languages.

"Okay, get them to size it up," Bill said. "But we can't underestimate it, I agree with Paul, this isn't an easy thing to get done."

"Is there any way out of it? I mean, did you really commit?" Paul asked.

"Well, I didn't put anything in writing, but I said I'd solve it. They're going to send us an invitation for a proposal, so we'll see what that says and I guess we could always just pitch the languages. But if we do that and they don't have an operating system then the whole thing doesn't fly. It's just another way to fail."

"So we need to either tell them right now to look elsewhere or we need to come up with a solution. I'll ask around the industry quietly and see if I can find anyone who's got a start. Maybe we can piggyback off something," Paul said.

"Great. Steve, what do you think?"

"This is more your guys' thing than mine. I don't understand how big a deal it is technically, but I'm with Kay. I think we have to grab the opportunities when they come along and this is one of them. If that means we need to write it ourselves then we should just hire some more people and get it done."

The meeting broke up and the three men left the room, strangely deflated after what should have been good news.

***

The next day they received a formal invitation to pitch from IBM.

IBM confirmed the outline specs of a machine they were going to present to the CMC in two months and asked Microsoft to provide 16-bit versions of all of their main languages.

And a 16-bit operating system to run them on.

***

Bill was standing with a group of programmers in front of a whiteboard in the open office when Paul ran over.

"Bill, Bill, we need a moment!" he panted.

"Give me a minute," Bill said to the programmers, throwing the marker he was using to the nearest person and pacing off with Paul. "What is it?" he asked when they were out of earshot.

"I've got the answer."

"The answer to...?" Bill looked puzzled. Despite how big a deal IBM was, Microsoft still had lots of balls in the air and Bill and Paul both worked directly on all of them. An 'answer' could have applied to almost anything.

"To the operating system for IBM. Tim's just called me. He's got a 16-bit OS ready to go."

"Tim?"

"Paterson, over at Seattle Computer."

Seattle Computer was a small outfit, exactly the kind of company that Harrington had been concerned about when they had first visited Microsoft. Set up by Rod Brock a couple of years earlier to manufacture memory boards, they had developed a 16-bit CPU when Tim Paterson, Brock's chief engineer, had been inspired by the same Intel 8086 chip that had got Bill so fired up about 16-bit chipsets.

Paul knew Tim Paterson from the development of the Softcard for Apple. Business never exactly boomed at Seattle Computer, and in one of their slow periods Paul had employed Tim Paterson part time to help Microsoft develop the Apple Softcard. When that was finished the two had kept in touch. Tim had even gone with Bill and Paul to the 1979 National Computer Conference where they had used his 16-bit CPU to demonstrate their newest BASIC.

"Seattle Computer need someone to develop a 16-bit operating system so there's a decent market for their CPUs, so I asked Tim if he knew anything about CP/M-86," Paul said, using the name of the, as yet illusory, 16-bit operating system that Digital Research were supposed to be developing. "He didn't. Apparently every time he speaks to Kildall's people they just keep promising it'll be out some time next year. Anyway, he said that he and Brock have pretty much given up waiting… so he's developed one himself."

Bill froze in place and Paul, lost in his monologue, overshot him by a couple of steps. When he noticed that Bill had stopped he scurried back. Bill's brain was whirring and whatever module of his brain that had been running his feet had obviously been shunted over to focus on the problem at hand.

"Go on," he said, nodding excitedly and rearranging his glasses compulsively.

"He said it's not as good as he'd expect the proper CP/M-86 to be, in fact he's called it QDOS for Quick and Dirty Operating System!"

"But it works."

"It works."

"And we could license it."

"No reason why not."

C:\PART\CHAPTER> 3.4

The day of the pitch, September 30th 1980, arrived and found Jack Sams sat on the IBM side of a long table in Boca Raton waiting for the Microsoft team to show up.

They were late. Well technically it was 09:58 and the meeting wasn't until 10:00 but Sams was nervous. It was weird but he'd come to identify with these guys over the month or so he'd been dealing with them and despite sitting on the opposite side of the table today he was privately routing for them.

Don Estridge looked at the clock on the wall and checked it against his watch.

"I reckon Gates is our answer Don," Sams said, mostly to fill the silence while they waited.

"I certainly hope so because if he isn't we don't have one and that means we don't have a working machine. I don't fancy going back to the CMC and telling them that I failed."

Don leant back in his chair and placed his cowboy booted feet up on the edge of the desk, something that would have been completely unthinkable in any part of IBM except one of the crack squad of trouble shooters like the ones he'd gathered around him to deliver this.

"I'm sure we'll have something credible for CMC," Sams said. "Microsoft are a great team and Gates is a force, you'll see."

"Well, John believes in him since he spoke to the kid's mother."

Sams was taken aback and the looks on the faces of everyone else at the table told him he wasn't alone. When Don referred to 'John' they all knew he meant John Opel, the man who had been president since 1974 and would become CEO of the company four months later. But what was he doing talking to Gates's mother?

"His mother?"

"Yeah, apparently they're on the board of United Way together or something. I was giving him a briefing on the project and I mentioned that we needed this Seattle company run by someone called Gates to deliver the goods on the software and he says, 'That must be Mary Gates's boy. She's great. If he's anything like Mary then we'll be in good hands.' so that's that. We'd better make bloody sure they can deliver today gents because John's watching." He looked at his watch again, "So where the hell are they?"

***

Although Don Estridge would never find out, the answer to where the Microsoft team were was: a Burdines department store not far outside Boca Raton.

Bill had made the trip to Florida with Steve Ballmer and Bob O'Rear, who was going to lead the development effort in Microsoft. The three of them had landed at Miami airport two and a half hours earlier assuming that would give them plenty of time to get to the IBM offices.

Wanting to look their best they had not worn their suits on the overnight flight from Seattle so once they'd landed they headed for the men's room to get changed.

Steve and Bob were both standing outside the gents, starting to get a little confused, when Bill finally came out.

"Where's your tie?" Steve asked with a frown.

"I haven't packed it, that's what took me so long. I was looking for it."

"In that?" Steve tried to lighten the mood by pointing at the now empty suit bag in which nothing could possibly hide. "Never mind. So you haven't got a tie?"

"No," Bill said. "Do either of you have a spare?"

"No."

"Sorry Bill, no."

"Damn it. Well it's too late now, let's go. Where's the rental place?"

Steve pointed and the three of them made their way to the rental agency's booth. It took far too long for the agency to find their reservation, then another age to collect the car.

Bill, who didn't have a watch on kept asking Bob the time.

"We can't be late."

"We know that Bill."

"I'll drive," he said, unnecessarily, both Steve and Bob knew him well enough to know there was never going to be any other option.

After what felt like an age they got on the road and Bill interspersed his questions about the time with curses at the traffic and the car.

"What is wrong with this stupid thing, did someone forget to connect the gas pedal? Why doesn't it accelerate?"

"We're going to be late," Steve said.

Better late than dead, O'Rear thought as Bill veered around the car in front but decided it was wiser to remain silent.

After a minute's silence Bill spoke as though halfway through a conversation.

"The tie is an issue."

"It'll be fine."

"Give me yours then."

Steve, riding shotgun, winced slightly. He thought he'd got it under control in time but Bill had seen it.

"Exactly. You'd look like an idiot. Do you think *I* want to look like an idiot?"

He stared at the road ahead and squeezed his lips together while he overtook a truck. When they were safely passed he shook his head.

"No. We've got to stop and get one."

"It'll make us late."

"We're already late," Bill snapped.

"It might be better to be a bit later if it'll make you feel readier," Bob said from the back seat in a reasonable voice. "You don't want to present feeling at a disadvantage."

Steve shot him a look over his shoulder but Bill hit Steve in the arm and smiled for the first time since the bathroom at the airport.

"See Steve, Bob knows what I'm talking about."

"Hey it's your call, you're the boss."

***

They finally arrived at IBM's office just before 10:30 and were shown into the room where the Project Chess team were waiting.

That's a lot of people, Bill thought as Sams made the introductions.

He already knew Sams of course and a couple of the others, Lew Eggebrecht and Pat Harrington had been involved in the early work, and he'd had one conversation with Don Estridge, Sams's boss, but the others he didn't recognise. Luckily Sams had given him a run down of the members of the wider team so when he heard their names he knew what they did and the sorts of positions they were likely to take.

When Sams had finished Bill stood and introduced himself, Steve, and Bob, and then opened with an apology.

"Again, I'm really sorry we were late."

"As long as it's not a sign of things to come Mr. Gates," Don Estridge said, raising a couple of gentle chuckles from the IBM side of the table and nervous smiles from Steve and Bob. "That will be fine. We all have the day blocked out for this."

Bill nodded to Steve who handed out copies of the reports, there weren't quite enough so Steve and Bob shared.

"Well, I'll try not to take up any more of your time than is necessary," he said. "If you'll turn to page two, I'll begin…"

And he launched into his presentation, starting with a high level plan that showed how Microsoft could meet the delivery deadline that IBM had shared.

His single previous conversation with Don had been a phone call to help come up with a schematic diagram showing how the various parts of Project Chess fit together. They landed on a system architecture diagram that had the user, shown by a big circle at the top, interacting with a set of applications like the new spreadsheet program VisiCalc, a word processor, and computer languages; all of which were underpinned by an operating system and lower level assembly language; which in turn rested on IBM provided hardware.

Like all conceptual diagrams it grossly oversimplified things but it was a neat representation of the thing they were aiming at and he knew Don was pleased enough with it that it would end up in Bill Lowe's final report to the CMC. So he used it now to structure his presentation.

He highlighted the various elements that Microsoft would deliver and timescales from the shortest for BASIC to a longer timeline for FORTRAN, and so on for each. He even cheekily highlighted the 'Applications' box and described how Microsoft would be providing their *Typing Tutor* and *Adventure* game released by their recent Consumer Products division.

And then he came onto the crunch point.

"I'm also happy to confirm that we have managed to source a 16-bit operating system."

He paused briefly and looked at Don intently. He was pleased to see the beginning of a smile appear on the project leader's face before it vanished again to be replaced by his professional mask.

"Who from?" asked another IBM team member whose name Bill was irritated to admit he hadn't caught.

He'd discussed this with Paul, Nishi and Steve after Paul first found Paterson's QDOS and to their credit they had decided to be open that they hadn't developed it themselves but to major on the fact that they'd manage it from here on in.

"It was developed by a small Seattle company who we can put you in touch with if you want. However, as I agreed with Mr. Sams, Microsoft will be happy to act as a single point of contact for you." He exchanged a meaningful look with Sams who caught the reference to their discussion of the optimum number of throats to choke. "We have agreed an unlimited sub-licensing arrangement with the company so there will be no legal issues, and if you turn to page twelve you will see that we have included a plan to manage integration with your BIOS and do the coding for any enhancements that are needed."

"What about CP/M, haven't I read that that is something of a de-facto standard for these microcomputers?" asked Ed Kiser from the foot of the table.

Sams rose slightly from his chair and, to Bill's surprise, actually fielded the question on his behalf.

"I'll answer that one Bill. As I explained to Don, Ed, we intend to continue pursuing a relationship with Digital Research to give our users a choice of operating systems when we launch, but unfortunately Digital Research weren't able to provide a schedule to develop the 16-bit operating system, in fact they wouldn't even commit to do it at all. There are also some legal issues to resolve regarding the sharing of information."

He sat back down and nodded at Bill to continue.

"Thank you Jack. I'd also just add," Bill said. "that our operating system mimics the APIs from CP/M so any users familiar with the program calls from CP/M will be able to use the same functions within our operating system."

"So they won't notice the difference?" Don asked.

"Isn't that a copyright problem?" Ed probed again.

Bill frowned slightly, anyone who had done any research on the young boss of Microsoft would have come across the anecdotes about his letter to hobbyists back in the MITS days. Ed must have known that and was needling him, albeit without any real venom. He managed to avoid rising to it and answered calmly.

"Absolutely not, at no point have we duplicated the code inside CP/M. We have merely replicated the calls it uses to make it easier for users to transfer their knowledge." *God, I hope that's true. I'll have to get Paul to speak to Paterson and confirm.*

When there were no other questions on the technology Pat Harrington cleared his throat and got everybody's attention.

"I know we asked you to include any key terms in your written proposal Mr. Gates," he said. "But are there any particular contractual items that you'd like to bring to my attention before I read it?"

Although he'd delivered it formally, Harrington's question was actually a bit of a layup, he and Sams had already told Bill that they preferred to get the heads of terms out early on to ensure there weren't any fundamental disagreements or nasty surprises down the line.

By this time Bill was relaxed enough to joke slightly.

"Only the money," he said, getting about as many laughs as Don had at the beginning of the meeting.

While the polite laughter rippled round the table, Bill steeled himself for an argument, he hadn't tested this next point with Harrington in advance and it might not go down well.

"Actually there is one," he said, taking the plunge. "We need this to be non-exclusive. All of our deals are non-exclusive."

He held his breath.

Retaining the right to sell to anyone was key to the company strategy that he and Paul had built into Microsoft. They had both agreed that they would never be tied to a single customer again. Even if that customer was as big as IBM.

"Fine by us," Harrington replied.

That's it? Did he just agree to it?

Not quite able to believe he had won what he saw as such a key point so easily Bill took the unusual step of providing the other side a way out.

"Well, we'll have to finalise contracts of course if your project gets the green light. So we can agree it then."

"Sure, but I don't think that particular point will be an issue," Harrington repeated.

Bill looked about the room to see if any of the other IBMers disagreed but there wasn't a flicker on any of their faces.

What Bill didn't know was that agreeing to leave Microsoft clear ownership of the code and the right to sell it to others wasn't a mistake or an oversight on IBM's part. They were keen to avoid anything that might appear to be anti-competitive. Since 1969 the company had been fighting an antitrust case against the US government that alleged that they had violated Section 2 of the Sherman Act (something that would become unpleasantly familiar to Bill in the future). The case had tied up an inordinate number of company resources, with over 30 million pages of evidence being provided and countless hours of executive time being given over to depositions. Although the thirteen year long case would be dropped by the Attorney General a little over a year after this meeting IBM had no desire to enter a new field and immediately open themselves to the same charges. So, while it was essential to Bill to retain ownership of Microsoft's code, IBM might very well have insisted on it themselves.

And, although nobody in the room then could have predicted the results, just like that the clause that would make so many Microsoft employees millionaires, and Bill, Paul and Steve billionaires, was agreed.

C:\PART\CHAPTER> 3.5

IBM delivered the first prototype machine, a mess of open chips and wiring in November 1980. Unlike all of the other manufacturers that they had dealt with up until now they insisted on complete security. There would be no keeping the test machine out on a table for anybody who happened by to tinker with, or for Bill and Paul to show to visiting executives of other companies. IBM's machine, codenamed the Acorn, would be kept in a room without windows, which had to be kept locked at all times, whether someone was working in it or not.

For IBM with its choice of buildings, a windowless room that you could reasonably expect people to work in was not hard to find, or if necessary build. That wasn't the case for Microsoft in their offices above the National Bank. The only room without windows they had available that they could secure was little more than a closet at the back of the suite, a ten foot by fifteen foot space with barely enough room for half a dozen people. And no air conditioning.

Still, as soon as the prototype arrived it was installed in that room and the glorified closet would become the beating heart of the Microsoft IBM project.

***

"Jesus, it's hot in here!" Bill said as soon as he, Paul and Steve had crammed into the tiny office to see what Bob was complaining about.

"Is it? I hadn't noticed, this is how I always dress in winter in Seattle," Bob replied with an irritated shake of his head.

Bill looked him up and down as though seeing him for the first time and took in his bermuda shorts, T-shirt and the sweat beading on his forehead.

"Alright Bob, we're all working hard," he said obviously offended. "We have to keep the door closed all the time. It's part of our commitment to the customer."

Although a large percentage of Microsoft were working on Project Chess in one way or another they tried to avoid using IBM's name to minimise the chance of slipping up when talking to outsiders.

"They can't get in to the building without us knowing though right?" Steve said. "Maybe we prop the door open and tell everyone else not to come back here. Then if the customer does show up we'll lock it up. Better, right?"

Bill didn't look convinced but Bob nodded gratefully and Paul seemed to be on the same page, so he let it go for now.

"Anyway, you didn't call us here to moan about the heat Bob, what is it?" Bill said, forgetting that it had been him who'd brought up the heat in the first place.

"It just doesn't work Bill."

"What doesn't work, DOS? BIOS? BASIC? You need to be more specific," Bill snapped.

The approaching deadline and even less sleep than usual had made him snappier.

"The machine. Look at it, it looks like Rube Goldberg built it. Wires drop out, chips break. Actually the wires aren't the problem, at least we can find them eventually. But when a chip goes because some Neanderthal used a soldering iron like a hammer, finding it takes forever. Look!" He pointed to a blue box the size of a notebook with a metre of ribbon cable snaking out of it to an exposed circuit board that was emitting an audible humming noise. "We've had to get an Intel circuit emulator specially. And that isn't helping with the heat either, I can tell you."

"Well, you're managing this part of the project aren't you Bob, have you told the customer?"

"Of course I've told them! I even wrote to them last week but they just blame the software. Sometimes it is of course, but it takes us days to prove it because the machine is just so damn flaky. We're supposed to deliver working versions of the OS and the first lot of languages by the middle of January. We're never going to do it at this rate."

"Oh, hold on…" Steve started to say but Bob was letting off steam and making the most of the undivided attention of both Bill and Paul.

"And they want to see progress every day. Every day, Bill! I mean it's not like we don't make progress every day, when the machine's working that is, but do we really need post them a floppy disk with the work on to prove it? Do you know what we did yesterday? We couldn't get Paterson's latest amends to play nice with the BIOS… you have days like that when you're churning out code like this. Hell, you know that… So I got Ed to reformat the disk before he sent it over to them so it was blank. They rang me this morning and I just played dumb. They weren't even too bothered, I said I'd send it with tonight's one and the guy I was talking to said that was fine he probably wouldn't have had chance to test it anyway!"

Bill's ears pricked up at the idea of a specific programming problem to get his teeth into.

"Have you sorted it? Shall we take a look?"

"No need, Ed cracked it overnight. I'll send it over to you with tonight's code so you can take a look. It was a neat little hack actually," Bob said looking wistful, then caught himself and got back on topic. "But that's not the point! The point is that they insist on getting them every day and they don't use them. It's just to *manage* us." He made air quotes around the word 'manage' and said it with naked disdain.

Bill who had been leaning with his back against the wall, pushed off it and bounced upright. Somewhere through Bob's long diatribe his irritation had melted away and he had shifted gears into problem solving mode.

"Okay Bob, I get it. We can't fix all of it, like the daily updates, I'm sure it's mostly pointless but they're IBM, there's only so much we can expect them to change about the way they work. But here's what we're going to do," he said, decisively. "Steve, send Harrington a letter telling them the January deadline doesn't count for anything until we get a reliable machine we can test on. Bob, when a new prototype comes in your job is to crawl all over it, test it every which way you can, I want to know that thing works one hundred percent before we let them start the clock again."

"Like C-Cubed all over again," Paul said, in a reference only he and Bill got.

"Exactly. The clock doesn't start ticking on us until they've delivered the goods. You find any issues, you raise it with them instantly so they know it's not happening. And if you get any grief bring it to me. I'll speak to Estridge. In the meantime keep Paterson, and everybody else who's working on the languages, cranking out their code based on the 8086 simulator. It'll get us pretty close so when they finally get us a working version of the real thing we'll just have tweaks to make." He clapped his hands together. "Make sense to everybody?"

"Yep."

"Yes, thanks Bill. That helped," Bob said, his posture noticeably more relaxed already.

Bill started to leave and then stopped with his hand on the door.

"Oh and Bob, I don't want to hear about Ed's little reformatting trick with the disks again." Bob looked shocked that Bill would disapprove so Bill, afraid that he'd misunderstood tried it again with a slightly different stress. "I don't want to *hear about* it, Bob. I speak to Estridge regularly and I'd hate to have to admit to anything like that if I was asked."

***

"I like what you've done with the place," Steve shouted.

He and Bill were at Bill's house in the Leschi neighbourhood of Seattle, a twenty minute commute from Microsoft and a key part of how he'd reduced his turn around time to seven hours. The plan was to meet Paul and Nishi for dinner but Bill had stopped by home for the first time in three days to get changed and grab some spare clothes to bring to the office.

Bill was in his bedroom getting changed and the conversation was being shouted from room to room.

"Huh?"

"The furniture and stuff. I like it," Steve waved his arms around.

"Oh, I hadn't really noticed. My mom picked it."

"Hm. I really should get my own place here soon."

"I've got a shortlist of decent neighbourhoods somewhere, I'll see if I can dig it out for you," Bill shouted through.

"Great. Thanks. Hey Bill, there was something I want to talk to you about."

"Yeah, what's that?"

"Staffing."

"Staffing?"

"Yes, we need forty more people."

Bill appeared in the doorway with one arm in a sweatshirt and a frown wrinkling his forehead.

"Forty people. Is this a joke? I don't get it."

"No, I'm serious. You asked me to take a look at the staff situation and I've done that. We need forty more people."

"Steve, we only have thirty employees in the whole company now."

"I know."

Bill shook his head, unable to believe what Ballmer was saying.

"No, you're taking the piss somehow but I'm missing the punchline. I was out of the room, start again."

"There isn't a punchline Bill, I'm talking work. I've looked at all of the projects we've got on, the deadlines, the number of people working on them and I'm telling you straight: We need forty more people."

"But that would more than double the size of the company."

"I know."

Steve waited. Silence was an unusual weapon for him to use and it threw Bill who was even more confused and decided again that it was a joke. "No, I just don't get it. Sorry."

"Bill, stop. I'm telling you this is not a joke, if we don't hire forty more people then we're going to start missing delivery dates."

When it finally dawned on him that Steve was indeed being serious, Bill exploded. He stormed through the lounge, past where Steve was sitting on the sofa without looking at him, and headed for the kitchen. A minute later he was back and thrust a little square yellow note under Steve's face.

"Do you know what this is?!"

Steve looked at it.

"It looks like a list of the current staff."

"That's right. It's a list of payroll we need to make. All of the staff and their monthly salaries. And this," he waved his other hand, in which he had another yellow note. "Is how much we've got in the bank. Do the math Steve. Tell me how long we could survive if we don't bring in more business."

"About a year."

"Exactly."

"Exactly what? I've never known a company with a cash pile big enough to make payroll for twelve months."

"Well, then you've never known a well run company have you?"

Bill moved to stand directly over Steve, who was still on the sofa. For just about any other new employee it would have been intimidating, but Steve was 6 foot 5, built like a football player, and one of the main reasons Bill had recruited him was precisely because he had never had a problem disagreeing with Bill. However loud it got.

He just threw his arms wide and laughed intentionally.

"Now who's joking? I worked at Procter & Gamble Bill, I don't think they're exactly badly run even if they wouldn't meet the almighty Bill Gates' standards!"

"Microsoft isn't Procter & Gamble!"

"I know that but it isn't Seattle Computer Products either!" Steve said using the only small computer firm he could think of as a reference.

Both men had been shouting but now Bill stepped back, took a breath and spoke as calmly as he could.

"The other day I heard that Pertec are closing MITS. For good. In the next couple of months they're just going to wrap up the Albuquerque factory. MITS was top of the heap two, three years ago Steve, and now they're gone. That's what can happen in this industry."

"I get it Bill. But you're being way too conservative."

"We're not hiring forty people," Bill said with an air of finality.

He started to turn away, considering the matter closed but Steve stood up and held his ground.

"We are if you don't want *us* to be gone in two or three years."

Bill blinked, shocked that Steve hadn't taken his word as final, but he was sucked back into the debate instantly.

"I didn't bring you here from business school so you could bankrupt us."

"No, you brought me here so I could help you grow the business. So let me help you. This is what we need to do, we need to take risks if we want to grow."

"We could go broke."

"Yes, of course we could. But we *will* go broke if we get a reputation for failing to deliver."

Bill started pacing back and forth in front of Steve.

For a minute he said nothing and just paced. Steve fought against every instinct in his body to press the argument, knowing that his best bet was to remain silent as well.

Before long Bill stopped pacing and looked at Steve, trying one last angle but his voice was completely calm and Steve could sense that Bill was almost convinced and any remaining fight was as much for show as anything else.

"And what if we lose business?" Bill asked. "We'd be putting all of those people out of work."

Steve simply shrugged it off.

"Who cares? We'll be giving them work in the meantime. No one thinks they're getting a job for life any more. And what about if we *don't* go out of business, we could be giving them work they love for as long as they want."

Bill paused again but he didn't start pacing and this time the pause only lasted ten seconds.

Then he nodded once, definitively.

"Okay so hire them. But let's be really picky. I want us to make sure we're only getting top notch talent. Just adding more heads won't speed us up if they're no good."

"I totally agree."

"We only want the best at Microsoft."

"I remember. It's why you hired me."

Bill laughed and the row was over as quickly as it had started.

"I don't want us to get fat though, I still want people working hard, we need to keep our edge."

"I'm with you. I've no intention of going easy on them. We'll find the right guys, guys we can trust, but then I'll ride them hard."

"Perfect." Bill looked at the clock. "Crap, come on let's go, they'll be expecting us."

"Okay," Steve said. "Hey, before we do, what is this thing?"

He pointed at the little yellow note Bill had thrown at him which was now stuck gently to the top of the coffee table by the faintly sticky strip on its back. He'd never seen anything like it.

"It's called a 'Post-it', they only came out a couple of months ago. Neat aren't they? I'm going to get loads for the office."

"Very cool. What's this one?" He pointed to one stuck to the window frame that had a list of colours written on it with a square next to each one.

"Ah, that one's from my Mom. I told her I wouldn't be able to have dinner with them for a while."

"Pity, I like your mom's dinners," Steve interrupted. "Not sure I'd have come to Microsoft at all if you hadn't included one of her dinners as part of the recruitment drive."

"I figured. So anyway, since I'm not going to see her as much she came up with this way of communicating. It's efficient. She leaves notes when she comes in if I'm not around. This one's about suits. I told her I'll need some to deal with IBM so she left this. I tick the box on the colour I want and next time she's in she'll pick it up and get them sorted for me."

"Ha! Neat, do you think she'll do mine?"

***

In April 1981 the space shuttle Columbia was due to launch from Cape Canaveral, and for geeks like the Microsoft crowd it was a momentous occasion.

Bill had been thirteen and Paul sixteen when the Apollo 11 astronauts landed on the moon, and for science and math guys like them it was exciting. It had been all they had talked about for days. Since then they, like most of America, had moved on to other things but the dream was still there lying dormant under the surface and the space shuttle, with its promise of the next big adventure in space, rekindled it for some.

***

Paul bounced happily into Bill's office, dropped into the chair in front of his desk and waited for Bill to look up from the contract he was marking up with a red pen. He was muttering as he worked and Paul caught the words "stupid", "dumb", and "who wrote this?"

After waiting a couple of minutes for Bill to finish in which he still didn't look up Paul realised that somehow he hadn't even noticed that Paul was there, so he just started speaking.

"Me and Simonyi are going down to Cape Canaveral this weekend to watch the launch. Do you want to join us?

"Launch?" Bill said, without looking up.

"Columbia. The space shuttle. It's a reusable spaceship Bill. It's made the news once or twice."

"Oh, yeah, I've heard something about that," Bill said distractedly.
Paul laughed.

"Heard something about it! You need to get out more."

He'd been joking but Bill flew off the handle. He threw down his pen and stared up at Paul, his eyes wide.

"Well, I can't can I?! One of us needs to take this stuff seriously!"

"Hey, what the hell does that mean?"

"You, you're just not interested like you used to be. We've got some serious stuff going on here Paul, it can't all be exciting new gadgets and playing your guitar."

"I knew that wound you up." Paul had left early a couple of nights before to have a jam session with some friends and had bumped into Bill as he left. His partner hadn't seemed happy but hadn't said anything about it until now. "If you've got a problem then you should have said something."

"I'm saying something now. You can't just swan in and out whenever you fancy."

"Are you having a laugh? I left two hours earlier than I normally do, and it was seven o'clock! Where else would we be having this conversation with someone who *only* put in an eleven hour day?"

"But Microsoft isn't anywhere else Paul, if we want to survive we need to move faster than everyone else, work harder than everyone else! We've always believed that!"

"No, you've always believed that. I think if we want to survive then we have to make better stuff than everyone else. See the future better than them and write better code than they do."

"It must be lovely in the world you live in," Bill said with a sneer. "How do you think this stuff gets sold? It doesn't just fly off the shelves because it's better than everyone else's. I'm out there working people constantly."

"I know that, I do it too, maybe not as much as you, I've always been more into the technical bits but if it weren't for me we wouldn't have a business at all, remember? It was me who saw the *Popular Electronics* mag, it was me who went to meet Roberts, it was me who kept the whole thing going while you stayed at Harvard."

"Oh not this again! We both made sacrifices, I worked on Microsoft just as much as you, I just did it while also doing a full time degree. And then I risked giving up Harvard for the company."

"What?! You can't have it both ways, either you did nothing at school because you're a genius or you worked really hard on both school and Microsoft. And from what I remember you were quite happy to leave Harvard because you weren't the cleverest person in the class. Like I warned you."

"Says you, how long did you last at Wazzu?"

Paul caught sight of their reflection in Bill's window and didn't like what he saw. He took a deep breath and tried to calm down.

"Look none of this changes anything, all I'm saying is it's okay to do other things than Microsoft every now and then."

Bill wasn't prepared to let it go.

"And all I'm saying is that it's only possible for you to think that because I'm here all the time making sure we deliver. Everything we're doing has tight timescales, all of them have contracts to negotiate," he waved the contract he'd been marking up. "You know, apart from Christmas, I haven't had dinner with my folks for six months? Hell, I've barely even been home."

"That's your choice Bill. Perhaps you should ease up a little. Get a girlfriend."

"I've had girlfriends."

"No, you've had girls. That's not the same thing." Paul threw his hands up in the air in exasperation. *This is just another argument that's going nowhere,* he thought. "Anyway, we're going. I only told you to see if you wanted to come with us but you can forget that now. We're going to leave Thursday night so we won't be here on Friday."

Bill frowned. "Friday? That's the company meeting."

Paul looked nervous for the first time since he'd come into the room. In the excitement of the shuttle launch he'd forgotten about the company wide meeting. Both men knew that it was something that Bill would never have done.

Bill sensed Paul's weakness and changed tack.

"Well," he said. "I guess it's up to you then isn't it? I can't stop you. If you'd prefer to go to watch the launch than be present at the first full Microsoft meeting that's your choice."

Paul had no idea how to respond to that without backing down, something he wasn't prepared to do in the moment, so he left without another word.

***

In the end Columbia's launch got moved to the Sunday, and Paul and Simonyi were able to go without having to choose between Microsoft (or Bill) and space.

They went to the company meeting on Friday and were in Florida to see the launch on Sunday. Bill didn't join them.

Paul never regretted it, he would later describe the launch as 'seeing history' and Simonyi loved it so much he would go on to visit the International Space Station twice as a fare paying passenger.

Back on earth nothing about Bill and Paul's relationship changed overnight. An argument between the two of them was nothing new, they had been arguing almost from the day they met, and in the past it had always spurred them both on to bigger and better things. Together. But now something below the surface had shifted. The cracks were starting to show and the growing staff at Microsoft was beginning to notice.

***

In May 1981 Tim Paterson came to work for Microsoft. Rod Brock over at Seattle Computer Products still owned the rights to the QDOS operating system Tim had written, but having the original developer at Microsoft meant he could work full time on the changes that were needed before the launch.

It meant one point of weakness had been removed but Bill was still worried about their reliance on a third party and, the night he returned from a trip to Japan to see Nishi, he called a crisis meeting with Paul and Steve.

Despite the increasingly visible fractures in Bill and Paul's relationship, Bill still viewed him as essential to any discussions of Microsoft's strategy.

"All that the Japanese manufacturers wanted to talk about was developing a 16-bit machine," he said.

"Oh, I bet it must have killed Kay not to tell them about the Acorn," Paul said with a twinkle in his eye. The ebullient Nishi wasn't known for being able to hold his tongue.

"Yeah, at one point he asked me to actually gag him! But it made me think, we've been banking on IBM opening up the 16-bit language market, but what if the operating system itself is where the value lies?"

"I thought the operating system just made the machine work. You said no one gets excited about them," Steve said.

But Paul frowned slightly, instantly seeing where Bill was going.

"Bill's thinking that other manufacturers might want to copy the PC completely, like they did with the Altair."

"Exactly," Bill said. "And if they do then they're going to need an operating system that works the same as IBM's."

"They could just reverse engineer it," Paul said.

"They could, but why bother when they could save time by buying exactly the same code?"

Then Steve got it.

"Which we can sell them because of the non-exclusivity clause."

Bill pointed his finger in a gun-like motion at Steve and grinned.

"That's it. That's what I was thinking."

Paul combed his beard with his fingers.

"Do you think the PC will really become the thing they all want to copy?" he said. "Why not the Apple II or one of the others?

"I don't know for sure, but the industry is bound to coalesce on something at some point, and this is IBM so if anyone's going to be the new standard then they're a pretty safe bet."

"You could be right. And if you are..."

"It could be a huge new opportunity for us," Steve said.

In an approach he didn't use with many others Bill had let Paul and Steve come to the conclusions he'd already reached on their own, but now he dropped the hammer quickly.

"Yeah, but it's an opportunity that leaves us exposed with Brock."

"Why?" Steve asked. "We've got the license to sell it that Paul negotiated."

"And as licenses go it's a good one," Bill said in a rare moment of praise. "But it's still just a licence, we don't own the software and if it does become a big thing then people won't need to come to us, they could go to Brock."

"Wait. Our contract with IBM let's them resell it as well," Steve said.

"I'm not worried about that," Bill said.

"No, they reserve the right but they're not going to have any interest in doing it. Roberts never did with the Altair. It's not in their interest to sell to competitors," Paul added. "The issue will be Brock."

"I want us to buy it from him outright. Do you reckon he'll go for it?" Paul nodded.

"Probably, for the right price. Tim thinks that Brock might be scaling things back anyway, refocusing on the hardware now that Tim has gone."

Bill checked his watch, it was gone eight o'clock at night.

"Okay, why don't you get in touch with him first thing tomorrow and make him an offer to buy all of the sales rights."

"I assume we're not telling him it's for IBM?" Steve said.

"Absolutely not. The NDA prevents it and I wouldn't anyway, it'll just push the price up."

Paul shrugged in a kind of half-nod. "Truth is he'd have held out for more money even on the current license if he knew who we were selling it to."

"He's going to be pissed when he finds out it's IBM," Steve said.

"I'm not bothered about him being pissed off. I'm bothered that we get a fair price," Bill said.

"For him or us?" Paul said with a smirk.

"Both, of course," Bill said, and turned his hands palm up in a gesture of mock openness.

"I'll speak to him in the morning," Paul said, and then added, "I don't want us to rip him off though."

"We're not. We're taking the risk here. He's getting the certainty of cash now, while we take a punt that we can turn it into something bigger. If we're right about the PC market then we'll do well, if we're not then he'll have done well. That's fair."

"That's capitalism," Steve said.

***

On 27th July 1981 Paul secured the full rights to Tim Paterson's Quick and Dirty Operating System, which by the end of the year, after Tim had made his changes to it, would be sold as both IBM PC DOS and Microsoft's MS-DOS.

Rod Brock wanted one hundred and fifty thousand dollars for it, Paul offered him thirty. In the end they agreed on a price of fifty thousand dollars.

The product that would eventually catapult Microsoft's market capitalisation far beyond IBM's was theirs to do with as they liked.

The 12th August 1981 would be a momentous day for the computer industry. Don Estridge led a press conference at the Waldorf Astoria in New York to launch IBM's new personal computer, the PC 5150.

At the same time they put out a press release:

Personal Computer Announced By IBM — for distribution on August 12, 1981.

IBM Corporation today announced its smallest, lowest-priced computer system — the IBM Personal Computer.

Designed for business, school and home, the easy-to-use system sells for as little as $1,565. It offers many advanced features and, with optional software, may use hundreds of popular application programs.

"This is the computer for just about everyone who has ever wanted a personal system at the office, on the university campus or at home," said C. B. Rogers, Jr., IBM vice president and group executive, General Business Group.

IBM has designed its Personal Computer for the first-time or advanced user, whether a businessperson in need of accounting help or a student preparing a term paper.

An enhanced version of the popular Microsoft BASIC programming language and easily understood operation manuals are included with every system. They make it possible to begin using the computer within hours and to develop personalized programs quite easily.

...

Advanced Operating Systems

IBM, in conjunction with Microsoft, Inc., has adapted an advanced disk operating system to support IBM Personal Computer programs and software development. It has also contracted with Digital Research, Inc. and SofTech Microsystems, Inc. to adapt the popular CP/M-86* and UCSD p-System* to the Personal Computer.

There were, of course, other machines that were comparable, after all that was why IBM had made their move. But having a brand like IBM attached to it instantly legitimised the PC as far as business was concerned. And once people became used to buying and using them in the office it wasn't long before computers started breaking through to the home as well.

It was a watershed moment and the industry as a whole recognised it.

What was less well recognised was quite how well positioned Microsoft was in the new arrangement. Even IBM didn't really see them as any different to their other vendors. Despite their name appearing more often in the press release (which is longer than the extract above and mentions Microsoft three times providing totally different functions) than any other company, IBM didn't even invite any Microsoft representatives to the launch party.

But then the scale of what this day meant to their future wasn't really understood at Microsoft either. Bill saw IBM as an important customer, sure, but not the single most important customer. Although the senior Microsoft team had considered the idea of PC clones as possible, it was a long shot bet.

When the announcement came through on the Dow Jones telex at Bellevue, Steve Ballmer ripped it off and posted it on the front door of the office and then everyone got back to work.

Bill himself wasn't even there. He was at Apple talking to Steve Jobs about the next big thing for Microsoft.

C:\PART\CHAPTER> 3.6

Bill had a lot in common with Steve Jobs, the chairman of Apple. They were both young, Jobs at twenty six was only six months older than Bill (who was about to celebrate his birthday with one of the soon to be infamous Microsoft parties); they had both dropped out of college to create a technology business with a friend; they had both made those businesses undisputed leaders in their field, Bill in languages, Jobs in hardware.

But where Bill was well known within the computer industry, Jobs had begun to come to the attention of the more general public. Following Apple's IPO in December 1980, he was one the country's richest men. He had appeared on national television and the covers of magazines (though not yet TIME, that would come six months later).

Truth be told Bill, at this stage, was a bit of a fan boy.

Bill and Jobs had already been working together for a number of years by then, but always at arm's length. That was about to change. Jobs had invited Bill down to California to get him on board with his top secret new project, a computer with a graphical interface.

The idea of a graphical interface was very much in the air in the late seventies and early eighties. Xerox PARC had developed the Xerox Star which demonstrated a number of the key features but they had failed to make it commercial. Bill himself had loudly banged the drum for them in May at a conference at the Playboy Resort in front of four hundred industry experts, but so far nobody had successfully delivered one.

In a move that showed how dysfunctional the company was behind closed doors, Apple had two competing projects underway to develop a graphical computer.

Their main effort was known as 'The Lisa'. It was an expensive machine which had been under development for a couple of years, but it had been repeatedly delayed due to underestimating the complexity and in fighting in the team.

Then there was the Macintosh, which was conceived as a cheaper 'bring computing to the masses' machine which would sell out of the box with everything you needed to be up and running quickly. When Jeff Raskin had initially come up with the idea, the Macintosh had been a text only machine like the PC, but recent events in Apple had changed that.

The Lisa was originally Jobs' own brainchild, a chance to stamp his personality on a machine, but following complaints about his style Jobs had been 'promoted upwards' to become chairman and responsibility for the Lisa had been taken off him.

Searching for a way to still make his mark he landed on the Macintosh project and reinvented it as a graphical computer with all of the functionality of the Lisa but at a more affordable price. Raskin was out and Jobs took over.

By the time Bill and the Microsoft team flew down to Cupertino, Steve had fully taken over and the Macintosh was on track to become his baby.

"You know Paul, of course," Bill said as they walked through the office and Jobs, who at this time was sporting a neat beard to try to look slightly older, nodded. "But I don't think you've met Charles Simonyi?"

"Hello," said the dark haired man walking beside Paul.

"European?" Steve asked, noting the accent.

"Hungarian," Simonyi replied. "Via Denmark and then Xerox."

Steve raised an eyebrow.

"Ah, well some of these ideas may be familiar to you then. We were quite inspired by some of the work at Xerox PARC," he said, patronisingly.

Simonyi bit his tongue having been briefed by Bill and Paul on the sort of behaviour to expect from Jobs.

Charles Simonyi had joined Microsoft in February that year and was known affectionately as the 'Mad Hungarian'. He was a certified genius and his deep knowledge of, and passion for, technology meant that he fitted in perfectly with Bill and Paul. He was more than able to hold his own in the ultra high bandwidth conversation between the two men.

"This is us," Steve said, when they reached a room at the back of the office.

He opened the door and ushered them inside.

In the middle of the room was a single table with what looked to Bill like a disassembled Apple II. There was a monitor and a disk drive which had both obviously come from the current Apple machine but connected to both was a breadboard stuffed with exposed components.

Behind the table stood a round faced man with glasses to rival Bill's.

Steve quickly placed himself between them and the table to interrupt their view.

"That's Andy," he said, cocking his thumb over his shoulder.

"Hey guys," Andy Hertzfeld said with a subdued wave.

"Everything ready, Andy?" Jobs asked.

"Yeah."

"And are you all ready?" he asked Bill with his arms open wide.

Bill stifled a smile, Jobs was nothing if not a showman.

"I think we are, Steve."

"Okay, let me introduce… the Macintosh." He paused and then when none of the Microsoft team reacted he brought them around to the other side of the table and let them get a look at the machine he had been blocking.

Despite the fact that the peripherals had been cadged from an Apple II it was clear even to Bill that this wasn't just an upgrade to the existing machine. As he seldom tired of pointing out, hardware just wasn't as interesting to him as software, but nonetheless he was pretty sure he recognised a Motorola 68000 chipset that he knew the Apple II didn't have. He glanced across at Paul and saw that he was drinking it all in, no doubt he was committing as much as he could to memory so they could discuss it later.

Andy took a seat behind the desk and, as the rest of them crowded behind him to see the screen, he pulled something from beside the keyboard.

"That's a mouse," Paul said, surprise evident in his voice.

"It is," Steve said.

Bill was familiar with the idea of a mouse, which had first been introduced by Doug Engelbart in the famous Mother of All Demos in 1968, and he knew that several manufacturers (including Simonyi's old stomping ground, Xerox) had prototypes, but like the graphical user interface none of them had yet made it into a real product.

Andy looked up at Jobs, who nodded.

"Okay Andy, let's show them what we've got here."

Andy turned on the computer and Bill was surprised at how quickly it sprang to life, having become accustomed to the boot time on the PC.

"No fan?" Paul asked.

"I don't like the noise," Steve replied.

"So how will the CPU not overheat?" Simonyi said with a puzzled expression.

"We'll use convection cooling."

Simonyi darted his eyes towards Bill which Bill took to mean that he wasn't convinced and he cringed to think the Hungarian might get into an argument with Jobs, but thankfully Andy was ready and prevented any more discussion.

"This is what we're calling the 'desktop'," he said gesturing at the screen with his left hand while with his right he moved the mouse.

The black and white monitor showed a grey background with a dialog box floating over the top titled 'Control Panel' and a series of rectangles representing windows.

Andy moved the mouse and on the screen the cursor, in the shape of a small watch, tracked his movements. He selected one of the icons and clicked on it with the mouse's single button.

The rectangle opened and became its own window which Andy enlarged.

Bill actually gasped when he saw the window, titled 'Macs' contained lots of small icons of stylised computers which immediately started bouncing around within the window.

"That's awesome!"

"Wait, there's more," Andy said.

He opened another window which contained a dozen or more crude alligators and dragged it over the top of the first window.

"Impressive," Paul said. "Can both redraw at the same time or is it only the active window?"

"Both, watch," Andy shifted the second window to show the Macs underneath zooming about their own window.

"Very cool,"

"Isn't it?" Steve said from behind them, drawing their attention back to him. "This is the future, we're going to change the world with this."

Andy meanwhile was opening the rest of the windows to show the capabilities of the machine and pretty soon the screen was covered in windows with robots, pepsi caps and even the Apple logo but as he tried to open the last window, ironically enough labelled 'Bugs', everything disappeared. Including Steve's smile. He frowned, causing Bill, Paul and Simonyi to turn back to the screen.

"What's happened?" Jobs demanded of Andy.

"I don't know, give me a minute, I think it's…"

"You think?! You think?! What the fuck is this?" Steve exploded.

The Microsoft team tried to edge from between the two of them but they were trapped. Andy looked desperate to escape as well but there was nowhere he could go so he simply shrank in his chair while Jobs shouted at him.

"These guys came all the way down here to see this and this is the best we can do? *This* is the best we can do? Thirty seconds and a frozen screen?! What the fuck is wrong with you?"

"It's okay Steve," Bill said. "It was a good demo and we get the idea."

"Yeah, yeah, okay." The rage left Jobs as quickly as it had come and he pointed to the back of the room where there was another table with half a dozen chairs arranged around it. "Here grab a seat."

Bill, Paul and Simonyi followed Jobs and sat while Jobs perched on the edge of the table and launched into what was obviously a well rehearsed pitch.

"We're going to change the world with this one. Really. It's going to be the computer that everyone wants. No, needs! We're going to make it so easy to use that we don't need to give people instruction manuals. Even your mom will be able to do it. Not your mom Bill, she can probably already write code, in fact she'll probably end up running the company. But everyone else's mom." He grinned. Bill was surprised Jobs knew anything about his mother but then perhaps he shouldn't have been. Mary Gates was an impressive woman and it wouldn't take much research about Bill to find out about her. But it was interesting that Jobs had done any research.

"Computers are going to become like toasters, easy to use, cheap and basically essential. Sure, you can make toast on a fire but why would you? No-one thinks of doing without a toaster and pretty soon no-one will think of doing without a computer."

As he spoke Andy sheepishly came over and joined them, having given up trying to get the demo going again, but Jobs was carried away with his excitement and seemed to have forgotten his earlier outburst.

"In fact we won't even think of them as computers any more. Computers only appealed to nerds like us. The Macintosh is going to be an information appliance. If you want information you'll use it like you use your toaster now to make toast. And they'll be everywhere, millions of them. Do you know about one in every thousand Americans have a computer? In the next five years we're going to get that down to one in ten and then eventually one in one.

"We'll build an Apple factory that's like a great big conveyor belt. We'll put it on the beach and tip sand in at one end and out the other end we'll get computers. Information appliances. It'll be astonishing. This is it guys, I mean it. You want to be involved don't you?"

It took Bill a moment to realise that Jobs was actually waiting for a reply, as soon as he had Jobs spoke again.

"I mean, I know you're in bed with IBM," he said. "But is that really what you want?"

"We're not in bed with them, it's not an exclusive arrangement. I'd be interested to hear what you have to say," Bill replied, finally managing to get in a word, but Jobs didn't seem to be listening anyway.

"I think it's going to come down to Apple versus IBM. And we can't let them win. If they do it'll be like, the Dark Ages, again. Everywhere they go they stifle competition." He fixed Bill with a stare. "Is that how you want people to remember you, as a lapdog of the oppressor?"

Again Bill resisted the urge to smile. He thought Jobs's Dark Ages reference was a touch melodramatic but he recognised the desire to win at all costs. And he knew a battle between the two computer giants with Microsoft supplying both sides could only help Microsoft's sales.

"I'm interested Steve, and it's a cool machine."

"World changing," Jobs nodded enthusiastically. "We're going to put a dent in the universe, aren't we Andy?"

"Absolutely," Andy replied.

"Yeah," Bill said, noncommittally. "GUI is definitely the way the industry has to go. What about that mouse though Andy, how does the hardware control the cursor?"

"It's not the hardware, it's all in the…" Andy started to answer, glad to be back in the conversation but Jobs instantly cut him off.

"Shut up!" he snapped and then, when everybody looked at him with open mouths, he smiled at Bill. "You can't expect us to give it all away on the first date, Bill. Nobody buys the cow when they can get the milk for free."

Bill laughed and everyone joined in, albeit slightly nervously.

"When are you aiming to have it ready for release?" he asked.

"End of next year," Jobs said, confidently.

"Okay, we're interested, let's talk contracts."

***

"What did you think?" Jobs asked.

Andy shrugged.

"I've never been that impressed with him."

"Gates?"

"Yeah. That Donkey programme on the PC is a joke."

Microsoft had written a number of simple applications that shipped with every PC and Bill himself, for a laugh, had written a small game in which the aim was to drive a car without hitting donkeys that would occasionally wander into the road. Given that the donkeys made an amusing noise when they were hit that was never how anyone played it.

"I think it's supposed to be a joke," Jobs said.

"Yeah, I get that, but the *coding* is a joke. And even joke programmes should have neat code."

Jobs shook his head. He knew his engineers weren't impressed with the PC, and he agreed, he'd joined in when they'd pulled apart the one they'd bought to test, but he thought Andy was missing the important point.

"Okay, but do you think they'll deliver what we need?"

"Yes, they got the concepts quickly, apart from Gates' question about the mouse. Odd that he'd think it was hardware when he's always banging on about software being the only important thing." He hesitated. "I'm sorry about that by the way."

Jobs waved his hand dismissively.

"Don't worry about it. But in future remember, you never give them more information than they need to do the job. You need to watch Gates. He's smarter than you think." Andy didn't look convinced so Jobs explained. "He was first in on the Altair and he used the air cover it gave him to position Microsoft cleverly. And look who was left standing when the dust settled. There's no MITS and Microsoft is the largest software company in the world. Now he's in with IBM and that'll give him air cover for even longer."

"Yeah, but being the largest software company is like being the biggest fish in a little pond. They have sales of what a couple of tens of millions of dollars? Apple is twenty times the size of them. Whatever he thinks of hardware, it's where the money is."

Since Apple had gone public Andy knew their sales figures, but he was guessing about the size of Microsoft because the information wasn't public. Even so, he wasn't far wrong, Microsoft's sales in 1981 were $17 million compared to Apple's over $300 million.

Steve agreed about the hardware but he wasn't prepared to write Gates off so quickly.

"Well, I wouldn't bet against him out manoeuvring Big Blue, but either way I'm certainly not going to let him have a chance to get one over on us."

"So should we be doing business with him if he's a threat?" Andy asked, sensing his boss's uncharacteristic reticence.

As soon as he'd said it though Jobs's competitive drive got the upper hand again.

"He's not a threat to me. You just need to keep him in his box and watch the lid carefully."

***

"What did you think?" Bill asked when they were in the car heading to the airport.

"There's nothing really new there, he's taken it all from Xerox, but it's well put together for a prototype," Paul said.

"Really well put together," Bill echoed with a far away look in his eye.

Paul snorted.

"It always surprises me that you think so highly of Jobs. He's not technical at all, you know."

"I know," Bill said and shrugged.

"Smart and technical don't occupy precisely the same space. They are overlapping sets."

Paul's brow furrowed. For years 'not technical' had been Bill and Paul shorthand for 'complete waste of space' but while technical-smart-guys like Simonyi would always be at the top of Bill's mental league, he'd started to realise the value that non-technical smart-guys in other fields could bring.

189

Paul wasn't having it though.

"But Jobs pretends he's technical. He likes people to think of him as a computer whizkid, but the Apple I was all Woz and now he's doing the same thing with the Macintosh, he's surrounding himself with guys who'll do the technical work for him."

"Yeah, I know all that, but he gets the concepts so completely. And he does manage to make it cool."

Paul looked at his friend. Bill had never cared what people thought of him but it was obvious that he was fascinated by something Steve had, some x-factor, that Bill couldn't fully process.

He was about to press it further when Simonyi interrupted and saved it from degenerating into an argument.

"The idea of not having a fan is going to come back and bite him," he said.

"Hmm." Bill nodded slowly then, with a trace of Jobs' enthusiasm still lingering, he said, "It's awesome to see they're doing it for real though, right? This is the stuff we've been talking about for years but nobody has made it happen. Is it me or does it seem a step closer now?"

"The demo was good. I can see them making this work," Simonyi agreed.

"He's a good salesman," Paul said, but he was just as impressed with the Macintosh as Bill was, and he didn't sound anywhere near as cynical as he'd been intending.

They rode in silence for a minute, each of them mulling over the fact that the future had gotten a little closer.

"So do we try to sell them the whole suite of languages like the IBM deal?" Paul said, eventually.

"No, it's the applications that are going to be the key," Simonyi said. "I mean, yes, of course, we sell them languages, but also applications."

Bill nodded and adjusted his glasses.

"I agree with Charles. It's the applications that are the opportunity if Jobs is right about his market. I can tell you now my mom is nowhere near as technically savvy as he seems to think, there's no way she'll be learning to programme BASIC any time soon. But give her a spreadsheet and she'll learn to use it to read budgets for the boards she's on. Give her a word processor and she'll use it to send letters. Applications are where we're going next."

"What do you think of his timeline?" Paul asked.

"Ambitious," Bill said.

"Particularly if we're going to write a whole bunch of applications."

"Maybe we focus on one or two at first. When we get back to Seattle, I'll have Steve send them a letter with a proposal for us to do a spreadsheet, BASIC, maybe a word processor."

***

The first computer application to attract any real attention had been debuted at the 1979 National Computer Conference.

While Bill was in the Microsoft booth using a borrowed copy of Tim Paterson's 16-bit CPU to demonstrate the 16-bit version of Microsoft BASIC, a previously unknown company was across the hall showing off a completely new idea: the spreadsheet.

Developed by Dan Bricklin and Bob Frankston, the spreadsheet, which they called VisiCalc, was revolutionary.

With its built in mathematical functions and ability to automatically recalculate whenever a number was changed, it saved a huge amount of time and effort for anyone who worked with large sets of numbers. Scientists, students, accountants, businesses, stockbrokers, the list of potential customers was huge and VisiCalc became the first 'killer application', convincing thousands of users that computers had a real purpose.

That had been two years ago and in the meantime VisiCorp, who marketed VisiCalc, became the undisputed leader in the realm of applications. In 1981 when they visited Jobs to talk about the Macintosh, Microsoft by contrast was still primarily a language company.

Both Bill and Paul had recognised the importance of VisiCalc early on, in fact in June 1979 immediately after the National Computer Conference, Bill had set up a Consumer Products division under his friend Vern Raburn. The division had produced and sold programmes like *Adventure*, a text based computer game, and *Typing Tutorial*, which as the name suggested taught people to use a keyboard. By 1981 both had been converted to be available for the launch of the new PC, but Bill's attention was focussed on the market that he was already dominant in. As we have seen, even the move into operating systems was intended largely to support the sale of languages.

Unusually for Microsoft, this time Bill and Paul's technical skills probably held them back, if they wanted a computer to do something they wrote a programme to make it do it.

However, it was becoming increasingly apparent that as computers became more and more accessible to a wider audience many of them would want to buy out of the box applications, rather than write their own.

Applications were the reason Bill had hired Simonyi back in February 1981, and it was the market that he wanted them to concentrate on now.

***

"We need a project name," Neil Konzen said, looking at the prototype that was taking up another office with newly papered over windows to keep out anyone not in the secret development group.

Jeff Harbers considered it. Jeff had worked on the IBM account and was going to be Microsoft's development lead for the Macintosh. He had brought Neil onto the team because he was familiar with Apple having worked there until joining Microsoft a few months earlier.

"What about 'Sand'?" Jeff said.

"Because of his factory in India."

Everybody who Bill was bringing into the Macintosh team had heard Jobs' metaphorical factory speech. While they were still excited by the machine itself, the hyperbole had come to be coloured slightly with the usual sarcasm that was never far away from these hyper intelligent young men.

"I don't think he ever actually said it was going to be in India."

"It's going to be though, isn't it?" Konzen said with a smirk. "India or California. Or maybe Tahiti."

"Sand," Harbers tested it out. "Wait, yes! S...A...N...D... Steve's Amazing New Device!"

Before the end of the day they'd gone out and found a tray, filled it with sand and tucked it away in the corner.

***

After a lot of legal to-ing and fro-ing Microsoft and Apple agreed contracts in January 1982.

The original agreement called for Microsoft to deliver a spreadsheet application called Multiplan, a database application called File and a graphics application called Chart.

Steve was concerned that Bill might use what he learnt from the Macintosh to develop windowing programmes of his own and sell them to other manufacturers, so he made sure that the contract had an exclusivity clause that he thought prevented Bill from doing so.

Bill, of course, was no stranger to contracts. He had been raised around the law; had written his first contract at age ten with his sister; when he was thirteen, instead of fantasising about girls he and Kent had been fantasising about running Fortune 500 companies; and when the mighty IBM sent in their contract law specialists to negotiate with Microsoft it was mostly Bill himself that they had dealt with; and although the rest of the world didn't know it yet, he had already used the freedom he had kept in that contract to sell several copies of MS-DOS to the makers of PC clones who would be releasing them soon.

Bill, the consummate contract writer, was happy to accept Jobs' exclusivity clause but naturally saw to it that it was limited in quite precise ways. The final clause was specific to the applications he had agreed to deliver to Jobs and, critically, it expired on New Year's Day 1984.

Unfortunately for Steve, his belief that the Macintosh would be released at the end of 1982 would provide Bill's next great opportunity.

C:\PART\CHAPTER> 3.7

In mid September 1982 Bill and Paul went to Europe together on a promotional tour. Multiplan for the PC had been delivered a month earlier and the idea was to visit a number of European cities to spread the word about the new application and Microsoft more generally.

They stopped first in London where Bob O'Rear had recently set up a new European arm of Microsoft, before they headed on to Munich and then Paris.

While they were in Munich Paul felt himself coming down with something. He felt exhausted and out of sorts.

In August, about the time of the Multiplan release, Paul had discovered a lump on the right side of his neck but it didn't hurt so like most men his age he had simply ignored it and expected it to go away. He didn't think too much of it and it never crossed his mind that it could be connected to how generally rundown he was feeling now.

At first he figured that he must be getting some sort of flu but, when he didn't develop a fever, he put it down to a combination of jet lag and his non-stop schedule and tried his best to push through it.

The roadshow carried on to Paris but by the time they had finished the first press conference Paul had to admit that he couldn't carry on. He still hadn't made the connection with the lump in his neck, but he was beginning to suspect that he might have something more sinister than the flu.

He told Bill he had to go back to Seattle to see his doctor and hopped on the next plane. That was a Monday.

By the Friday he was under general anaesthetic and the surgeons were performing a biopsy on the lump in his neck.

***

"Can we shut the door?" Paul said when Bill returned to the office after the European trip finished.

"Of course," Bill answered, sensing his friend had something uncomfortable to talk about. "Erm, how did the doctors go?"

"That's what I wanted to talk about." Paul dropped into the sofa in the corner and looked at Bill. He knew he needed to hear this but he didn't really want to talk about it. "I've not had a great time while you were away."

Bill shifted in his chair.

"I had a lump in my neck and they took a biopsy."

"Christ, Paul. What were the results?"

Paul raised his hand to slow Bill. "Can you just let me tell this my own way? It's a lot to deal with."

"Sorry, go on," Bill said and closed his mouth. A moment later when Paul was still collecting his thoughts Bill interlaced his fingers and a moment after that his index fingers were tapping uncontrollably.

Finally, Paul began to speak.

"My doctor rushed me into hospital and I got a biopsy the next morning. When I came round the surgeon said he thought it was lymphoma," Paul explained. Bill opened his mouth a fraction and then made a visible effort to stop himself. "It took another day for them to get the results, but when they came back they said it was Hodgkin's lymphoma. Do you know anything about it?"

"No," Bill shook his head quickly and Paul was struck by how young he looked.

"It's a type of cancer, but it's one of the better ones you can get. They actually said that. One of the better ones. I'm going to need treatment but they said I should live."

Bill swallowed and looked like he wanted to speak again, Paul nodded to give him permission.

"Did they give you any numbers?" he asked.

"If it's early stage like mine then the cure rate is apparently in the mid-nineties."

Bill breathed out as though the diagnosis had been his.

"Okay," he said. "So we're going to be okay."

He took his glasses off and for the first time in Paul's recollection started cleaning them on his sweater.

"I'm going to need some time off," Paul said.

"Of course, of course. But you're going to be okay. So... so that's okay. We'll just carry on. If you need to take a bit of time off for the treatment that's fine, isn't it?" He took another deep breath, put his glasses back on and reached for a printout on his desk. "The early Multiplan reviews are in, do you want to hear a couple?"

"It's a six week course," Paul said, his voice flat.

Bill blinked rapidly, as though briefly uncertain what Paul was referring to, then his brain found purchase and he frowned slightly.

"Every day?"

"Five days a week."

"Christ," Bill said again.

Paul sat quietly, unsure of what else to say.

C:\PART> 4: RIDING HIGH

C:\PART\CHAPTER> 4.1

"Charles, you've got to come down here."

Bill's knuckles were white from his grip on the phone and Simonyi could hear the agitation in his boss's voice.

"Hi Bill. Where are you?" Simonyi asked.

"Where am I? Comdex of course!" Bill snapped.

"No, I mean where are you calling from? It's very noisy."

"I'm in the lobby. I had to come out here to call you. Look, who cares where I am, I need you down here now."

"Now?" Simonyi was surprised. "I've got a meeting tomorrow with…"

"I don't care who it's with. Get down here as quickly as you can. Get Miriam to sort you a plane ticket."

"Bill, slow down. What is it?"

"It's all going too fast and we're going to miss the boat. VisiCorp, have released a GUI for the PC and some guy called Mitch Kapor who used to work for VisiCorp is showing off a spreadsheet that everyone says is much better than VisiCalc or even Multiplan. I was actually standing there when this idiot in front of me said that."

"Okay Boss, I'm on my way."

It was Fall Comdex 1982 and Mitch Kapor's spreadsheet was Lotus 1-2-3. It would come to dominate the application business for the next few years and in the process become one of Bill's next targets.

***

A couple of days later Steve Ballmer was sitting in Bill's office and listening to his friend pour out his thoughts in a stream of consciousness.

Steve had often thought that what drove Bill was his ability to walk a knife's edge between confidence and worry, right now though the worry seemed to have the upper hand. He had calmed down since his panicked phone call to Simonyi, but he was still convinced that Microsoft was going to go the way of MITS.

Steve suspected it was because he was worried about Paul and didn't know how to handle it.

"Was it useful having Simonyi there?" he asked.

"Yeah, Charles is super-smart, you know that. But I usually have Paul at these things. Paul might have had some ideas."

Bill knew he wasn't Steve Jobs. In a good way. He knew that Paul was right about Jobs, he was a designer, not a hands on technologist. Jobs needed Woz. Bill didn't *need* Paul in the same way. He understood technology, he could out-code most of the people in Microsoft. God, he had written BASIC in a matter of weeks! But without Paul to bounce things off at Comdex and with the bad news from both Lotus and VisiOn, VisiCorp's GUI, he'd felt lost.

"Well you can still speak to him can't you?" Steve said.

"No, it wouldn't be fair. He's at home."

"I thought he was going to work part time."

"He is. When it all settles down."

Ballmer was quiet for about thirty seconds as he thought. A long time for him.

"Okay, here's what we're going to do. We'll get you, Simonyi and a couple of others and lock you away somewhere until you can come up with a plan."

"It's two plans, they're attacking us on two fronts Steve. GUI and applications."

"Okay, two plans. So who else could you use?"

"Raikes."

"Okay Raikes. I'll set it up."

***

"I read an article in *Inc* that said it was the biggest Comdex yet. There were fifty thousand people there," Steve said to Simonyi while they waited for Bill to arrive.

"I didn't know it was fifty thousand but it was definitely crowded," Simonyi replied in his soft spoken Hungarian accent. "Their convention center covers an area seven times the size of a football field and it was crowded with computer people!"

"Yeah, and they all wanted to see VisiOn," came Bill's voice from the doorway.

The group wasn't much bigger than Bill's original list, there was Steve, Simonyi, and Jeff Raikes, a former Apple employee who'd worked on VisiCalc for the Apple II and joined Microsoft a year earlier. For good measure Ballmer had added a couple of programmers, Rao Remala and Dan McCabe who together would lead much of the early GUI work.

"Tell us about it then," Rao said.

Bill strode across the room and stood in front of them, pacing while he spoke.

"It has just about everything that the Macintosh is going to have, natural language descriptions, windows…"

"Overlapping or tiled?" McCabe asked.

"Overlapping."

Everyone in Microsoft was used to the rapid fire nature of these sorts of discussions. If you couldn't keep up you'd effectively be frozen out of the meeting and more importantly, if it happened more than once, you'd be out of Bill's circle.

"Do they have icons like the Macintosh?"

"Not from what I saw, it was all text. Charles?"

"No, the demo was completely text based and I didn't like to ask the question in case it moved them in a better direction."

"So, all text, but mouse driven, point and click menus. And they kept going on about how it was like a real world desktop. Most of what he said could have been lifted straight from the speech I gave at Rosen eighteen months ago about using terms the customers know from stuff they've used before," Bill said, forgetting that he, just like Jobs who would also forget when it was convenient, had taken the ideas from Xerox PARC. "And it sits between the applications and the operating system to provide an integrated application set."

Rao let out a low whistle, expressing how they all felt. None of them could really believe the VisiCorp folk had pulled it off so quickly.

"And it was up and running? On a PC, not a Macintosh prototype, or maybe a Xerox Star?" Raikes asked.

"It was," Bill said. "I even challenged their chairman Fylstra about whether it was running on a VAX in the background and he just laughed. I heard this one guy tell someone he was with that it must be a video." He saw the glimmer of hope on the faces of his team and quickly squashed it. "It wasn't."

"We can't let them run away with GUI like they have with VisiCalc," Steve said.

"Exactly."

"How come we never heard of it?" Steve asked. "They can't have developed it overnight."

"They're not a manufacturer so we don't really have any way in. We need to think about that for the future but for now we need to concentrate on the immediate challenge. We sell languages, operating systems and we're moving into applications. VisiOn is an attack on all three fronts."

McCabe cleared his throat and ventured a challenge. He knew Bill encouraged disagreement, although Microsoft veterans would have told him to pick his moment carefully. Unfortunately none of them had ever told him how to identify the right one.

"But isn't it really just another application?" he said, tentatively. "Computers still need operating systems, if anyone wants to make a PC compatible machine that means coming to us. Programmers still need programming languages, VisiOn isn't doing that, so people will still need to come to us. And if it fits between the applications and the operating system then we can still sell Multiplan and our future applications to sit on top of it."

"You're not getting it!" Bill said throwing his hands up in frustration. "Today anybody using a PC has to interact through DOS, and what do they see at the top of the screen? A nice big Microsoft copyright label."

Following the recruitment of Rowland Hanson to lead the company's marketing, Bill was beginning to think about Microsoft's position in people's minds, and the senior team had started to see a move into retail marketing as essential.

"We lose that straight away if all the user sees is VisiOn," he went on. "And that's not the worst of it. I see three scenarios if VisiCorp own the interface space. Scenario one, we become invisible to end users but manage to stay in business selling languages to programmers and cling on to the operating system business. We won't have any easy way to leverage our existing market share into the application space. Microsoft tops out at the kind of growth we have figured for next year."

All of them shook their head, they knew that was not Bill's plan.

"And that's the best case scenario. Scenario two, VisiCorp decide to make one of your primitives inaccurate."

"Which one?" McCabe asked.

"That it allows third party applications. They're an application company, once they've insinuated themselves between the operating system and the application layer why would they continue to allow that? They'll turn it into a closed environment that will only run VisiCorp applications or license it at a cost that means we'd make no money from applications."

"Holy shit."

"Exactly. We go back to where we were before we released Multiplan and the application strategy is totally dead. But scenario three is the shit storm. VisiCorp turns VisiOn into a fully fledged operating system. Whether they move into that space on their own, or manufacturers drag them in doesn't matter to us, it's got to be a likely move. Why would you have three control layers? DOS already runs on top of the BIOS, and applications run on top of DOS. Now VisiOn will run between applications and DOS? I don't believe that will last long and anyone who does is just dumb. And we all know graphical interfaces are where the industry is going so which one do you think falls away? I'll tell you, DOS!"

Bill was waving his arms about as he spoke now, working himself into a frenzy.

"And that puts us squarely back to the company I was running two years ago. I'm new to this business thing Dan, I've only been running companies since I was sixteen but I don't think that's how you're supposed to do it!"

"No, Bill."

"And that's before I came up with the nuclear option. Some sort of graphical programming interface."

He paused dramatically but McCabe didn't rise to it, having decided belatedly that discretion was the better part of valour, instead Rao asked for them all.

"What's that?"

"If everything's going graphical, then why wouldn't programming go the same way? Point and click, build up a programme from common elements. Like object oriented programming but with predefined functions the user just assembles."

Simonyi tilted his head to one side like a dog who'd heard a whistle in the distance.

"I've never heard of that," he said, intrigued. He'd written his PhD thesis on a new programming technique he'd invented himself and thought he'd surveyed all of the existing ones to do it. It surprised him that he could have missed something so revolutionary as what Bill was proposing.

"It's just an idea I had on the drive in this morning," Bill said, dismissing it as quickly as he'd raised it and calming down almost instantly. "It would need the GUI to be a lot more advanced and programming functions to be standardised but it's at least possible, right? One to keep on the radar. I don't really think it's as likely as the others that's why I didn't include it as a specific scenario. But obviously if it did happen then we'd have absolutely nothing left. In any case, whichever scenario we land on we suffer, so we have to do something about it. Charles," he said and fell into one of the chairs, pointing at Simonyi to take over.

"On the plane on the way back Bill and I came up with our solution: Interface Manager. We're going to incorporate the mouse that Paul's working on…"

"How is Paul?" Jeff asked. Paul wasn't broadcasting his illness to everyone but the senior managers had all been told as they would notice his absence from Microsoft for any length of time.

Simonyi looked at Bill who waved the question away.

"Fine, fine," he said, quickly. "He's getting treatment, he'll be back soon and everything will be back to normal."

Simonyi hesitated briefly then thought better of whatever he had been going to say and went back to the plan he and Bill had outlined.

"Interface Manager will occupy the same space between DOS and applications that Bill has just described VisiOn does. Longer term we see ourselves replacing DOS altogether with a graphical operating system but we need to react to the need of the marketplace as soon as possible."

Simonyi headed for the whiteboard and started drawing to illustrate his points.

"The point of today is to start to flesh out the ideas but we've got some basic principles. We need to be able to have multi-tasking. Or at least the appearance of multi-tasking. VisiCorp haven't got it for real, they just cleverly park information in a holding pattern while the processor works on one application at a time. We could do the same.

"Dan, to your earlier question, we prefer the idea of icons rather than text like VisiCorp are using. We need this to be a visible break with what's gone before. And we think it will be important to find a way to make sure that all existing DOS programmes can still run on it. It will save us reengineering our own application development projects and, if VisiCorp do go down the closed environment route, then it'll be a differentiator that makes us more attractive."

Bill stood back up and Raikes, Remala and McCabe all looked up from where they had been scribbling in their notebooks.

"It's a two pronged plan. We obviously need to design the real thing, but I want to get something up and running fast so we have something to show people. Rao, you can do that." Remala nodded. "I've already told the sales people to mention it whenever they're talking to customers."

Raikes did a double take.

"Bill, how are they going to sell it if we haven't even designed it?"

"They're not selling it, they're introducing the idea," Bill said, pulling a face that betrayed deep disappointment. "If the customers who already trust us to deliver DOS to them know we've got a windowing system coming out well, maybe they'll hang on rather than take a risk on buying VisiOn."

Simonyi took over again.

"Comdex wasn't all bad news, I counted five manufacturers hawking PC compatible machines they are about to release. And most of the software on sale was for the PC, which was a total switch from last year when it was all Apple stuff."

Bill nodded but couldn't resist reiterating his point about their impending doom.

"That give us a bit of space, as long as there's a drive to make things compatible with the PC then we'll be selling DOS, but we don't want it to be the long term direction of the industry. Remember our application strategy depends on there being multiple systems that we can use Charles' p-code compiler on to port our applications on to. If we don't get GUI right then we're out. This has to be the company's top priority. So start shouting out features for Rao to build into his demo."

C:\PART\CHAPTER> 4.2

"I see Paul was in this afternoon. That's good."

It was about 8pm one night not long before Christmas 1982 and Bill and Steve Ballmer were in Bill's office chewing over the day. It was a habit they'd got into as a way to ensure they were both in touch with whatever the other was doing when their diaries were full. Microsoft had rolled out internal email widely earlier that year so Bill normally used the time with Steve to work through some of the less important emails that had arrived at his new 'billg' internal email address.

Steve had installed himself on Bill's couch with his feet up and was flicking through a sales report.

"Yeah, his therapy ended a week or so ago," Bill said.

"You know he mentioned to me that he might start something new of his own one day," Steve said idly, turning a page of his report.

Bill stopped typing and looked up from his computer.

"Outside of microsoft?"

Steve felt the temperature in the room drop, swung his feet off the couch so he was sitting up and put the report down beside him.

"Yeah. I guess so," he said.

"Hmph. We need him here you know."

Steve nodded. He had always known how much Bill and Paul got from each other, he wasn't quite so sure that Bill knew. At least consciously.

"He certainly adds a lot," Steve said. "All of the engineers think he's the business."

"Easier to talk to than me, right?" Bill said with half a smile.

Steve returned the smile at his usual full intensity.

"Hey, you said it, not me."

Bill looked back at his computer screen and his hands danced across the keyboard in a staccato rhythm as he banged out a reply to someone.

"How do we convince him to stay?" he said, punctuating the question with a particularly loud tap on the ENTER key.

"Whoa, we don't know for sure he's planning to leave. It might have been a throwaway comment. I think it was after you guys had had a fight."

They fell silent again and Steve picked up his report but the lack of typing coming from Bill's keyboard meant that he couldn't concentrate. After a minute Bill broke the silence.

"He's been here less and less."

"He's had his radiotherapy to deal with."

"It's finished now though."

Steve shuffled uncomfortably on the couch.

"I think it takes a while to recover from that kind of thing," he said. He put the report back down and looked at Bill. "Maybe we could ask him if he wanted to go part time permanently."

"But once he's better he'll want to come back full time, surely?"

"Maybe, yeah. Maybe. I'm just thinking that it's been a bit tense between you two anyway, don't you think? Perhaps going part time might let him concentrate on some of the other stuff he likes. You know, his music and stuff."

Bill adjusted his glasses.

"My worry is that it sets a bad example," he said. "Him coming and going whenever he wants."

"We could formalise the part time hours, so there was a regular pattern to it. Everyone would know where they stand. Some of the secretaries are part time."

"None of the secretaries have stock."

"True," Steve replied.

Bill looked pensive and Steve could tell that he wanted to solve what he saw as the problem, but he fundamentally couldn't understand why Paul wouldn't just want to come back.

"Hey, maybe I'm wrong anyway. Perhaps in the new year he'll come back and you guys can have a talk, he'll be feeling better and you can get it all back on track."

"No, you're right. We've always had differences of opinion, Christ we've worked together for fourteen years it'd be weird if we didn't disagree, but in the past we were an amazing partnership. This last year that's started to feel different. When we fight it's like he just gives up. Like he doesn't care any more." Bill took his glasses off and rubbed his eyes. "But I don't see how part time would work. Besides, now we've introduced the stock options it could demoralise the other stockholders if they see him as coasting and still getting rich off the growth in the company."

***

Neither Bill nor Steve were aware that Paul was walking past Bill's office at that exact moment and, in a cruel twist, that he had heard the very worst part of their conversation he possibly could.

"...coasting and still getting rich off the growth in the company..."

Paul stopped, brought up short by the horrible feeling that they were talking about him.

He moved closer to the door and listened.

***

"What if we find a way to lock his shares in the current position?"

"How?"

"I don't know yet... Maybe we could issue additional options but just to some people not everybody," Steve said.

"What people?"

"Well... everybody but Paul, I guess. Or we pick a project like Windows that really matters to us and incentivise the people working on it with a new stock scheme."

"Or we could do it based on hours worked," Bill started to say. "That would be fair but it would still reduce his..."

He stopped abruptly mid sentence as the door flew open and crashed against the wall.

Paul stood in the doorway, holding his briefcase and bright red in the face.

He pointed at both men one after the other, unable to find any words. Finally he looked straight at Bill, his rage written all over him.

"This is unbelievable!" he screamed. "It shows your true character, once and for all."

"Paul, hold on!"

But he turned on his heel and left, slamming the door shut behind him.

***

Paul resigned shortly afterwards.

Bill sent him a long letter asking him to reconsider, pointing out how closely they'd worked and how much he valued him, but Paul had made his decision.

Paul's Hodgkin's lymphoma went into remission, however, on 18th February 1983 he left Microsoft. He remained part of the board but his involvement in day to day operations at the company was at an end.

C:\PART\CHAPTER> 4.3

In July 1982 Bill had hired James Towne as Microsoft's president. The idea was for Towne to focus on the operational running of the company and for Bill to concentrate on the software development and sales.

Towne had been a vice-president at Tektronix and was supposed to bring a wealth of general management expertise. It was the right idea but the wrong person. Towne and Bill did not click.

Hired on 6th July 1982, he left on 16th June 1983.

Towne hadn't worked out but that didn't mean there was anything wrong with the idea, so Bill began looking for alternatives and found what he was looking for quickly in Jon Shirley the vice president of computer sales at Radio Shack.

Bill and Jon had worked together on the Tandy Model 100 and had sat opposite each other across the negotiating table several times. Despite the fact that they had always been on opposite sides of those negotiations, it had given them a knowledge of, and respect for, each other. They knew what they were getting into.

Shirley joined Microsoft in August 1983.

In common with the original idea, Shirley looked after the managerial side of things and Bill looked after software and deal making. It was a partnership that worked in part because Bill and Jon had complementary styles, Jon was a decade older than Bill (and most of the company's staff for that matter) but he was no less driven than they were to make Microsoft a success. However, where Bill would attack any problem head on with a fair degree of noise, Jon brought a more measured, calm approach to a situation.

Jon would remain the president at Microsoft for seven years before retiring.

***

The Red Lion Inn wasn't the most salubrious retreat the Microsoft team had rented recently but this three day workshop wasn't about rallying the troops or impressing customers, this was a crisis meeting and the conference room at the Red Lion was acting as a temporary war room.

Bill had called the off site meeting after he had been presented with that quarter's sales figures for Multiplan. He wasn't happy.

Bill stood at the front of the conference room, manning an overhead projector himself.

Despite the fact that everybody present, Charles Simonyi, Jeff Raikes and a programmer named Doug Klunder, already knew the numbers, Bill had insisted on opening the meeting with a reminder of where they currently were.

"We're a month away from launching Word and announcing Windows," he said.

"Windows?" Doug Klunder asked.

Bill looked annoyed at being interrupted so early but Doug knew that pretending you understood something you didn't was a cardinal sin in Bill's book. He might be irritated to have his flow interrupted but if it became obvious that Doug had sat there and let something he didn't know pass by then it would be a lot worse.

It was Jeff Raikes who answered him.

"The new name for Interface Manager, Hanson in marketing has rebranded it. He says all the magazines are calling GUIs windowing systems so if we call ours 'Windows' it'll mean we own the idea."

"Thanks. Sorry Bill, carry on."

"Thank you, Doug," Bill said sarcastically and Doug was tempted to rethink his previous assessment of the benefits of speaking out, but he knew it was just Bill being Bill. "So as I was trying to say, Brodie has done brilliant work getting Word ready to release in just seven months. It will give us a presence in the word processing category to go alongside what should be an already established spreadsheet in Multiplan. And when we announce Windows, we'll be formally setting out our intention to move into the GUI space. Which is all good, right?"

Nobody was stupid enough to fall for that trap, they all knew why they were here, so they said nothing.

Bill slid a transparency on to the overhead projector and a chart was beamed onto the wall ahead of them showing sales volume against time, with two coloured lines that rose steadily over time. The lines were close but in recent months the blue one had edged ahead.

"Sales of spreadsheets since we released Multiplan a year ago. This line is sales of Multiplan," he said, pointing to the blue line.

Then he laid another transparency on top of the first showing a red line appearing at the start of the year. "And this red one that almost needs another page to show it, is Lotus 1-2-3."

He tapped the new line at the point at which it rocketed past the first two and glared around the room at his team, daring them to speak. None of them did. The silence stretched out again until eventually Jeff spoke.

"At least it's higher than VisiCalc," he said.

"It's embarrassing, is what it is!" Bill slammed his hand down on the table, knocking the transparencies so that the angle of the lines changed again. Raikes noticed that it made the 1-2-3 line look even more dramatic but he chose not to point it out.

"Who are Lotus? They didn't even exist two years ago. We should own this space. So we're here to work out what we're going to do about it. We're not going to let this carry on, by the time we leave this room I want us to have a plan that gets Multiplan above 1-2-3 by the end of next financial year. In fact, I want Lotus out of business. I want them gone." He made a fist and smashed it into his other palm on the word 'gone'. "If anyone tries to buy a copy of 1-2-3 next year I want retailers everywhere to look confused and ask them what it is."

He turned off the projector and looked at his team.

"Everybody understand what we're here for?"

There was a mumbled chorus of agreement.

"Okay, let's start with what we know about 1-2-3. Why is it doing so much better than us?"

"They're doing TV ads," Doug Klunder said, tentatively.

"Hanson says TV advertising is a stupid way to market software. He says it doesn't lead to any sales because the overlap in audience and the computer market at the moment is too small. Even if he's slightly wrong it can't be making the difference we're seeing here."

"We know that in lots of ways Multiplan is better than 1-2-3, but 1-2-3 is faster than Multiplan. And speed matters. Kapor has done a good job in terms of speed," Simonyi said.

"It wasn't him, he's a DJ for God's sake, it was Sachs," Klunder said.

Doug was right, the majority of the coding on Lotus 1-2-3 had been done by Jonathan Sachs, but it was unfair to call Mitch Kapor a DJ. Sure, he'd been a DJ once upon a time, as well as a Transcendental Meditation instructor, but he was also a pretty mean coder. He'd made his fortune writing a data analysis and graphing programme which he then sold to VisiCorp before parting ways with them in 1981 to set up Lotus Development Corporation.

"Anyway, it's only faster because they wrote it just for the PC. We built Multiplan to be able to port it to any operating system," Jeff said.

"Well that's good news isn't it?" said Doug to the room. "It means he's placed all his chips on IBM. He can't sell it to other manufacturers who don't follow the PC operating system without reworking it."

"I don't think it was a proper plan, I think they just built for the biggest market at the time," Jeff said.

"What if we rewrite Multiplan just for the PC?" Doug asked.

Simonyi winced and shook his head.

"It would mean a complete rewrite, do you know how many versions we've got out there? Almost a hundred. Our whole application strategy is based on quick portability to other operating systems."

Bill had listened to the discussion quietly, now he adjusted his glasses and his eyes narrowed as he ran through scenarios in his mind.

"Maybe it's time to change that strategy," he said a few seconds later.

Simonyi looked surprised. He'd been key to the portability strategy when he first arrived at Microsoft, he'd given a presentation to a group like this one that included what had come to be called 'Simonyi's revenue bomb'. It had helped convince Bill he was the right kind of thinker and it was based completely on the advantage they'd get from building portability in from the ground up. But if Bill was thinking of shifting approach then there was no point in Simonyi holding onto it too strongly.

"Go on, what are you thinking?"

"Look how many manufacturers are coming out with PC clones now. Paul and I always thought it was possible that one system would win out, that was what drove the best possible upside on DOS. Portability was the right bet at the time to cover all possibilities. But what if we've ended up in a world where there aren't lots of conflicting operating systems. What if there are just a handful? Then we'd be better off using the same approach as Lotus."

"Writing specific versions for each of them so they're optimised for that operating system."

"Exactly."

"It exposes us to the same problem as we had a year ago, which ones do we bet will win?" Simonyi thought aloud.

"The PC, obviously, given where the market has gone."

"Maybe the Commodore 64?"

Although it is only a memory now, the Commodore 64 was introduced in 1982 and became the fastest selling home computer. It remained a dominant force in computing through the eighties.

"And the Macintosh," said Jeff.

"Yes," said Bill "Jobs is later than he wanted to be but he's going to launch soon, he's pushing for the end of the year and it's a good machine. It could do well."

There was a pause while everyone thought but nobody suggested any other candidates. That alone spoke volumes to Bill. If this group couldn't come up with more than three likely candidates then consolidation seemed like it had legs.

"It would certainly be the easiest way to increase the speed of our applications," Simonyi said, running through the same thought process as Bill.

"Okay, let's keep it in mind. What else have we got?"

"We're going to launch Word next month, that will help with sales more generally," Jeff said.

"It won't help with sales of spreadsheets," Bill snapped. "And your plan is to what? Just abandon the spreadsheet market altogether, right?"

Jeff looked irritated by the rebuke but didn't react.

"No," he said simply.

"No, obviously. If you haven't got anything intelligent to say Jeff, don't say anything at all. I *meant* what else do we know about 1-2-3 that explains their sales."

Simonyi steepled his hands in front of his face and pinched his lips.

"Hold on," he said, prompting a look of relief on Jeff's face. "Maybe there's something in what Jeff is saying. Not to abandon spreadsheets completely, but maybe we don't try tweaking Multiplan, maybe we introduce a whole new spreadsheet. Designed for GUI from the beginning."

"Like Word is," Bill said.

"No. Word will be a step towards graphical but it basically just adds some menu functionality to encourage mouse use. I'm thinking we skip over the character based systems entirely and concentrate on writing a spreadsheet for Windows."

There were raised eyebrows all around the room, including Bill's.

"Windows is a year away at best. We'd be sacrificing a category for twelve months," Bill said.

"Perhaps it's better not to be in it at all if we can't win it. We could get Hanson to write something explaining how we're going to concentrate our efforts where we perform best, the future. I don't know, some market-y speak stuff, he'll know how to spin it."

"I don't think that's a good idea," Raikes said. Everybody looked at him, slightly surprised he'd been bold enough to try again after his first two kickings. "I mean, I think the first half is good, I just think we shouldn't withdraw Multiplan. We know it's better than 1-2-3 in lots of ways, and if we pull it there's a risk we'll lose credibility. It would be like admitting that we think Lotus made a better product. Microsoft has never done that and I don't think we should start now." Bill was nodding so Jeff grew more confident. "I think Charles is right, we should start developing something new but we should carry on pushing Multiplan in the meantime, try closing the gap as much as possible, but mostly keep our name in the category."

Bill nodded, from his discussions with Hanson he knew it was the sort of thing he'd say. In fact it even rang true from his earliest conversations about marketing with Steve back in his days at Proctor & Gamble, always try to dominate a category, that had been the magic of Steve's sideways detergent boxes!

"Okay, that sounds right. Let's check it with Rowland when we're out of here but I'm not inclined to abandon Multiplan until we have to. It's an income stream even if it isn't a winner. For the next three days let's assume we're keeping Multiplan but in parallel we're looking to develop a whole new offering for Windows and leapfrog character based spreadsheets. Any threats to that plan?"

The team thought quietly for a moment.

"What if Lotus develop a graphical 1-2-3?" Doug said.

"For the PC or Macintosh?"

"Either."

"If they want to do it on the PC they'd have to use Windows and since we're the ones building Windows, we should have a head start on how it works," Jeff said.

"Is that right? Are we allowed to do that?" Doug asked, nervously.

"Why the hell not?! It's my company we can do what we want," Bill said, bristling. "It's not like there's a Chinese Wall between our development groups. We'll make Windows interface calls available to other software companies, we want them to be able to develop on it. But we'd be idiots not to use what we know to be a little ahead in some areas."

"Okay," Doug said, sounding less than convinced. "But they could do it for the Macintosh," Doug pushed.

"Actually they can't," Bill replied. "I worked a clause into our contract with Apple that forbids them from getting anybody else to write a spreadsheet, or anything else we're providing, until the exclusivity period ends. Basically I protected us from exactly this situation."

"Neat," Doug said, impressed by Bill's foresight.

Bill accepted the praise, even though in truth he'd been thinking of VisiCalc when he wrote that clause into the agreement with Jobs.

***

By the end of the three day long session, the group had set the direction for the next Microsoft spreadsheet, designed to crush 1-2-3.

They would kick off a project, codenamed 'Odyssey', to develop a Windows based successor to Multiplan and aim their first version at the PC market.

It was the first departure from the previous portable application strategy and the first of Microsoft's applications intended from the outset to be fully GUI based.

The spreadsheet would come to be called Excel, and while it would experience changes along the way, it would become a mainstay of Microsoft's application suite for the next thirty five years (and counting!)

C:\PART\CHAPTER> 4.4

"Good to see you're still here Rao," Bill said, sticking his head into Remala's office. "Only the cool kids at this time, hey?"

Bill had stopped by the Windows developer's office on his way home for the night. It was gone ten pm but Bill's example had long since seen to it that Microsoft was a twenty four hour a day operation. People usually rotated in and out of the office to suit themselves, or the deadline of whatever project they were working on, with little regard to 'normal' working hours. And sometimes, of course, the same people would see the whole twenty four hours through.

"Ah, Bill, good to see you," Rao said, sitting a little straighter in his chair.

It wasn't unusual for the Chairman and CEO to drop in on developers but it still didn't happen to any one of them often enough to stop them feeling slightly on edge when he happened by.

Bill smiled at Rao, walked past the programmer's desk and stood in front of the window looking down. It was dark outside, but the lights of Bellevue could be seen below them. To show everyone how important the Windows project was he'd ensured that Remala had been moved to an office with a panoramic view, quite the luxury before the company moved to Redmond a couple of years later.

Rao spun his chair to look at his boss but Bill continued to look out of the window.

"We need to announce Windows now," Bill said, without turning.

Rao's eyes bulged and he was glad that Bill had his back turned. Then he caught himself, no doubt his hyper intelligent boss was watching him in the reflection of the window. He made an effort and composed his face.

"But we're nowhere near ready Bill," he said, as calmly as he could.

Bill turned and smiled again.

"We've got the demo you built."

"The demo is barely anything more than a video. The only code in it is what I use to display the windows themselves, there's no actual applications under any of it."

"Rao, don't worry about it," Bill came forward and put his hand on Rao's shoulder. "Nobody's ready when they announce. VisiCorp showed VisiOn at Comdex last year and they still haven't even released it. But if we don't announce it now then we'll look like idiots and I'm not having that. It's bad enough already, think how much worse it'll be in the new year when Jobs announces the Macintosh. If we haven't got something for people to wait for then they'll just flock to Apple."

He'd walked back to the door as he spoke and he paused halfway across the threshold, his hand on the door frame.

"Anyway, I just thought I'd stop by and tell you that I'm going to be getting our marketing people to plan something big, so it'll probably turn up the pressure a bit on your group. Thought it only fair to let you know. Well, got to go, I've got a date tonight and it doesn't do to keep them waiting, hey?" He grinned and left, then stuck his head quickly back round the door. "As always, if you hit any problems, you know where I am."

He left, this time for good, and Rao sat there stunned before reaching for one of the bouncy balls that he kept on his desk. They'd become something of a stress relief around the office recently, he didn't know who'd first introduced them but they were fun and sometimes it was good to lose yourself in the rhythmic bouncing when you'd got a deep problem to solve.

He did it now, bouncing it in short hops on the desk, his hand only six inches above the surface and his eyes never actually looking at the ball.

Bill had been smiling the whole time and Rao was pretty sure he was in good standing with the boss but what could he possibly mean 'turn up the pressure'? It was ten o'clock now, Bill was only just leaving and Rao hadn't even started to think about packing up.

He wasn't sure he liked the idea of the pressure being turned up.

***

Bill rang Rowland Hanson's home number as soon as he got back to his own place. Hanson had the good sense not to comment on the hour.

"But I thought it wasn't ready yet," Rowland Hanson said when Bill had given him the news that he wanted to launch Windows. "Don't your guys need to, like, develop it?"

"Never mind about that, that's not the way the computer industry works. Everybody announces stuff ahead of it being finished."

Bill had brought Rowland on board from Neutrogena to help Microsoft set its brand apart from other computer software companies.

In their initial interview Bill had impressed Hanson by commenting that the only difference between moisturiser that sold for one dollar an ounce versus moisturiser that sold for forty dollars an ounce was the marketing. Hanson was thrilled to have found someone who would appreciate the value he could bring and joined Microsoft a few months later.

"I've been invited to give the keynote at Comdex and I want to announce it then."

"That's only a couple of months away!"

Bill, excited by his idea, misunderstood Hanson's tone.

"I know! Everyone is going to be blown away when we announce so soon after releasing Word. So in terms of how we do it, I want something totally different, like you did for Word."

"It'll be harder to give away copies of something that doesn't exist."

Hanson had agreed with David Bunnell, now the editor of *PC World* and who Bill had known since the MITS days, that the magazine could give a way a sample copy of Word to each subscriber in the October 1983 issue, the formal release of Word would take place on the second day of Comdex, 29th November. It was run of the mill in the cosmetics world that Hanson had come from but a first for the software industry and Bill was convinced it was going to set tongues wagging when it came out.

"That kind of thing I mean, something that gets everyone talking. I want us to own Comdex."

"Okay, let me think about it."

"Great, that's all I ask. Now, I've got to go, I'm late for a date."

"Night Bill."

"Yeah, night Rowland."

Hanson hung up.

***

Hanson didn't have to think for long. He came back to Bill a few days later with a strategy.

"I'm going to need to hire a guy I know, he's a bit radical but he'll help me flesh this out, but the short version is that I think we do two things."

"Two?"

"Yeah, I've looked at the usual channels that are available at Comdex, more floor space for a bigger booth, advertising boards, that kind of thing…" Bill pulled a face but Rowland held up a finger and carried on speaking without giving him the chance to interrupt. "But it's too short notice to book any of them and besides, I don't think it's what you really want. So I've come up with some ideas I want to run by you."

"Okay."

"But they're all a bit different and there's a risk they'll fall flat, which is why I'm proposing we have two launches. We'll do a formal announcement before Comdex and then we'll try to turn Comdex into a Windows party by stealth."

Bill looked excited and Rowland could hear his foot tapping beneath the desk. "Tell me about it," he said.

"Hold on, as I said I've got some ideas for it but first we need to get the formal announcement out of the way. I want us to have an old style press conference that's spiced up a bit by renting somewhere nice and getting the manufacturers all up on stage together."

"Won't it take the punch out of the Comdex announcement?" Bill said, pulling the same disappointed face he had earlier.

"Yes," Rowland said and Bill blinked, he hadn't expected such candour. This is why he liked Rowland. "But that's a risk we have to take to make sure the message lands in case the Comdex noise isn't as successful. It'll still be a big deal, trust me."

Bill did.

"Okay, so what about Comdex then?" he asked.

Rowland paused.

"I'm thinking we blitz the place."

"Comdex?"

"Vegas. Well, the strip. There's nothing formal we can do through Comdex itself because of the timing but they don't own the whole of Las Vegas so my plan is that we do things around the edges. All of the normal conference advertising has been done before anyway so if we want to make a mark we'll need to do something different. I'm thinking Windows advertising on the taxis so you can't get from the airport to the conference without seeing one. And things like discount vouchers for local restaurants with Microsoft advertising all over them, swag bags, partnerships with local hotels to deliver Windows branded stuff to attendees rooms. Basically I want everyone attending Comdex to be immersed in Windows. They'll go away thinking Comdex was all about Windows regardless of what's in the actual halls themselves. What do you reckon?"

***

The two launch strategy was an unmitigated success.

In New York on 10th November 1983, Bill held a press conference in the prestigious 55 storey, Helmsley Palace Hotel on Madison Avenue.

With more than twenty manufacturers standing beside him, Bill announced that Microsoft, who as he reminded the audience already provided the MS-DOS operating system for 95% of 16-bit computers, were going to release an extension to that operating system that would run on all of them and provide a graphical user interface for those existing machines without needing new hardware. Its name: Windows.

Calling it "…a landmark in making computers easy to learn and use…" Bill promised that existing DOS software would continue to run on Windows and it would make transferring data between applications easier. Why buy a new machine or consider going to another GUI?

And the launch date for this epoch defining milestone? April 1984.

By the end of 1984, he predicted, 90% of personal computers would have made the switch to Windows.

And then, at the end of the month, he took the show to Vegas for Comdex.

Running from 28th to 2nd December Comdex drew eighty thousand visitors that year and all of them, as Rowland Hanson had planned, were bombarded with Windows merchandise almost every minute that they weren't actually inside the convention center.

In the end, with the help of the creative genius he had recruited, Hanson's campaign had swollen to include Windows keychains given to anyone renting a car at the airport; a game involving collecting a Microsoft button from the convention booth of any of the manufacturers supporting Windows and finding someone who had one with a matching number; and even Microsoft Windows pillows placed in the hotel rooms of Comdex attendees.

Hanson spent half a million dollars on the campaign, including tens of thousands of dollars on tips to bellboys and other hotel staff to help blanket the hotels with Microsoft marketing material.

On 28th Bill gave the first of what would over the years come to be many keynote addresses.

Despite its outwardly supremely confident chairman and successful marketing blitz, there was actually a subtle reminder hidden in the crowd during that keynote that Microsoft was still a relatively small company punching above its weight. In the unlikely event that any of the conference-goers knew the wider Gates family they would have spotted another Bill Gates there that day.

Bill Sr. was there providing his son with not just moral but technical support. He was the one running the slide projector for Bill's presentation.

As a high powered Seattle lawyer and by then the head of the National Conference of Bar Presidents, he was probably over qualified but he must have done an okay job. Bill's address went off to rapturous applause.

***

Not everybody was quite so happy with the launch of Windows.

IBM had refused to take part in the manufacturer line up in New York and held off endorsing it even at Comdex. Perhaps beginning to sense their increasing reliance on Bill, the management at Big Blue were starting to look to develop their own windowing system and were even flirting with endorsing VisiOn.

However, while IBM chose to express their objections through a silent refusal to join in the marketing game, the objections coming from another quarter were, predictably, a lot noisier.

***

"Get Gates down here, now!" Steve Jobs shouted as he paced around the room like a caged tiger. "What the fuck does he think he's doing?"

"Shall I get him on the phone Steve? I'm sure he can explain."

"No! I want him here in person explaining why it's okay to have fucked me over like this."

"Okay, I'll speak to him, Steve, see how quickly he can get down here."

Steve paused by his desk, grabbed up a notepad and flung it against the far wall.

"Don't *'see how quickly he can get down here'*. Get him here tomorrow!"

***

The next afternoon Bill was sitting calmly in an Apple office while Jobs vented his anger.

He had come alone expecting a one on one conversation with Jobs, but Steve had had other ideas. In a room that was just a little too small for them all to fit in comfortably, there were ten Apple employees and Bill.

When he'd arrived he'd been escorted to this room by a secretary who had resisted all of his attempts to engage her in conversation. She'd obviously known that he was there for a dressing down and had walked as quickly as possible, desperate to spend as little time as she could with someone she considered toxic.

She'd dropped him off in this room where all of the Apple team had already assembled and were waiting for him to arrive.

The room had been arranged so that the tables formed a single long barrier down the middle of the room. The Apple team were all sitting on the other side with Jobs once again pacing backwards and forwards behind them.

Nobody invited him to sit down but Bill took a seat in the middle of the table anyway, directly opposite the empty seat that he assumed was Jobs', should he intend to sit down at all in this meeting.

Jobs didn't waste any time with pleasantries.

"What the hell do you call this?" he said, scooping up a printout from the table and throwing it across at Bill.

Bill glanced at it and saw that it was a copy of Microsoft's press release from 10th. He fought an urge to be sarcastic.

Unlike Jobs, Bill had known this moment was coming for months and so he stayed calm throughout.

He also knew that he hadn't done anything wrong. Certainly not contractually, and as far as he was concerned, ethically as well.

"It's Windows, Steve."

Jobs looked like Bill had insulted someone he loved.

"Stupid name," he said dismissively and then with as much passion as a wronged spouse he said, "How could you have betrayed us like this?"

"Well, I don't think that's quite fair."

"Fair?! I tell you what isn't fair, stealing from me. Stealing from Apple. You've stolen the idea of Windows from us."

Steve stalked around the desk and stood looming over Bill. Steve, at 6 foot 2 inches was four inches taller than Bill even if Bill had been standing, but this was a man who had gone toe to toe with his six and a half foot tall father when he was a pipsqueak twelve year old. He wasn't about to be intimidated by Jobs.

"That's one of way of looking at it Steve, I have another way. I think it's more like we both had this rich neighbour named Xerox and I broke into his house to steal the TV set and found out that you had already stolen it."

"Don't try to be clever Gates, neither of us had a contract with Xerox. You and I had a contract that said you couldn't develop a GUI."

"No we didn't," Bill said without raising his voice.

Jobs frowned and looked briefly over at his people, when none of them reacted he turned back to Bill.

"What?! Yes, we did. In fact we still have and you're in breach of it."

"No Steve, we've got a contract that says I won't build a graphical spreadsheet or any of the other applications we're developing for you. It says nothing about an operating system. And in any case it says we won't sell them before the end of the year. Windows won't be out until next April so either way there's no breach of contract."

Jobs stood stupefied for a moment, his lips moving slightly as he thought of different retorts.

"This is still a distraction. You're supposed to be working on applications for the Macintosh."

"We are, they'll be delivered on time, you have my word."

"Your word, pah! His word!" he said playing to the captive crowd of Apple staff, one or two of whom sneered. It was the first contribution any of them had made so far.

"Yes, my word. You'll have Multiplan ready for launch as we promised and the others shortly afterwards. Look, Steve, Windows isn't a threat to you, the Macintosh is a great machine, and it will be out before Windows is, so anyone who wants to buy one isn't going to wait for Windows. But there are customers who don't buy Apple stuff, you're never going to sell to them anyway. It's a different market. What Windows does is bring those customers into the GUI world that we both think is the future." Steve's shoulders relaxed slightly and he lowered himself into the chair next to Bill. "In fact getting them hooked on a GUI on a PC might even make it more likely that they'll switch over to a Macintosh in future."

"Hm."

That was a thought that Bill had made up on the fly and Jobs didn't sound convinced but at least he wasn't fuming any more.

"But hey," Bill went on. "I get that you were angry at how you found out, I should have spoken to you guys about it first so you knew what was going on. But I assure you they're different developers we've hired specially, there's no conflict here at all. Your own guys will tell you that we're delivering our code on time and to a high spec."

Bill looked across at the Apple team and pointed at the man responsible for managing the relationship with Microsoft. He looked incredibly uncomfortable to have been dragged in, nonetheless he nodded.

"It's true," he said, quietly. "They're on track. Multiplan is in testing now."

Feeling that Jobs had mellowed, Bill pressed his new found advantage.

"Listen, let's put this aside for now, Windows will trundle on in the background but let's all concentrate on getting ready for the launch of the Macintosh. Are you all sorted?"

Jobs pulled himself more upright in the chair and put his elbows on the desk and faced his team. He didn't seem to notice that he was now sitting beside Bill grilling his own people.

"I'm having to fight in here, you don't know what it's like. You're so lucky not having a public company Bill."

"I can imagine, all those hoops to jump through when you just want to release great stuff. Is there anything else we can help you with?"

"Is there anything Bill can do that will get us across the line?" Jobs studied each of his team in turn and then looked pointedly at one of them. "What about BASIC?"

"Yeah, we're a bit behind on the BASIC."

Jobs gave him a withering look. "You've been 'a bit behind' for months. Are we going to get it done or do we need to get Bill's guys on it?"

By the time they finished the meeting Bill, in a move he'd perfected since his earliest days in Albuquerque, had taken an irritated customer and upsold him something else.

C:\PART\CHAPTER> 4.5

Bill got back into his house, surprisingly tired. He had left the office much earlier than usual and the traffic had been much worse than he was used to.

Why does anyone bother leaving early? he thought.

Still, being home early meant he could make the phone call he hadn't managed yesterday. He checked the time, 9pm. Perfect, his mom would be still up.

"Congratulations Mom," he said when she picked up. "First woman head of United Way's national executive. Not bad."

"Thank you Trey, but it's not really that big of a deal," Mary replied.

"You're joking! How many Boards do you serve on now, three, four, five? Dad's going to have to become a stay at home husband."

"Don't be silly Trey. Anyway why are you ringing, you could just pop round?"

Bill's parents still lived in the Laurelhurst home he'd grown up in and earlier in the year Bill had bought a place just down the road from them. It looked out on to Lake Washington and even had its own dock, not that he used it.

"I've only just got in and I've still got a load of work to do. When I come round I want to be able to relax."

"And have me make you dinner?"

"Well, you or Dad when he gets his new apron fitted!" They both laughed, imagining Bill Sr's giant frame in an apron. "I'm ringing because I needed to sound something out with you, a couple of things actually, and they're about United Way."

"Oh, okay, go on then," Mary became all business like the flick of a switch.

"You know Jon Shirley? I've mentioned him, my new president."

"Yes, the one who used to be at Tandy."

"That's right, well he's suggested the company starts a charity matched-giving programme. For every dollar one of our employees raises we'll match it, up to some limit we've not agreed yet."

"Oh, that's fantastic Bill, I've been saying for years you need to do something in the charity sector."

Bill had a flash of frustration.

"I know Mom, and I will, but right now I'm focussed on running the business. It won't help if I give everything away and the company fails, will it?"

Mary stayed quiet, this was a conversation they'd had repeatedly and there was no point going over old ground. Particularly not when Bill seemed to be moving slightly anyway.

"Anyway," Bill carried on when she didn't reply. "Jon has suggested that we could target the programme towards United Way. How do you feel about that?"

"It sounds great," Mary said without hesitation.

"And it's not a conflict of interest with your new position?"

"No, of course not, we're all supposed to fundraise. I didn't have anything to do with suggesting it but if anyone thought I had then it would be fine."

"Okay, that's good. That brings me onto the other thing. John Akers from IBM is on the board with you isn't he?"

"Yes."

"Well, he's telling me I should join the board as well."

"Ah, so that's what you're really worried about as a conflict of interest."

"I suppose so, yes, what do you think?"

"I understand the concern but you don't get anything from it, it's just a way of giving back to the community," Mary said. He didn't tell his mom that one of the biggest selling points in his mind was that, as Shirley had pointed out to him, he'd be able to get time with Akers when they met for Board meetings. "Besides, it wouldn't be up to me, you'd go through the normal selection process. But as chairman of a good sized company you'd stand a fair chance if you weren't my son, so I don't see why it should count against you that you are."

"Okay, that's great. I'll put my name forward then."

"Good, I'd like that. Hey did you know that my dad was on the Washington United Way board? Well, it was United Good Neighbor then, but you'll be following in his footsteps. Gam will be pleased. When are you going to see her next?"

Bill moved the phone away from his mouth and sighed, he knew he needed to make more time for his grandmother, she was an amazing woman but she wouldn't be here forever.

"I don't know Mom, things are really busy here but I'll try to get up to her before Christmas. And I'm going to spend a Think Week with her in Spring."

Since returning to Seattle, Bill had tried to get away from the office for at least one week each year. He called it his Think Week and he spent them with Gam at her place on the Hood Canal out of contact with everyone except her. He would take armfuls of books and spend the week reading and thinking deeply about the direction of the company, then return to Microsoft and deluge his people with the ideas he'd had while away.

***

On 22nd January 1984 Apple played an advert during the Super Bowl that would become infamous. More than one hundred million viewers saw Apple's portrayal of IBM as Big Brother from the Orwell novel *1984* and watched as a sledgehammer wielding (and inexplicably vest top wearing!) peroxide-blonde woman, runs through crowds of grey-clad bald drones and storm troopers, before smashing a giant screen broadcasting the face of the enemy.

The minute long advert finished with: *On January 24th, Apple Computer will release Macintosh. And you'll see why 1984 won't be like "1984."*

The Apple Board hated it, but Jobs loved it and for the time being at least, Jobs would sometimes still get his own way at Apple.

While he was definitely conscious that the relationship was becoming a lot more even-handed, Bill realised that Apple was still a pivotal relationship for Microsoft and if the industry went the way that he was now expecting, i.e. consolidation around a small number of standards, then he expected the Macintosh to be one of them. He wasn't just spinning Steve Jobs a line when he'd said it was a great machine. He really believed it.

In fact the Macintosh would not sell anywhere near the numbers that Jobs had forecast, a failing that would lead in part to his ousting from Apple a year later, but it and other Apple computers would continue to make up a significant portion of Microsoft revenues for years to come.

***

Jon Shirley and Bill had had an hour long meeting scheduled from 2pm so, knowing that it was unlikely that Bill would have eaten, Jon had suggested they do the meeting at Burgermaster in the hope that it would soften the blow of the message he had to deliver. Bill, never one to turn down a cheeseburger, had jumped at it. He had suggested driving but Jon said the ten minute walk would give them a chance to get some air. And him to enjoy a pipe on the way back.

When the two of them sat at one of the few outdoor picnic benches, the only part of the drive-in restaurant that didn't need you to sit in your car, Jon got quickly to the point.

Jon finished his burger before Bill and started to tamp tobacco into his pipe. This was August 1984 and a year later smoking would be banned in restaurants, Jon was hoping that at least outdoor areas like this would still be legal, he enjoyed a smoke after a meal.

"You're too much for them," he was saying. "There's been a couple of..." he swayed his head and waved his half filled pipe.

"Complaints?" Bill completed the sentence, sounding hurt.

"Well, some people think your style is a bit aggressive."

"What people? No, never mind." Bill caught himself. "I'm not aggressive Jon. You know me, I like high bandwidth communication that's all. If you can't think fast you've no business being a programmer."

"I get that Bill, but they're not all programmers. You're running a big company now, it's not just you, Paul and a handful of programmers who think exactly the same way you do."

Jon had been President and Chief Operating Officer for a year and the two of them had established a great working relationship. Bill had learnt that Jon was worth listening to even when he had ideas that Bill didn't like. Which he suspected was about to happen now.

"Okay Jon, cut to the chase, what do you think we need to do?"

"A reorganisation. We'll split the company into systems and applications groups."

"Hive off part of the company?"

"Absolutely not. This is still one Microsoft under you as chairman. I'm just talking about having separate operational divisions."

"Who'd have day to day leadership then?"

"Steve on systems, you'd keep applications until we can find someone to take it over from you. But we'll be actively looking. You need to be able to dedicate yourself full time to the chairman role. When the new CFO comes on board, you will need to spend time with him." Jon said, referring to his already ongoing search for a Chief Financial Officer.

Bill allowed himself a diversion.

"How's the search going?"

"I've got a strong candidate, Frank Gaudette, but we haven't sealed the deal. I'll introduce you when we're closer."

"Okay, that'll be good we need someone to get a hold of that whole area," Bill took a slurp of his Diet Coke, having made the switch a year earlier after his mom had ragged on him about how much sugar he was having with his can-an-hour habit. "So back to your taking-my-company-from-me plan."

"Bill!" Jon scrunched up his face. "That's not what this is and you know it. You trust me, right?"

"I do." Bill nodded. "I'm just joking. Half joking. It does feel a bit like that though. Have you discussed it with the board?"

"Of course not! If you think we can make it work in a different way then I'm all ears, this isn't about taking over, it's about setting Microsoft up for success. Getting a structure that is sustainable and could even set us up for an IPO."

"I'm still not sure I want to do that."

"I know, but at some point we're not going to have a choice, we might as well be ready." He finally lit his pipe and popped it in his mouth.

"Okay, tell me more, what happens when we replace me on the applications side? What do I do then? I'll have nothing to do."

"You'll be full time as chairman, other board chairs find it a full time job."

"Other board chairs think four hour days are full time," Bill mumbled, then added in a normal voice, "But what specifically will I do?"

"You'll carry on with the external representation you've been doing and the key customer accounts…"

"So like I already do."

"That's right. And you'll set the company strategy and overarching direction, which products are we going to make, which markets are we going into."

Bill shook his head but he was clearly thinking, rather than disagreeing. So far.

"There's no way we can afford for me to step away from the design stuff…"

"…Not my intention…" Jon said while Bill continued to speak.

"…Particularly Windows, we need to get that out fast and I can help. How do I do that if it's under Steve?"

"Because we'll formalise your design role across both divisions as part of the chairman's position. I'm really not talking about some sort of honorary chairmanship where you retire quietly and have a title. You'll do design across both divisions, provide guidance and review to applications and systems teams. You'll still be totally involved in the products, but instead of being the builder you'll be the architect. What does Simonyi call it… a meta-programmer."

"I'm not hearing much different from today." It had been some time since Bill had actually written a piece of code so in that regard he'd stopped being a 'builder' already.

"Well, this would formalise most of what we've already done," Jon took a slow pull on his pipe. "And you wouldn't have any actual direct reports, of course."

Bill smirked, tying it all back to Jon's original point.

"Ah, because of the complaints."

"No. And they weren't *complaints*. But it does have the dual advantage of both freeing you up from boring people management to focus on where you add more value, and giving the teams a manager they can moan to after you've given them your 'direction'." He laughed. "Look, speak to Big Bill and your Mom, see what they think about it. I think it's for the best, but I promise you I'm not going to do anything or even raise it again until you tell me you're on board."

Bill regularly relied on both Bill Sr. and Mary as a sounding board for decisions but this was one he didn't need their input on, he was quiet on the walk back to the office but before they'd reached the front door he'd decided. Jon was right. He told him so and Jon announced it in a company wide email the next day.

C:\PART\CHAPTER> 4.6

Through the first quarter of 1984 Windows continued to generate excitement in the press and manufacturers continued to get on board in response to the Windows-heavy sales pitches that routinely accompanied any interest in buying Microsoft software of any kind.

In the meantime though other software companies were announcing and even releasing their own graphical systems and to Bill's intense irritation the Windows delivery date kept getting pushed back.

Around the time of the New York announcement Bill had recruited Scott McGregor, another ex-Xerox PARC employee who Charles Simonyi had known, to head the team.

McGregor brought both knowledge and experience of windowing systems from PARC, sadly what he didn't bring was a magic wand.

April 1984 came and went and Windows was nowhere near ready.

The release date was pushed back to fall 1984 and Bill started getting Steve Ballmer more and more involved to help ensure the deadline was met. It turned out Steve didn't have a magic wand either and in the summer, when it became obvious that the fall date would be missed as well, he was sent on a tour of manufacturers and the press to grovel about the delay and commit to a new deadline. Spring 1985.

By January 1985 it was clear that Windows was not going to hit even the vaguely articulated 'spring' deadline and Bill lost all patience.

McGregor left Microsoft, making him the fourth product manager to head up Windows and fail to deliver.

In an attempt to bring the errant project under control Bill split the management role, tapping up Tandy Trower who had worked previously on Microsoft's languages to head the technical side of it and giving Steve full responsibility for getting the product out of the door.

By April 1985 the Windows team had shifted into full sprint mode. People were staying later than ever, coding at their desks to loud rock music until the early hours of the morning before stumbling out of the door and either heading straight home to collapse into bed; trying to cling on to some semblance of normality by going out in groups to grab pizza or take in a late showing of a movie; or simply giving in to the inevitable and sleeping at their desks.

Bill wasn't involved in the coding of Windows or the late night partying, but he'd have recognised the hacker spirit from the days when he and Paul would do the same thing. And while it wasn't quite official company policy to encourage it, everybody knew that their programmer-chairman would not have seen it as a bad thing.

Bill's reputation as one of the few company leaders who could genuinely hold his own with his staff made him something of a legend with the developers. They were killing themselves to deliver for the company, but above all they were doing it for him.

***

Tandy Trower and Rao Remala, still on the Windows team through all of the product managers, had prepared themselves as much as possible for what was starting to become known inside Microsoft as the 'BillG' review.

The review was an opportunity for Bill to cast his eye over every product that was under development and be sure that it was heading in the right direction, and at the right speed.

When it came to Windows, nobody in the room was going to be surprised that the answer to the second of those questions was, 'no'.

In later years, when Microsoft moved to the Redmond campus, the BillG reviews would usually take place in the executive board room, in 1985 at Bellevue things were still a little less formal so the review had been scheduled in one of the normal conference rooms.

Rao and Tandy arrived together accompanied by a couple of their developers, and they all took a seat. There were already about a dozen people there including Steve Ballmer and surprisingly Bill. Bill was notoriously late for meetings since he was usually running from one to another but in what should have been a warning sign for Tandy he was there early for this one.

They'd arrived at the end of a story Bill was telling to the assembled executives so the Windows team stood awkwardly, waiting for it to finish.

"… I said if it bothered him that much he should repurpose the chipset into base three."

Rao had no idea what the story was about but Bill's executive team obviously found it amusing enough as they all burst out of laughing.

Bill smirked and took a swig of Diet Coke while the room gradually fell silent. He became aware of the team standing in the doorway and frowned slightly. He gestured to the empty chairs with a quick flick of his hand.

"Sit, sit," he said.

Taking a seat next to Tandy, Rao saw a yellow legal pad and a stack of paper that was easily an inch thick, on the table in front of Bill.

He recognised the paper, it was the detailed spec and timeline for Windows that they had sent him the night before in readiness for this meeting. He was surprised to see that the top page had some notes in the margin.

Wow, he thought, *he's actually had chance to take a look at it.*

He'd assumed that Bill's assistant had insisted on them sending over all of the documentation they'd refer to so that Bill could use it in the meeting. He hadn't expected him to have had chance to skim it before hand.

Bill pulled his legal pad towards him and divided it into quadrants then pushed it back out of the way and pulled forward the spec, flicking through the pages to find something specific

Rao's eyes widened when he saw that not only had Bill skimmed the spec, he'd read it throughly. On practically every page Rao could see that the margins were covered in scribbled notes and questions. Detailed questions.

Bill stopped flicking about a third of the way through and tapped a note he'd scribbled in the margin.

"I'd like to start with how we're running old DOS applications."

"Okay," said Tandy who was slated to do the majority of the talking. Rao and the rest of the developers were there in case a more detailed question came up that he couldn't answer. "We've developed an application we're calling WINOLDAPP, it's basically a window that emulates the command..."

"Yes, yes, I know all that," Bill cut him off. "I've read it. What I want to know is how we're handling the memory grab."

That caught Tandy on the back foot.

"The memory grab," he fumbled.

Rao tried not to let his face show how sorry he felt for his team leader as he watched Bill scribble something on his pad with his left-handed scrawl. Tandy had prepared a presentation and it looked like he wasn't going to get chance to cover any of it.

There was a time not too far in the future when these meetings would become legendary, and everyone would know what they were getting into when they got an invite. But this was a transition time, Microsoft's structure was still incredibly flat for a company with revenues of $140 million and when Bill had concerns or questions about a product he would still drop by the developer's desk with no regard for the hierarchy and quiz them on an arcane piece of detail about what they were doing, somehow demonstrating an encyclopaedic knowledge of what they were working on. It was potentially more challenging but at least you didn't have time to worry about it in advance.

Before long the BillG reviews would settle into a regular process in which Bill would pepper his product managers with progressively more challenging questions. The goal was to answer them well enough that he walked away with confidence that the manager had a grip on things and he could leave them alone.

It was a way of resolving the tension between the control freak nature of the boss and the limited time he had available to be involved in every decision in an ever growing company. If the product manager could prove that they were able to stand up to a grilling then they were free to run their area with a fair degree of latitude.

In combination with his combative style it made for some pretty tense meetings and nobody expected to get out of them without at least some bruising but, as had always been his way, he appreciated those who pushed back and he could be won over when you proved to him he was wrong.

Unfortunately for Tandy, the unspoken rules hadn't quite been established by that point so it took him by surprise, but he had worked with Bill for three years now so he knew the boss well enough to adapt, and after the first left field question he began to hold his own. Eventually he even managed to bring the discussion around to a subject he needed to get Bill's agreement on.

"I think we need to include some small applications for free with Windows when we launch," he said. "You know the little programs that ship with the Macintosh for free, something like that."

"Sounds interesting," Steve said. "What had you got in mind?"

Bill didn't look as happy as Steve but for now he kept quiet and humoured Tandy.

"Dan McCabe is working on a little graphics programme he's calling Paint, that would be good to include. And we could do a calendar, a calculator, and even a stripped back word processor."

That was the end of Bill's ability to hold off.

"A word processor?!" he exploded. "That is the stupidest fucking thing I've ever heard! We sell a full fledged version of Word, why would we want to compete with ourselves by giving away something that isn't as good for free?"

"Word isn't a Windows programme," Tandy said, keeping his voice level. "I've spoken to the team developing the Windows version and they tell me it will be a year before they're ready."

"Well, they're wrong and anyway there's no way we're doing two," Bill said.

"We want to be able to offer comparable functionality to the Macintosh."

"You can run Word for DOS in the WINOLDAPP window."

"True, but we know other software providers aren't exactly knocking down our door yet to build applications for it. If we don't include something ourselves then there'll be almost nothing available on it."

"They'll develop more when you pull your finger out and release test versions they can code against."

"I think there's something in it Bill, Borland released something similar recently for DOS. It would be good to move ahead of them and show it could be done on a GUI."

"We'll be cannibalising our own sales."

This went on for some time, but Tandy stuck to his guns and in the end Bill backed down and agreed. Microsoft Write would be released with Windows 1.0.

Other arguments didn't go as well and Tandy found himself getting more and more annoyed through the meeting until finally, during an argument about the memory constraints they were working within, he lost his composure.

He had suspected from the beginning that Windows was a poisoned chalice and that Bill and Steve were only giving it him as a way of easing him out of the company. He'd even raised it with them when they first suggested he do it. They had assured him that was nonsense, and they thought he was the best man for the job, in fact they'd both actually laughed when he'd asked them about it. He had believed them at the time or he would have never taken the job, but now, exhausted from the tiny amount of sleep he was getting and feeling browbeaten by Bill, he was starting to wonder again and his nerves were fraying at the edges.

"It's taking us more time than we'd like to handle all of the display types, it's tricky to fit it all into the memory we have available," he said.

"Ridiculous," Bill snapped. "You just need to write it more carefully. Do you know how much memory I had to work with on the Altair?"

Tandy was frustrated enough to bite back but he had heard plenty of variants on the 'I could do it myself' argument over the years and knew they were right often enough that there was no point challenging Bill about them, so he focused on what he figured was the safer factual point.

"I'm not writing it Bill, I manage the team that writes it," he gestured to Rao and the others sitting beside him.

Bill threw his hands up in the air.

"Why the hell not? You need to be coding as well, no wonder we're behind."

"That's not my job, that's not why you put me on this."

"To tell the truth, I'm beginning to wonder why I put you on this."

That was when Tandy lost it.

"Hey, I can always leave, it's not like I'm going to lose all of those amazing stock options I don't have, is it?!"

He didn't know when but somewhere in the middle of his rant he had stood up, and by the end he was shouting, his chest heaving from how hard he was breathing.

Bill, suddenly calm again, just shrugged.

"You know where the door is."

He had no intention of getting rid of Tandy but he wasn't about to submit in front of the wider team. Luckily Steve intervened and saved them from themselves.

"Okay, guys, let's take a breath here," he said, his voice uncharacteristically calm. "Tandy sit down. Please. We've had this conversation before, nobody wants you to leave. Can we just get on with the review?"

Bill made a mental note to drop by Tandy later and check in on him and decided it was time to focus the spotlight on Ballmer.

"Good idea. So what about this timeline then, Steve?"

At this point the new launch 'date' was being touted as fall '85.

"I think we can do it," Ballmer said, his voice was still calm from his Mother Theresa move a moment ago and he was openly surprised when Bill turned on him.

"You think?! I don't want to hear that you think, Steve. I want a fucking guarantee. I'm done with this, it's embarrassing."

"Yeah. No. I get it. We'll ship in the fall."

Bill looked at Rao as Steve spoke and saw a look flit across his face.

"Your developers don't look convinced."

Steve looked at Tandy and Rao for support. "We can do it, can't we guys?"

The more junior developers looked like rabbits caught in the headlights. Rao started to agree, feeling like he didn't have an alternative but Tandy stopped him by placing a hand on his colleague's arm.

"It might be wise to have a little bit of contingency," he said, carefully. He didn't want to betray Steve but the last thing that he wanted to do was commit to another unachievable deadline when there seemed to be a chance to shift it.

Steve looked hurt but Bill nodded. It was curt but at least it was an acknowledgement. He turned back to Steve.

"Okay, add some contingency, this fall was an internal goal anyway, we haven't formally announced it anywhere. Steve I want you to work out a realistic plan you all agree on and come back to me with a final launch date. An actual date." He stood and collected up the spec papers, knocking them on the desk to get them back into a neat pile. He started to leave and paused above Steve, putting his hand on his friend's shoulder. Steve looked up at him and Bill looked him square in the eyes. "But let me be very clear Steve, Windows leaves this company by the first snowfall or you do."

Then he left the room.

***

Of course, Windows wasn't the only thing underway at Microsoft in the summer of 1985. Excel launched in September. Following another change in strategic direction that resulted, much to the development team's dismay, in another significant rewrite, it actually launched first on the Macintosh. A PC version to run on Windows would have to wait until November 1987.

And another development also started that summer. A kind of development that was less familiar to Bill and his fellow coders but much more familiar to the world at large. Ground was broken on the new Redmond campus on August 4th 1985.

By the mid-eighties Microsoft's sales were doubling every year and, despite Bill's inclination only to hire the best and not to grow too fast, the company was expanding its staff at a rate of knots. At the end of December 1985 there were nine hundred ninety eight members of staff (of whom two hundred and seventy one were programmers) and they were starting to outgrow the Bellevue offices.

Years earlier Bill had confided in Jon that he had always wanted to build a site for Microsoft along the lines of the best college campuses. Somewhere that would encourage 'his' people to mingle, interact and share great ideas. And with many of the employees having come straight from college, a similar environment would make them feel at home and help with recruitment.

With space at Bellevue becoming an issue, Shirley went to Bill and proposed that instead of renting another building they start from the ground up and build the campus he had dreamed about.

Bill was excited.

So Shirley auditioned local developers to identify sites for a new base for the company and surveyed the current employees to see how far they would be willing to travel. When he found that none of the employees would abandon ship over the fifteen minute additional travel into Redmond the choice was made, and he secured a five hundred acre site in Redmond that remains the headquarters of Microsoft today.

The new campus expanded over time but the first phase would cover thirty of those acres, feature plenty of outdoor space and have special X-shaped buildings designed to ensure as many people as possible could get their own office with a view. It would come to solidify Microsoft's relationship with Seattle.

The move in date was set for Spring 1986 but there were a couple of little items to get out of the way first. Windows was still not released and the public status of the company had to be decided.

***

On 28th October 1985 Bill turned thirty. To celebrate he held a roller skating party for his friends and Microsoft employees.

Less than a month later, on 20th November Windows 1.0 was finally released.

It would have been hard to match the marketing blitz from two years earlier when the idea of Windows was announced at Comdex '83, but now that the thing had actually arrived they had to do something. So, timing it again to coincide with Comdex, Microsoft celebrated the launch by sponsoring a roast of themselves with a demo of Windows baked into the middle of it.

More than three hundred industry insiders were invited to the roast, hosted by *PC World* magazine's John Dvorak, to watch the tuxedo clad Bill and Steve's double act.

Stewart Alsop, the editor of *InfoWorld*, presented Bill with the Golden Vaporware Award in honour of Windows' many missed release dates. But for the most part Steve was the butt of the jokes while Bill handled the more serious side of the presentation.

Steve opened by reflecting on the journey Windows had taken to get to the launch.

"Actually there's been a lot of change for me since Windows was introduced, at the time we started Windows development I was the financial guy. I was the guy who reviewed the investment decision. I said, 'Okay, six man years, no problem; one disk, no problem.' We're now eighty man years later and were selling a $99 product with five disks... They moved me into a new job."

He pointed out that he had become a joke inside Microsoft when he had run a personal advert in the company newsletter to sell his house and the editor had titled it, 'Ballmer's house for sale: Has Windows. Ballmer does not.'

And then finished by holding aloft a window squeegee and bucket and shouting, "At Microsoft we're damn proud to have done Windows!"

When Bill, with unusually well combed hair, took to the podium for his presentation, Steve ran back on and the two of them sang a couple of lines from *The Impossible Dream*, after which Bill took another pop at Steve.

"First I'd like to thank Steve because Steve's really been a part of the whole process. We used to have a lot of meetings where we'd sit and say, 'Look we've just gotta cut features, we've just gotta cut features, we gotta get this thing out. What can we do?' So Steve's kind of a non-technical guy so he came up with this idea that we could rename the thing Microsoft Window... And we woulda shipped that a *long* time ago."

Then Bill, smiling like a little kid throughout, ran through a demonstration of the functionality of the new Windows, showing that it could run old DOS software (he even used the cursed 1-2-3 to do it), making a strength of the decision to use tiled instead of overlapping windows and finally, since there still wasn't any other graphical software to actually *use* on Windows, showed off Tandy Trowers' mini applications.

Although it was fairly obviously a defensive manoeuvre to take the sting out of any criticism others might care to make about the delay, the launch went over very well.

Windows would come in for a lot of criticism in the coming months and years until Microsoft finally reached an acceptable version with Windows 3.0, but on the day it was well received. And to be fair, most of the criticisms were really about the difficulty of realising the vision of a truly revolutionary GUI on the technology of the time.

True, the Macintosh had a slicker interface, but Windows showed that it would be possible to implement those same ideas successfully on the PC.

C:\PART\CHAPTER> 4.7

Bill waited until the day of his thirtieth birthday before he finally notified the Board that he was prepared to take Microsoft public. In theory it was a decision for the board as a whole to make but with 49% of the shares and by far the loudest voice, nobody was going to do it until he was happy.

There had been pressure to float the company for years, both from the press and also the staff who held stock options, and it had only intensified when Lotus and Ashton-Tate had gone public in 1983. But Bill had resisted. He had heard horror stories of the pressure of an initial public offering (or IPO) from Lotus's Mitch Kapor, and feared the distraction and increased demands on his time that going public would inevitably bring.

"The whole process looks like a pain," he said. "And an ongoing pain once you're public. People get confused because the stock price doesn't reflect your financial performance. And to have a stock trader call up the chief executive and ask him questions is uneconomic. The ball bearings shouldn't be asking the driver about the grease."

And as if all of that wasn't reason enough, only a couple of months earlier in May 1985, he had seen what could happen to a founder who lost control of his board.

In a row that became very bitter, and very public, the Apple board had sacked Steve Jobs.

Eventually though Bill decided that Jon Shirley was right. It was better to jump than wait to be pushed. And if they didn't do anything then they would be pushed very soon.

Since 1981 stock had been issued to a growing number of employees and once that number passed five hundred the SEC rules meant that the company would have to be floated publicly. Microsoft were forecast to cross that threshold at some point in 1987.

So, despite his reluctance, by the time October 1985 rolled around Bill had come to the conclusion that the time had come.

***

The job of shepherding the company through the IPO fell to Frank Gaudette, the Chief Financial Officer hired by Shirley in 1984.

The fact that Microsoft had no debt, fifty seven and a half million dollars worth of working capital, an absence of venture capital partners looking to cash in, and a chairman who was reluctant, meant that Frank was able to turn the tables on the usual way IPOs worked.

Unlike most companies in the run up to an IPO, Microsoft held most of the cards. And Frank didn't let potential underwriters forget it. He made the investment bankers who wanted to underwrite the offering come and pitch for the work, making it clear that they wanted the business, not the other way around.

Bill was happy to leave most of the schmoozing and choosing to Frank but, once they had chosen the underwriters (Goldman, Sachs and Alex. Brown), the delicate matter of the initial share price had to be resolved and that wasn't something Bill was going to sit quietly on the sidelines for.

The way Bill saw it, the opening price was sensitive for a couple of reasons.

Firstly, the volume of trading that takes place of a company's shares is considered a mark of health and confidence in the company, and while Bill might not have particularly wanted to play this game there was no way his competitive nature would let him lose at it.

And then there was the matter of how much money the underwriters and institutional investors stood to make. A low price for institutional investors and a high price when the shares were released to the public would mean that the investors would pocket the difference. And that offended Bill's principles. After all, what had these investors done to create the value they'd be collecting. Nothing, that's what.

So the price had to be very carefully set.

At first the underwriters argued that a price range of $17 to $20 would be right, but Bill was concerned that they were overvaluing the company, which was only ten years old at that point and in his view had some serious risks that should be taken into account. He argued for a range of $16 to $19.

The underwriters were astonished, companies do not usually insist on *lowering* their valuation. Particularly when it would cost the man who was making the argument about $11 million.

But Bill insisted.

And so they agreed.

***

The most obvious casualty of the IPO was the relationship between Bill and his Japanese opposite number, Kay Nishi.

Things had been strained between the two men for some time. They had always disagreed about Kay's flamboyant lifestyle, Bill had never liked the fact that Nishi would fly first class on his regular trips shuttling between Tokyo and Seattle, but they had gradually grown further apart as they started to disagree over business as well.

Prompted by Nishi, in 1983 Microsoft had introduced a standard architecture for 8-bit machines called MSX, but as we have seen Bill was focussed on the 16-bit market. He felt that Nishi was distracted by MSX and a longstanding desire to move into chip manufacturing that didn't fit with Microsoft's vision.

The fact that Nishi had a partnership agreement with Microsoft rather than an employment contract meant that he had more latitude to pursue these things but that didn't mean Bill had to like it. And if Bill didn't like something then there was a fair chance people would hear about it.

Nishi was no different and the two men had an increasing number of vocal disagreements throughout 1985.

Most accounts point to the final straw being when Nishi spent a huge amount (some say half a million dollars, some say a million) on a giant automated statue of a dinosaur to advertise MSX, but the IPO clearly brought matters to a head.

The prospectus detailed two loans totalling half a million dollars that Microsoft (for which read Bill) had made to Nishi over the years for his side investments and which they were now writing off.

Bill offered Nishi a permanent job with Microsoft but Nishi wasn't prepared to leave his other interests. The two of them met and tried to find a way forward but were unable to come up with anything they could agree on.

In February 1986 Bill opened a new Japanese subsidiary, Microsoft K K, and severed his relationship with Nishi. It would be years before they spoke again.

***

In December 1985 as part of the preparations to go public, Bill Neukom, who for years had represented Microsoft through Bill Sr.'s law firm, Shidler McBroom Gates & Lucas, moved formally to become Microsoft's VP of Law and Corporate Affairs.

Neukom pulled together a first draft of the prospectus working with outside counsel from his old firm and then the underwriters spent the remainder of January working with senior managers in Microsoft to flesh it out and try to identify any problems before the document was released to the world.

Finalising the prospectus needed Bill's time but it was a team effort, most of the leg work was done by the underwriters and the information came from Bill's team. But once it was ready it became necessary for Bill to get more involved again.

As part of any IPO, the company's top executive officers, the CEO, CFO and COO, are expected to put on a roadshow to prospective investors, and as CEO, chairman and the only remaining founder, Bill couldn't avoid it.

Predictably, he wasn't impressed.

"We need to go in for a rehearsal for the roadshow," Frank said, in early February.

"Jesus," Bill said. "What is this?" He knew the process full well but was still not convinced it was worthwhile. "Neukom says I can't say anything that isn't in the prospectus anyway."

"You can't."

"Well, then what's the fucking point of me going?! I've got a company to run here. If they want to have anything to invest in then they should just leave me to it."

"Does it really need all three of us, Frank?" Jon asked.

"It's the way it's got to be I'm afraid," Gaudette said in his Queens, NY accent. "If they're going to invest in us they want to get a good look at you."

"What is this, the stone ages?! What difference does it make what I look like? All of the information they need is in the prospectus. And if it isn't then we should sack Goldman."

"It's just how it's done, Bill. Not all industries are as up to date as tech," Frank said.

Despite his reservations Bill, for the most part, towed the line and only allowed his irritation to show through on a couple of occasions. Like when one of the investment bankers told him that he could make his presentation on the financials more lively and he commented snarkily, "You mean I'm supposed to say boring things in an exciting way?"

Eventually though, everyone was satisfied and Bill, Jon and Frank jetted off on February 18th accompanied by the Goldman, Sachs and Alex. Brown folks, to start the international roadshow covering eight cities in ten days.

***

By the time the three chief officers returned from hobnobbing with investment bankers in Europe, the Bellevue staff had moved into the Redmond campus.

Bill, sitting at his new desk overlooking the carpark which coincidentally gave him a good view of who was in the office, was starting to question the lower price range he had pushed for. The market itself had moved positively and the interest from institutional investors during the roadshow had been very strong. In fact Goldman described it as the one of the strongest books they'd ever seen.

The day after they got back he called Jon and Frank into his office to discuss it.

"Goldman are saying now that it will probably trade at $25," Bill said. "What do you think Frank?"

"You can never be sure of these things but yes, I think they're in the right ballpark."

Bill shook his head. In an IPO the lead underwriters, in this case Goldman and Alex. Brown, allocate shares to the institutional investors and Bill didn't like the idea of giving money away to them.

"So if the IPO price is $19, these guys who happen to be in good with Goldman and get some stock will make an instant profit of $6."

"Yeah, that's the way it works."

"I don't get it. Why are we handing millions of the company's money to Goldman's favorite clients? We should raise the IPO price higher."

"We need to be careful not to alienate them too much Bill," Jon said, his voice reasonable. "If we set it too high then they won't bite."

"Set it at $23 and they'll still make 10% in a matter of weeks." Bill, disinterested in the whole process at first, had had his need to win ignited.

"We've got more control than usual here Bill, and I can push them around some, but we've got to leave some money on the table or they'll walk. These guys aren't used to being told what to do. Push hard enough and they'll walk away even if it means losing out on a profit. And they'll hope that enough of their colleagues will do the same to give us a bloody nose."

"They're like you Bill," Jon said with a sardonic smile.

Bill nodded, as perverse as it was that actually made sense to him.

"Alright, but they don't need to make $6 a share. I bet we can move the price higher and not lose them."

Jon turned to Frank.

"We could use Goldman's initial estimate. What was that Frank, $17-20?" he said.

"Yeah, we could back that up by pointing out that they came up with it."

"It should be above $20," Bill said.

After more to and fro the three of them settled on a price of $21-22 and it was up to Frank to call the underwriters and convince them to play ball.

They weren't easily convinced.

Eric Dobkin, the Goldman's partner dealing with the offering argued with Frank, pointing out that SUN Microsystems had just gone public and seen their share price drop from the initial offer price on the first day of trading on the market. The executive team wouldn't want the market to show a similar lack of confidence in Microsoft, would they?

Frank, amused by Goldman's discomfort dealing with people who wouldn't let them run the show without challenge, held his hand over the phone and winked at Bill and Jon.

"They're in pain!" he said.

He uncovered the phone again and laid out his position.

"Eric, I don't mean to upset you, but I can't deny what's in my head. I keep thinking of all that pent-up demand from individual investors, which you haven't factored in. And I keep thinking we may never see you again, but you go back to the institutional investors all the time. They're your customers. I don't know whose interests you're trying to serve, but if you're playing both sides of the street, then we've just become adversaries."

There was a silence on the other end for a beat and then Dobkin said, "I'll need to speak to my partners."

"Great, you do that Eric, but we're on the clock here remember," Frank said, and hung up.

Dobkin rang back within minutes and tried once more to convince Frank that it was the wrong move but Frank cut him off.

"I've listened to your prayers," he said. "Now you're repeating yourself, and it's bullshit."

For Goldman's this was not business as usual. They were used to thinking of themselves as the smartest guys in the room, but Bill, and by extension the rest of Microsoft, was not prepared to concede that ground to anyone easily.

In the end they agreed on a range of $20-22 but with a caveat that Goldman's would be telling investors that the target was $21 and nothing less.

***

Microsoft's stock was released to the public on 13th March 1986.

Goldman's estimate of $25 for an opening price had been accurate. The first sale they made was at $25.75 and any fears that it was overpriced were quickly put to rest. Retail interest was as strong as the institutional investors' had been before it, and by the end of the day two and a half million shares had changed hands and all that interest pushed the price higher still. They closed the day at just under $28.

Several of the early institutional investors did exactly as Bill had predicted and sold off blocks of their shares to realise a quick profit. That combined with the options exercised by employees meant that by the end of the financial half year about a third of Microsoft's public shares were held by individual investors.

The floatation meant that for the first time it was possible to put a market value on the size of the holdings that the Microsoft team owned, and although nobody jumped ship as Bill had feared, most of the major shareholders did sell some shares as part of the IPO.

Paul Allen sold the most, liquidating just over $4 million of his stake in the company he co-founded eleven years earlier and retaining a stake that was worth $172 million dollars by the end of the first day.

Steve Ballmer sold only $630,000 keeping the overwhelming majority of his $46 million in the company; Charles Simonyi also sold a small percentage, taking home $200,000 and holding $8.2 million, not bad for the boy who had run away from Communist Hungary twenty years earlier on a temporary visa; Jon Shirley, so much closer to retiring than the rest of the team, sold 15% of his stake bringing in $1.2 million dollars worth but still leaving him $9.5 million.

And Bill had, of course, taken care of his parents. Even after they had realised $693,000, Bill Sr. and Mary had more than $2 million worth of their college dropout son's stock, including the shares that were held in a trust that he had set up for them.

But by far the largest beneficiary was the man who probably cared least of all about it, Bill himself.

He sold eighty thousand shares at the IPO price of $21, bringing him in more than $1.6 million in cash, but the real news was his 'net worth' as a result of the 45% stake he didn't sell. Going public had given Bill paper assets worth $308 million and catapulted him securely into the middle of the Forbes 400 list of richest Americans. He now had a fortune almost twice the size of Steve Jobs's (which can't have gone unnoticed).

But weeks later he was still fretting about the impact of going public.

When he saw a stock chart pinned up in a Microsoft developer's office he stopped and asked, "Is this a distraction?"

"No, it's just nice to know how much I'm worth, Bill."

"Why, are you thinking of leaving?"

"No! Of course not, I don't want to leave Microsoft," the employee said, thinking Bill was threatening his job when in fact he was mostly just bemused.

"So what difference does it make what the stock price is? Let's say the stock dropped in half or a third. Big deal. I would still order the same hamburger. I'm not thinking about the stock price, I'm thinking about software products. And you should be too."

***

By the end of 1986 Bill was the chairman of a public company; had replaced Steve Jobs as the technology industry's wunderkind (if you could still be a wunderkind in your thirties); was in charge of more than a thousand members of staff, on his dream campus; had been on the cover of just about every national business or technology magazine; and was the youngest, self-made person on the Forbes 400 (there were two other thirty year olds but both had inherited their wealth).

Not bad for a thirty year old, and he could have been forgiven for thinking that 1986 was going to be about as life defining a year as they could get.

But in 1987 Bill would meet someone who would ultimately have a much deeper impact on his life than anything that had gone before.

C:\PART> 5: PERSONAL MATTERS

C:\PART\CHAPTER> 5.1

Melinda French was born on August 15th, 1964 in Dallas. In 1987 she graduated from Duke University having earned a bachelor's in computer science and economics, and an MBA.

Despite having done summer internships with IBM and being almost guaranteed a place there, she applied to Microsoft as well, recognising that it might be easier to advance in a smaller company than it would in the giant IBM. Microsoft was growing quickly but with about 1400 staff in the middle of 1987 it was dwarfed by IBM's 389,348 employees.

When Melinda got the call (or more accurately, when her mom took the message) from Microsoft's recruiter to offer her a place on their first ever class of MBAs, she jumped at the chance.

She had been in the company for three weeks when she was sent to a meeting in New York. Whenever Microsoft staff travelled they shared hotel rooms to keep the costs down and Melinda ended up sharing with a woman who was one of about thirty staff attending a trade show. The trade show contingent were meeting up for a meal that night so her roommate suggested that Melinda join them after her meeting.

***

Melinda ran the last few steps to the restaurant, then paused to catch her breath. It was embarrassing enough to be late, but she didn't want to join her new colleagues as a sweaty, panting mess.

Once she'd composed herself she entered the restaurant and asked the maitre'd to show her to the room that Microsoft had rented for the evening, then stood in the doorway scanning the room.

"Hi Melinda!" her roommate shouted and waved to get her attention, as she stood in the doorway scanning the room.

"Hi! Sorry I'm late. My meeting overran."

"No problem, we've just ordered. Grab a seat and the waiter will be back round."

Her roommate, the only face she recognised, was flanked by people she obviously knew well, so Melinda took one of the only two empty seats left. They were at the other side of the table, about as far from her roommate as possible.

Well, at least I'm not the last one here, she thought.

She introduced herself to the man sitting next to her who acknowledged her politely, then instantly turned back to continue the conversation he was engaged in with the woman on his other side.

Five minutes later Melinda had only spoken to the waiter and was starting to regret coming when the door to the private room opened again and two conflicting thoughts ran through her mind in less than a second.

Oh good, someone to talk to. Then she saw who it was. *Oh crap, no! Don't sit here, don't sit here!*

But there was only one chair left, if the newcomer was planning to stay, he was going to end up sitting next to her.

Bill Gates made his way around the room stopping every couple of seats to speak to people as he went, like a king at some medieval banquet.

Maybe he's not stopping, maybe he'll just work the room a bit and then leave. God, I need to have something clever to say. She wished her meeting had been about something more material, what the hell did you say to the man running the company when you'd been there less than a month?

She ran out of time.

"Hello," Bill said, pulling back the chair next to her and sitting down.

She nodded and smiled but didn't speak.

He didn't stop looking at her, evidently waiting for her to reply before realising it wasn't going to happen and the corners of his mouth twitched up in a half smirk.

"Alright, don't go on!" he said. "If I'm going to be stuck with you all night I'm going to want to get a word in."

She laughed.

"Sorry, I didn't know what to say."

"I believe 'Hi' is what most of the humans use when they're trying to blend in. Shall we start again? Hi, I'm Bill."

He stuck his hand out formally and allowed the smirk full reign over his face.

"Hi, I'm Melinda."

"Nice to meet you Melinda. I don't recognise your face, I'm pretty sure I'd remember you." He tilted his head slightly and closed his eyes. "Melinda… Melinda." Then his eyes blinked open and he spoke quickly, "You're one of the new MBAs."

Melinda was surprised.

"You know all of the staff?"

"Honestly, no. But I see all of the new names. And there aren't any other Melindas in Microsoft. It's not that common a name."

"It was in the top 150 names last year."

"How do you know that?"

"I like data."

His eyes lit up and his competitive nature flared.

"In the top 150 means it was higher than 100. What number was it?"

"147," she replied without hesitating and Bill laughed. "Hey, I didn't say where in the top 150. It was 113th when I was born."

He looked at her appraisingly, "And when was that?"

"1964. August 15th."

He nodded and was silent for a fraction of a second then seemed to snap out of wherever his mind had gone.

"That's cool," he said. "I don't know how popular my name is. Pretty common I imagine."

"I imagine."

"So, you're our first female MBA."

"I am."

"What's that like?"

"I'm used to it. There weren't many women in my class either. And computers weren't really the obsession of choice for most girls growing up in Texas."

"No, I guess not!"

Melinda was surprised at how much she enjoyed the dinner with Bill. She already knew his reputation in Microsoft and the industry as someone not to be messed with, and one of the first talks her Microsoft MBA intake had received had been about how to stand your ground in a BillG review. But there was none of that during dinner. Sure, he was extremely high energy and there were a number of times during their conversation when it felt like she was in some sort of rapid fire interview. Like when he asked about the beginning of her interest in computers.

"First computer?"

"An Apple III. My dad bought it when..."

"Apple III?! I thought only people who worked for Apple bought them!"

"I got into coding at school on an Apple II, and my mom and dad had a small rental business on the side, so my dad bought an Apple III to do the accounts on."

"First programming language?"

"BASIC."

"On the Apple II at school?"

"Yes."

"Cool! That will have been Applesoft BASIC. I wrote that you know."

That wasn't quite true. Applesoft Basic was originally ported from Microsoft's BASIC by Ric Weiland and then a number of Apple employees had worked on it. But Bill had written the first version of Microsoft BASIC on which it was based back in his early sprint with Paul Allen, so it was more of an exaggeration than an outright lie.

"That's neat," Melinda said before he switched topics again and moved onto the next rapid fire challenge.

But she sensed that the verbal probing was just an extension of his natural curiosity and he seemed perfectly happy for it to run both ways.

And, above all, he was funny.

They had talked almost non stop since he had sat down, pausing only to chew their food (and not even every time then, in his case) so when he fell quiet over dessert it was a bit odd. She began to wonder whether she'd said something wrong at some point without noticing, when he suddenly blurted out what he was thinking.

"A bunch of us are going dancing after this, do you want to join us?"

She hesitated.

"I don't know, I've got an early meeting again in the morning."

"Come on, I promise not to tell the boss."

***

Two months later Melinda had finished up in the office and was walking to her car.

"Hello!" a voice called from behind her but she kept walking, it was a Saturday and none of her team had been in that day so she assumed whoever was shouting didn't want her until they shouted again, louder. "Hey! Melinda!"

She looked over her shoulder and saw Bill half walking, half running between the cars to catch her up. The carpark was busier than most offices would be on the weekend but it wasn't completely full and Bill was scooting between the spaces.

She smiled involuntarily. She hadn't seen him since the meal in New York.

"Hello Bill," she waved.

He slowed down.

"Hey, come here often?" he asked, matching her smile.

"All the time, the bosses are slave drivers."

"I've heard. You should have gone to IBM, they're a bunch of slackers."

She laughed.

"What about you, why are you here on a Saturday?"

"I'm always here," he said, frowning slightly as though puzzled by the question, then he shook it off and got back on track. "It's funny bumping into you, I was thinking about you the other day."

"Oh yeah?"

"Yeah."

"What were you thinking?"

"I was wondering if you'd go out with me."

She looked him up and down openly.

"Well, that would depend if you were asking me hypothetically or for a specific date," she said and raised her eyebrows.

"Okay, I'm asking you specifically. Would you go out with me, two weeks from Friday night?"

Melinda recoiled, the smile dropping from her face instantly.

"Two weeks from Friday?! Who knows their calendar that far out? Why don't you call me closer to an actual date and ask me again?"

Bill adjusted his glasses.

"That's not a 'no' though," he said.

Melinda looked at the man in front of her and suddenly the billionaire boss melted away and she saw the nervous geek with his colour coordinated slacks and jumper, and big glasses, and realised that this was difficult for him.

"It's definitely not a 'no'," she said, taking pity on him and wanting to be clear. "But I'm never going to say 'yes' for a date a fortnight in advance. I might be dead. Or married. Girls want a bit of spontaneity Bill."

"Okay, well maybe I'll give you a call another time then."

"That would be nice," she said. He smiled in a much more conscious polite fashion than she had seen before and turned and headed for his car. Having a flash of panic that she was making a mistake she added loudly, "*Real* nice."

She was pretty sure his shoulders moved but he didn't stop walking. She watched him go for a moment before she realised how embarrassing it would be if he turned and saw her watching him so she got quickly into her car and drove off.

***

Less than an hour afterwards she was back at her apartment, trying to decide what to have for dinner and the phone rang.

"Hello," she said distractedly into the phone, her eyes and mind on the inside of a cupboard hoping inspiration would hit.

"Is this spontaneous enough for you?" the voice at the other end said.

She turned from the cupboard and rested her elbows on the work surface, smiling.

"I guess that depends what you say next."

"I have two Microsoft things that I have to go to tonight but I'll be done by about ten. Would you like to go out for a drink with me then?"

She grinned but tried not to let it show in her voice.

"Yes, that sounds good. I could do that."
"Cool. I'll pick you up about ten then."

***

It was a good date. They laughed a lot and they both loved to dance.

The only awkward moment came when something he said made her realise that he'd asked his mom, who was still a Regent at UW to use one of her connections on the board of Duke to do a bit of digging into her. But she let it go and rather than ruin the fun she didn't let on that she'd worked it out.

***

Bill wandered into Steve's office the next morning without knocking and dropped into the chair opposite his friend.

"You're in late this morning," Steve said.

Bill opened his Diet Coke and took a swig before he answered.

"I've met a girl."

"You've met lots of girls."

"Yeah but I like this one."

"I seem to remember you've liked lots of them."

"This one's different."

"We'll see."

"She works here," he took another swig and stared straight at Steve looking for a reaction. "That could be a problem."

But Steve wasn't focussed on her employment status.

"How did you meet her?"

Steve was getting serious with his own girlfriend Connie and, while Bill clearly enjoyed being single, Steve had been worried for a while that his friend's growing fame and lack of a significant other left him open to gold diggers.

On occasion one or two girls around the office had even worn 'Marry Me Bill' T-shirts. It had been done as a joke but Steve knew that Bill's lack of social skills meant he might be the last to spot it when it wasn't.

"We met a few months ago in New York and we bumped into each other again yesterday in the carpark."

Steve rolled his eyes, but he was pleased to see that Bill was pursuing this girl, it took away his worry that she was only after his money. "Oh, you just happened to be there at the same time, right?" he said.

"Yeah."

"You, who knows everybody's number plate so that you can tell what time they get in."

"That's not true," Bill said, with a convincing air of outrage.

258

"Yes it is! You told me yourself. In fact I lost a twenty dollar bet with you on it."

Bill acknowledged the point with a smirk and then shrugged.

"Okay, well maybe it wasn't a total coincidence that I was leaving when she was. But that's not the point. The point is, do you think it will be a problem if I date someone from Microsoft?"

Now it was Steve's turn to shrug.

"You've done it before," he said.

"Years ago, when we were much smaller and we weren't public. And it was never serious."

"How do you know this is serious? Maybe she just wants a bit of fun."

"Maybe I do."

"Yeah, sounds like it. You're the one who brought it up."

"I don't know what I want."

"So hold on, just see how it goes. You're not about to compromise the business for a girl you've just met. But maybe in the meantime keep it quiet. It could make things difficult for her if people knew about it."

"Hm, good point."

***

Bill and Melinda started dating regularly, but kept it light for a year or so.

Melinda was still young and wanted to keep her options open, after all Microsoft was full of eligible young men. Perhaps none of them had quite the same material prospects as Bill, but money wasn't her driving force.

Bill himself had Microsoft to focus on, and he wasn't quite ready for it to be exclusive either, a committed relationship would require a level of time and energy that he wasn't prepared to invest just yet.

While things between them were still relaxed they did their best to keep it quiet. At first they hid it inside Microsoft but eventually she became his usual date at company events and even the stupidest of the intelligent people Bill employed must have known what was going on.

C:\PART\CHAPTER> 5.2

"On the whole I think it's good for the staff, but one or two of the senior managers think it might be getting out of hand," Jon said, chewing his unlit pipe.

Bill snorted.

"Only because they don't like getting thrown in the pond."

"You mean Lake Bill."

"Lake Bill?"

"That's what the staff have started calling the pond."

"Oh… Okay. That's cool, I guess."

Jon nodded. It was 1989 and, thanks in part to having Jon's calm and steady hand at the wheel, Microsoft had risen to more than 4000 employees. Two thousand of them on the Redmond campus. Most of them had signed up to a cult-like worship of Bill and naming the pond between Buildings 3 and 4 'Lake Bill' was just one example.

Not long after the move to Redmond somebody had thrown their manager into Lake Bill during a project closedown party, and at one point Steve Ballmer had been forced to swim the length of the fifty metre pond when he lost a bet that his team would complete all of their bug fixes on time. By 1989 a dunking or swim in Lake Bill to celebrate milestones (or commiserate missing them) was a firmly entrenched tradition.

"Yeah, but that isn't what's bothering them. They're okay with the dunkings, they think it helps the teams blow off steam."

"So what's their problem then?"

"They think that it might not show a professional image when we have customer meetings. And it's definitely a risk. Last time I had IBM here we passed two developers on unicycles."

"Juggling?" Bill asked.

Juggling was such a common pastime around Microsoft that the company meeting the year before had featured hundreds of employees juggling on stage to the tune of a specially composed song, 'We Can Make It All Make Sense'. In what was probably unintentionally illuminating, the words to the first verse went:

We're the Redmond kids, we've got software plans;

We've got ready hearts, we've got steady hands.
We can churn out code till our eyeballs glaze,
And the endless nights turn to endless days.

And, another verse included the line: *I am here so much, I don't need a house.*

"No," Jon replied. "They weren't juggling. They were jousting with sticks."

Bill's eyes lit up.

"On unicycles! I wish I'd seen that."

"Actually it was pretty neat. But it kind of makes the point that I've been hearing for a while, maybe it's setting the wrong image."

"As long as it isn't impacting productivity I think it's good. We want them to enjoy being here. Work hard, play hard, you know?"

"Productivity? Ed Fries couldn't get into his office the other day. In fact he couldn't even find it, one of his team had sheet rocked over the door! He had to go and ask Facilities if there was a building remodel going on, and where his new office was. They'd blended it in with the walls so well he figured it was an official thing. He lost an hour while the guy from Facilities checked with his boss before someone finally admitted what they'd done and they ripped down the new wall. "

"Brilliant!"

"And the lost hour?" Jon said, trying very hard to remain serious.

"Oh, Ed won't have lost an hour, he'll just have worked later."

"True."

"So what do you think we should do?"

"I'm not saying we should do anything yet, just watch it."

Bill looked thoughtful, then smirked.

"You know what I heard they did to Steve? He got back from his trip to the Valley and someone had made it look as though his office was completely filled with bouncy balls."

Jon smiled openly.

"Yeah I heard about it. Did you actually see it?"

"No, I couldn't, could I? He stormed up to me really pissed and said that he was going to work out who'd done it. I figured if I went and saw it I'd burst out laughing and that wasn't really the kind of help he was looking for!"

Jon chuckled.

"Don't tell him, but I know who it was. Hans Spiller."

"I should have guessed."

"Well, not just him, he reckons about a third of the developers were involved in the end."

"Poor old Steve!" Bill said. "You know a couple of years back Spiller replaced all of the drinks in the fridges? I went to grab a Coke and it was filled with Mr Pibb. And not just regular Mr Pibb, Diet Mr Pibb! Who the fuck drinks Diet Mr Pibb?!"

"That was probably the point!"

The two men laughed so hard that there were tears in their eyes. Finally Jon sighed and smiled gently at Bill. Bill pursed his lips together and nodded slowly, they both knew that the smile was unconnected to the joking around. It was a signal that they'd come to the real reason for the conversation.

"You didn't really come here to discuss pranks."

"No."

"I'm not going to make it easy for you, Bill."

Bill took a deep breath.

"I don't want you to leave Jon."

"I know. But I need to. I told you when I joined that I wasn't going to hang about until retirement age. I'm fifty two, for God's sake, most people here are under thirty. When I leave the average age will drop a year."

"Frank's older than you. And Maples is an old guy."

"Mike's forty six, Bill! He's not old."

Mike Maples had joined Microsoft the year before from IBM and, like Jon, had managed to combine bringing a more mature experienced approach to Microsoft with an ability to fit into the younger company's culture.

"Come on Jon, what will you do without Microsoft? You'll be bored out of your mind in no time."

Jon opened his hands.

"You know some of us weren't born just waiting for computers to arrive. I'll play with my vintage cars, maybe do something more in the arts." Shirley had long been active in the art world, and was responsible for the art around the Microsoft campus.

"I love fast cars as much as the next guy Jon, but really, how long can you spend racing them round in a circle? Particularly old ones, it's barely even racing." He hesitated, before saying simply. "We need you... *I* need you."

"You don't need me, Microsoft is all grown up Bill. I've done what you brought me here to do."

"Microsoft won't be the same without you."

"Yes, it will. It wouldn't be the same without you, you're the heart of the place, I'm the boring behind the scenes guy. There isn't a Lake Jon, is there?"

"We can rename it."

Jon smiled again and shook his head.

"I'm not staying Bill. Listen, part of me doesn't want to leave either, I've loved my time at Microsoft, but I've got to live the rest of my life. I'll help find you another boring behind the scenes guy."

In the end Bill convinced Jon to stay on the board and even to consider being a special consultant when necessary, but nothing he could say changed his decision to step down.

***

On December 27th Microsoft issued a press release confirming that Jon Shirley was leaving the role of president on 30th June 1990.

Michael Hallman, who had been president of Boeing's Computer Services division, joined as Shirley's replacement in April. But Shirley was a hard act to follow. Hallman lasted only two years before Bill dismissed him and decided, for a while at least, that a president might not be exactly what Microsoft needed while it still had such an active Chairman.

Hallman was replaced by a committee formed of Steve Ballmer, Mike Maples and Frank Gaudette, and of course, Bill himself. They kept their day to day roles as well but the four men, known within Microsoft as the Boop, Bill's Office of the President, met for half a day a week and handled any cross-company business and anything that was strictly 'presidential'.

***

Microsoft had introduced corporate email in the eighties and Bill had arranged for his mom to have a company email account not long afterwards. By the early nineties, email had replaced the post-it as Mary's usual means of communicating with her son when he didn't have time to speak.

Having grown up in the '30s Mary had naturally brought a letter writing grace to her early emails but Bill, who would credit the brevity of email as one of the secret ingredients to Microsoft's ability to move fast, had kept pushing until she saw it as an ongoing conversation rather than a formal letter. He had gradually weaned her off the need to sign every email, but she still started each one with 'Dear Trey' and he didn't have the heart to stop her.

Despite Melinda's growing presence, Mary was still very actively involved in Bill's life, pressing him to give back to the community and socialise more generally just as she had since he was young. In mid June 1991, she did exactly that, pushing him to meet someone regardless of his initial resistance. It would come to be one of the defining moments of his life and something he would always be glad he gave in to her about.

From: maryg@microsoft.com
To: billg@microsoft.com

Dear Trey,

Dad and I are having a little get together with some friends on 5th July. I hope you'll be able to make it.
You know how I like to show you off to my friends.
It'll be good for you to take a break.

From: billg@microsoft.com
To: maryg@microsoft.com

Mom,

I'd love to but I'm not sure I can make it. There's a lot going on here right now.

From: maryg@microsoft.com
To: billg@microsoft.com

1. Don't lie to your mother. You wouldn't love to.
2. There's always a lot going on there, you can make time.

Please, it'll be fun and your sisters are going to be there. They're looking forward to seeing you.
Besides, there's someone I know you'd like to meet.

From: billg@microsoft.com
To: maryg@microsoft.com

Very cryptic Mom, who?

From: maryg@microsoft.com
To: billg@microsoft.com

Meg Greenfield is coming, she's the editor of the WP and she's bringing Katharine Graham and Warren Buffett.

Katharine Graham the legendary ex-editor of the Washington Post, had long been someone Bill had wanted to meet. He knew of Warren Buffett because however much he tried to ignore the lists of rich people on which he appeared, it was impossible to miss the fact that the Nebraskan investor had been a regular entry on those same lists.

From: billg@microsoft.com

To: maryg@microsoft.com

Cool. Graham. Let me see what I can arrange.

_____

From: maryg@microsoft.com
To: billg@microsoft.com

That's nice. You won't come for your aged mother but you'll come to
see Katharine Graham.

_____

From: billg@microsoft.com
To: maryg@microsoft.com

You're not aged mother. But yes, I'm coming for Graham. I can talk to
you any time :-)

_____

From: maryg@microsoft.com
To: billg@microsoft.com

So is that a definite 'yes'?
And I'd like you to speak to Warren Buffett as well, he's a friend of
Kay's and I've spoken to him a couple of times. He reminds me of you, I
think you'd get on.

P.S. What is :-) ?

_____

From: billg@microsoft.com
To: maryg@microsoft.com

Yes, it is a definite 'yes'.
I'm sure Buffett is clever Mom, you really don't get to where he is
without being clever but we wouldn't have anything to say to each
other. I'm not interested in investing and I don't suppose he's interested
in computers.

P.S. Lean your head to the left and look at it sideways.

_____

From: maryg@microsoft.com
To: billg@microsoft.com

Warren is a very nice man, very down to earth. And from what I can tell he is interested in lots of things. Just like you, like I said. Anyway, have a quick talk when you're here and you can decide for yourself.

P.S. Oh, that's clever of you!

From: billg@microsoft.com
To: maryg@microsoft.com

Okay Mom, I'll speak to him if you want. I'm sure he's a lovely guy.

I can't take credit for :-) it's not one of mine Mom, lots of people use it.

Got to go now, I've got some work to finish off before I turn in for the night.

I'll be over on Sunday for dinner if I can. Love to Dad.

Love, Trey.

Mary was holding her fourth of July weekend party at Gateaway, the compound Bill had built for his family on the site of Gam's beloved Hood Canal holiday home.

Between their emails and the holiday weekend Mary had kept up the pressure on Bill to make sure he didn't wriggle out of the party. He hadn't but he had drawn the line when she had tried to persuade him to take time off and spend the whole day with her guests.

Instead he arranged for he and Melinda to fly in by helicopter, not so that he could make a flashy entry but rather so that he could make a quick getaway. As he flew his mind was still on the almost-finished Windows 3.0 which would be launching in a couple of months.

He was confident that this would be the version which finally convinced everyone of the value of the GUI.

His eyes were closed as he played over his most recent technical review in his head. He had woken this morning with a couple of last minute thoughts that he wanted to share with the development team and he wanted to be sure they hadn't already addressed them, so he was running through his memory of the review.

"Can we really not stay longer?" Melinda's voice came through his headset.

Bill opened his eyes and looked at Melinda, and found himself smiling automatically. Interruptions usually frustrated him but about six months earlier he had come to the realisation that he loved her. He'd told her as much, not necessarily expecting anything return, and to his surprise she'd said she felt the same way.

"You can if you want. She's trying to set me up with Warren Buffett and I could do without it to be honest."

"Oh?"

"Does some guy who picks stocks for a living sound like someone I'm going to get on with?"

"I don't know, I hear he reads a huge amount, maybe you'll have more in common than you think."

"You sound just like her!" he shook his head. "I mean, where's the value added in shuffling money around? He's not creating anything like we do at Microsoft."

"Okay, well just tell her you're not interested then."

"Oh yeah, I'll just tell her, that'll work," he rolled his eyes and Melinda laughed easily.

Their relationship felt even more natural because of the easy way that Melinda got on with his mom, but that didn't mean she didn't know what she was like.

"Well, maybe I'll stick around longer than you then, if you don't mind."

"Why would I mind? I'll need to take the helicopter but I'll get my dad to sort you out a lift back to Redmond."

"Great, that sounds good. Check before you leave though, I'll see how it's going."

"Okay, I'll let you know before I go and you can decide if you're coming. My plan is just to stay for a couple of hours. Long enough to meet Kay Graham, get my mom off my back about Buffett, and then fly back to Redmond."

It didn't go to plan.

***

Bill got to meet Kay Graham that day but only briefly, and it wasn't her fault or even Mary's, or if it was Mary's it was only because she facilitated his introduction to someone who would become one of his greatest friends.

"…And this is Warren Buffet; Warren this is my son, Bill, and his girlfriend, Melinda."

Bill looked at the older man in front of him (on 5th July 1991 Bill was 35 and Warren was one month away from his 61st birthday), took in his cardigan and Omaha Royals baseball cap with greying hair sticking out from the sides, and for the last time ever, thought he'd been right about the man.

"I've heard a lot about you Bill," Warren said sticking his hand out.

Bill shook it. "And I've heard a lot about you, sir, nice to meet you."

"Microsoft, isn't it? Perhaps you could help me understand something about your computer world."

Bill gripped Melinda's hand ever so slightly tighter and she saw his shoulders slump and she knew exactly what he was expecting next. *I've got this problem with my computer, can you fix it?* She'd had it herself. Everyone who'd ever had any job connected to computers had had it. Requests from non-technical relatives to make the computer work when the problem was the person not the computer.

"Of course, what's the problem?" he said and Melinda was astonished by how polite he sounded, he really was trying for Mary.

"Computer companies come and go. Why is that? When I invest in a company I look at the fundamentals. But these computer companies seem to obey different rules altogether. Look at Ashton-Tate, they went public three years before you did, at a valuation of tens of millions of dollars and now I hear rumblings that they're going to be taken over."

"Ashton-Tate are an unusual case. Mr Tate had a heart attack and died at his desk the year after they floated."

"That's unfortunate but a company should be able to survive the demise of its founder," Warren said and then his eyes fluttered closed for a fraction of a second as he thought aloud. "Ah, unless that is the key difference... over reliance on a founder figure because of the youth of the company and sector together."

He opened his eyes and stared hard at Bill, waiting for him to respond. Bill didn't disappoint.

"I wouldn't say 'the' key difference. But it's a factor. We are a new industry."

"And that could make it harder to value."

"But surely that's not unusual? All companies have an uncertain future when they float."

"True, but there are good models for it in the other companies in the same sector. Investors value companies based on the predicted earnings over its lifetime."

"But the lifetime of the company is an unknown value," Bill frowned.

"Precisely. That's why different investors place different value on a stock, but they're all using broadly one of two models, momentum investing or fundamentals. Let's ignore momentum investors for the purposes of this conversation, they're just..."

"Noise in the system?"

"Yes, precisely!" Warren waved his finger at Bill and beamed. "So if different investors use similar models to predict the underlying values, they should land on similar valuations."

"Tech moves faster, you could reasonably expect a higher rate of growth so that should be factored in…"

"It will be. In fact it is, though not as much as I'd expect. But if the sector as a whole is too immature to reliably predict any amount of longevity for a company then investors' models will disagree significantly. They're basically gambling."

"Leading to more volatility. The money will follow whatever is hot at the moment with little appreciation of your 'fundamentals'. I've been telling my staff the same thing, they should ignore our stock price for at least a decade."

Warren chuckled.

"I don't imagine you've had much success with that."

"No. But if what you've just said is right then basically even the 'fundamental' investors in tech are really following tends, so they're basically doing momentum investing as well."

"They're a new category we could call them 'trend' investing. They believe they're looking at fundamentals but they don't have real informed data to base it on, and they're only investing in the sector as a whole because it is as you said, 'hot'. I think I need to up date my model."

"You have a model?" Bill, already more intrigued by Buffett than he'd expected, was even more drawn in. "What do you model it on?"

Warren looked confused for a second and then smiled when he realised what Bill meant.

"Ah, you mean a machine. No, I meant a mental model. I like to create mental frameworks to explain things. It saves time treating each circumstance as though it is unique."

"Efficient."

"Absolutely, but it's essential to ensure that your mental model stays attuned to reality. So, the other thing I couldn't work out, is why can't IBM just crush you? They have much deeper pockets than you do…"

Midway through the conversation Bill had let go of Melinda's hand, and as Buffett spoke about mental models Bill had leant almost imperceptibly closer to him. *Almost* imperceptibly but it had been perceived by one other person besides Melinda, Mary caught her eye, bobbed her head quickly in Bill's direction and winked at her before retreating to stand alone at a safe distance. Melinda detached herself from Bill's side and followed.

"They seem to be getting on," she said when she'd reached the other woman.

"I knew they would, he can be so stubborn."

Melinda wisely didn't comment on where he might have inherited that trait.

"Let's leave them to it. I'll introduce you to some other folk. Come on."

***

An hour later Melinda came back to see if Bill needed rescuing. They weren't hard to find, the two men were standing exactly where she had left them, apparently unaware of the party going on around them. Warren was standing with his hands behind his back, the peak of his cap bobbing up and down occasionally. Bill was stood in front of him in full rocking mode.

As she got closer she could hear them speaking in quiet tones.

"Now tell me about Microsoft, you split your stock just last week," Warren said.

"A week yesterday in fact, I'd be interested to hear what you think actually. I felt that the stock had…"

"Sorry to interrupt gentlemen," Melinda said with a smile.

Bill stopped mid-sentence and looked surprised to see her but Warren stepped in to answer.

"Not at all, I'm sorry, I'm keeping you from Bill."

"Oh that's alright, I see him all the time! I just came to say that Mary asked me to tell you the croquet is about to start if you wanted to join us. And Bill," she positioned herself so that Bill could see her face and widened her eyes meaningfully. "I think you had that thing you needed to get done today?"

He blinked.

"What thing?"

"I think Melinda is asking if you need to go back to the office," Warren said. "Your mother did mention that you might only be here briefly."

"Oh!" Bill remembered his get away plan. "No, I'm okay at the moment. Thanks for checking."

Melinda struggled to contain a smirk. Bill seemed oblivious to how obvious he was making it that he had intended to ditch Buffett as soon as possible. And it was even funnier because Buffett seemed to be the only other person it wasn't obvious to.

"Okay, so will you both be joining us for croquet?"

Bill looked at Warren, who looked horrified at the thought.

"Well, if you're happy to carry on our conversation?" the older man said.

"Absolutely," Bill replied with enthusiasm.

Melinda watched with amusement as both men instantly withdrew again and she had a clear impression of herself fading from their view as she stood there.

"I was going to explain the rationale for the stock split," Bill said and adjusted his glasses.

She turned away from them and allowed herself the luxury of the grin she had been holding back.

***

Bill spent the day with Warren, the two of them lost in conversation that ranged from the future of the newspaper business, to the similarities and differences between Microsoft and IBM.

Bill tried, and failed, to persuade Warren that he should get a computer.

"You could follow the stock market," he said.

"What do I care about the daily prices of stocks?" Warren answered, cementing his position in Bill's mind.

Warren carried out one of his favourite thought experiments with Bill, choosing a company with the largest market capitalisation from an historical decade and seeing how it fared each decade on. Bill loved it. It got to the heart of Warren's value based approach to investing and tallied perfectly with Bill's own belief that the stock market was basically a distraction from running a company well.

In the mid afternoon, having discovered that they were both voracious readers, they drifted away from the party for a walk on the nearby pebble beach and spent an hour just discussing books.

Finally Bill Sr. came to politely insist that they rejoin the others for dinner and perhaps even try engaging with someone else.

They managed the first part, but failed at the second.

When Bill Sr. asked the assembled guests what they felt was the biggest factor responsible for their accomplishments to date, Warren and Bill both instantly said 'focus'. Most people might have considered the word 'obsession' more accurate, but both men recognised that day that they had found someone with a mind like their own. While they had different centres of attention, the mindset they employed was almost identical.

An hour before sunset Bill dismissed the helicopter pilot, having decided to stay through the evening.

C:\PART\CHAPTER> 5.3

At first they had kept their relationship secret, they'd even worked out a signal in which Melinda would put a light on in her office so he'd know he could come by without coming across other Microsoft staff. Over the years it had gradually become more and more of an open secret around Microsoft, however Melinda's name was still being kept out of the public eye.

By early 1993 though he was considering a step that would mean their relationship would become public.

And for a man who only months earlier had been described by Forbes as the richest man in America, and the youngest ever to top their list, any announcement he made was going to be *very* public.

"I think I want to marry her."

"That's great news," Steve took his eyes off the road for a second and studied the side of his friend's face. He frowned. "Isn't it?"

Bill had asked Steve to join him for a drive so they could talk in private and somehow Steve had ended up driving.

Bill didn't reply, he was lost in thought.

"Bill? I said it's great news but you don't look convinced."

"You know my mom and dad, they're so…" Bill waved his hands in the air. "Together. I don't know if I can be that committed to someone."

"Hey! If you put half as much energy into it as you do into everything else then you'll be great."

"But that's exactly it, should I put that much energy into it? No-one's got unlimited resources and I have to focus on Microsoft."

"Have I slowed down since I married Connie?" Steve expected to get a sarcastic comment back from that, so when Bill passed up the opportunity he knew it was serious. He pulled the car over and parked so that they could speak properly.

"Look," he said, taking his seatbelt off and turning fully in his seat to face Bill. "All I can tell you is that she's great and she brings out the best in you."

"Correct," Bill said, robotically.

Steve flashed back twenty years to their days at Harvard and saw the high IQ geek who had calculated all of the angles in poker before playing a hand. He'd been fun, and super smart, but emotion had never been his strong point. That was part of what Melinda helped him with.

"You make each other laugh, she's razor sharp so she can keep up with you. And above all else where are you going to find someone else who will put up with your shit?"

Bill, his mind working overtime to process what he knew was a huge decision, didn't even get the humorous tone under his friend's words.

"But the question isn't, *Is she the right woman?*, Steve; the question is, *Should I commit to any woman?*"

Steve gave up trying to bring any humour to the situation and went to the place he knew Bill would work better with.

"Why don't you make a list of all of the pros and cons. Get it straight in your head."

Finally Bill turned to look at him.

"Good idea," he said, then visibly put the subject aside. "Right, let's get back to the office, we've got work to do."

***

Bill proposed to Melinda on 20th March 1993 in San Diego.

Amazingly, despite the fact that a couple of months earlier she had stumbled across the pro and con list he had written on a whiteboard in his bedroom, she said yes.

On the flight home to Seattle, Bill had a surprise in store for his new fiancé.

He had the pilot give occasional updates on the Seattle weather throughout the flight but, unbeknownst to Melinda, that wasn't their destination. To avoid her getting any clue, he drew the window blinds and brought out a jigsaw he'd brought along specially, something they loved to do together.

When the plane touched down and the cabin door opened Melinda was astonished to see Warren Buffett and his companion Astrid waiting for them at the end of a red carpet.

"What's this?" Melinda said quietly to Bill.

"Beats me, I guess we'd better go say hello."

They walked together along the red carpet until the last ten yards, when Warren opened his arms to Melinda and Bill hung back a little.

Melinda sped up and hugged Warren. She might be surprised to see him but it was nice, while he and Bill were especially close, over the last few years the three of them had become firm friends.

"Hello Warren, what brings you here?" she said as she let go of him and kissed Astrid on the cheek.

"I came to say congratulations to my favourite couple," he said nodding at Bill who had caught up.

Melinda beamed.

"I can't believe you came all the way to Seattle just to say congratulations. You really are something else."

"What makes you think I'd come to Seattle? Dreadful rainy place, isn't it Astrid?"

"Oh goodness, yes. Terrible, never gets any sun."

Melinda looked confused and turned to Bill for an explanation. Bill broke out into a grin.

"When I told Warren that I planned to propose to you this weekend he asked what I was doing about a ring. I told him I thought you'd like to pick one out yourself, so he suggested that we stop by Omaha and he'd take us to a little jewellers he knows."

"We're in Omaha?!"

"Yeah, come on. Let's go put a dent in Bill's wallet," Astrid said.

Warren took them to Borsheim's, a fine jewellery shop that had been a favourite of Omaha's wealthy citizens since it opened in 1870. It was usually closed on a Sunday but Warren was able to fix that for the newly engaged couple, he had bought a controlling interest in Borsheim's four years earlier.

On the way to Borsheim's Warren kept needling Bill.

"You know we have a metric of love in Omaha, don't you? I've worked it out and I spent 6% of my net worth on my wife's ring. I don't know how much you love Melinda, but 6% is the yardstick in Omaha."

Forbes had estimated Bill's wealth at the end of 1992 as $6.3 billion so Warren was jokingly suggesting that Bill buy Melinda a $378 million engagement ring.

Sadly for Borsheim's (and Warren as its largest shareholder) they didn't have anything approaching that price. In fact nobody did, the most expensive engagement ring in the world until then had been Elizabeth Taylor's which sold after her death for nearly $9 million. Quite a way off Warren's 'Omaha benchmark'.

***

Two days later, with Melinda sporting her new engagement ring, the couple announced their engagement and Bill suddenly fell off the list of most eligible bachelors. It made headlines around the world, confirming the more private Melinda's fears that marriage to Bill would drag her into the public eye. Not all of the attention was unwelcome though, in September a group of industry friends threw them a fancy dress engagement party.

The closed group meant that they were able to relax and have fun. Bill went dressed as Gatsby from Fitzgerald's *The Great Gatsby*, his favourite novel, and Melinda went as Daisy Buchanan, Gatsby's love interest.

***

The wedding was set for New Year's Day 1994.

Some months earlier the family had learnt that Mary, who was just 63, had developed breast cancer. Nothing was spared in trying to treat her, but the illness progressed too quickly and the previously indefatigable Mary was forced to step down as Regent of UW after serving for eighteen years. But nothing would stop her attending her son's wedding and she was determined that her illness would not overshadow Bill and Melinda's day. Despite how ill she was most of the guests were unaware that anything was wrong.

The couple had decided to have the wedding on the island of Lanai in Hawaii.

If money is no object, and obviously it wasn't in Bill's case, Lanai is perfect for a quiet marriage away from the prying eyes of the press. The majority of the island is privately owned, and there are only two hotels, the Lodge and the Manele Bay. Bill booked them both out entirely.

Guests were instructed to make their own way to Honolulu, from there they were flown to Lanai by a Boeing 737 that Bill had chartered.

There were more than one hundred people at the wedding but a small handful of them had particular meaning for Bill. In each phase of his life he had tended to have a strong relationship with one other person and now that he was to embark on the most important relationship of all, they had come to support him. Steve Ballmer was there as Bill's best man; Paul Allen had sailed his super-yacht to Lanai specially, the two old friends having made peace some time before; and Warren Buffett had managed to come even though it was his friend and partner Charlie Munger's seventieth birthday on the same day (Warren had asked his wife Susie to attend Charlie's birthday on his behalf, and luckily for him Charlie was an understanding man). The only friend who was missing, of course, was Lakeside's Kent Evans.

On New Year's Eve, with the guests all on the island, the group split for lunch. The men lunched at the Lodge while Melinda and the rest of the women had a bridal tea at the Manele Bay.

During the tea Mary, despite her illness, stood and read aloud a letter she had written to Melinda. Looking her future daughter-in-law straight in the eye, she finished with a paraphrase of a verse from the Bible.

"From those to whom much is given, much is required."

By the time of the wedding her son, and by extension his soon-to-be wife, had been temporarily knocked to a mere second place on Forbes' list of America's wealthiest. The top slot had been taken by none other than his friend Warren. For Mary, who had given of herself her whole life and had been pushing Bill to increase the philanthropic work of Microsoft for years, that would not have mattered at all.

Mary had felt blessed her whole life, born into an already lucky family, she and Bill Sr. had done well for themselves even before Trey had risen to the dizzying heights that meant they could all enjoy this island paradise. But she had never lost sight of the importance of giving back and helping those less fortunate than she was. Knowing that she may not be with them for much longer, she wanted to ensure those same values would be carried forwards.

To most of the guests Mary's letter was touching, and it's final message an important one, but hardly revolutionary and not necessarily one they'd take away with them. To Melinda, who knew the effort it took the seriously ill Mary simply to stand there and deliver it, it was incredibly powerful and poignant, and it made a lasting impression.

When Mary raised her glass for a toast, Melinda held her gaze and smiled back at her almost-mother-in-law and hoped that her guests would assume the tears in her eyes were down to the emotion of the wedding.

***

In the evening the two groups got back together for the rehearsal dinner and then made their way down to the beach below the hotel for a combined New Year's and wedding luau on the beach.

There was dancing and drinking around the fire, and at ten o'clock there were fireworks to see in the new year.

In the middle of the night Bill stood beside the fire and got everybody's attention.

"Hi... well, I guess... first, thank you all for coming. It means the world to Melinda and I that you're here with us." There were cheers and applause so Bill waited for it to die down again before continuing, "Anyway, I erm... Melinda loves music and I wanted to do something special for her so I thought maybe I'd sing a song for her. She loves country music... But you know the problem is, I can't sing. So I thought I'd take some lessons. But I kind of work a lot, and if I'm not at work I'm with Melinda so that's tricky. Then I thought hey, we're all friends, you'll listen to me whatever I sound like right?" He paused and then laughed. "But then I thought, actually I like you all too much to put you through that. So finally I hit on the answer. I've asked another friend to sing a song for me."

Bill gestured towards a small group of palm trees at the edge of the beach and everybody turned to see Willie Nelson, Melinda's favourite singer, walk out from behind the trees, guitar in hand. Melinda screamed with delight, she had had no idea Bill had planned it.

Nelson walked towards them and started singing,

Blue skies
Smiling at me
Nothing but blue skies
Do I see...

Bill smiled with unadulterated joy and ran over to take Melinda's hand for a dance, while Nelson held the crowd spellbound.

As soon as Bill and Melinda started dancing the guests all paired off and joined in.

Nelson played for hours and later, when Bill and Melinda had sat down for a quiet moment together, Bill spotted his mom and dad dancing slowly in the sand. Bill Sr.'s tall form enveloping Mary almost completely.

Bill sighed and put his arm around his bride to be. A minute later they were swaying gently in time to Nelson's music.

"This is perfect, thank you," she said, quietly.

"No. Thank you," he said to her, not taking his eyes off his parents.

There would be no end to the speeches the next day but really as far as he was concerned almost nothing more needed to be said.

He knew the impact she had on his life and the idea of spending the rest of their lives together filled him with more gratitude than anything else he had achieved in his life so far.

C:\PART\CHAPTER> 5.4

On 10th June 1994 Bill got the tragic news that his mother, Mary Maxwell Gates, had passed away.

Honours and memorials poured in from the thousands of people whose lives Mary had touched, but none could diminish the family's sense of loss.

Bill's laser like focus on Microsoft meant that Mary had stayed involved in the day to day minutiae of his life right up until her illness stopped her. Emails from the office and home, daily phonecalls, weekly visits for meals and discussion, family holidays, company events that she had helped coordinate at Gateaway. The sheer volume of their interactions even on purely practical matters was huge. Of course, her absence was no worse for that, but it did mean that there were reminders hidden all over his life.

And for Bill Sr., Mary's husband of more than forty years, those reminders were even more common. The absence of his wife left a huge hole in his life that, however hard he tried to hide it, the whole family noticed.

Months later, Bill and Melinda were waiting in line at the cinema with Bill Sr. when he brought up a topic that none of them had mentioned since Mary's death, philanthropy.

"I expect you still get lots of requests for money," he said, out of the blue.

"Yes, Dad, we do."

When Bill Sr. didn't say anything else for a moment Melinda prompted him.

"What are you thinking, Bill?"

"Well, I wondered whether it would be worth me taking a look at some of them and seeing if there was anything worthwhile in there."

Bill looked pensive and his dad hurriedly added, "I don't have to if you think it wouldn't be appropriate. It's just, I've got some time since… you know."

"Yeah, I get it. Let me take a look this week Dad and I'll let you know what I find."

"Okay, well, like I said, don't worry if you don't think it's a good idea."

That night, when Bill and Melinda were alone at home she brought it up first.

"I think it's a great idea. But why not make it more formal? We could set up a trust or something for him to operate."

"Yeah, I've been thinking about it since the cinema. I like it, I'll speak to the accountants tomorrow and see how we set it up properly."

A week later Bill and Melinda diverted $100 million into the William H. Gates Foundation and put Bill Sr. in charge of deciding how the money was best spent.

At first it was a very low key affair, and the grants were all made in response to people who had written to Bill asking for support for one cause or another. Bill Sr. would review the requests and decide whether he thought it would be wise for the Foundation to grant them, he'd jot a note or two down and when he had enough of them together would send them over to Bill in a wine box to see what he thought. Bill would review his dad's comments, write his own and send the box back.

Whenever they agreed on a worthy cause Bill Sr. would write a check and draft a quick letter to the recipient.

It was a far cry from the globe spanning operation that the Foundation would evolve into over time, but it was the first formal step into organised philanthropy and it made a difference, both to the grant seekers and to Bill Sr.

C:\PART> 6: ANTITRUST

C:\PART\CHAPTER> 6.1

1995 saw two milestones for Bill. Windows 95 launched on 24th August.

It included some significant steps forward in Bill's dream of a GUI, for the first time arguably placing PCs on a level playing field with the Mac in terms of user operability. And, after all of the debate about the move from 8-bit to 16-bit software in the eighties, Windows 95 represented the company's first move into 32-bit software.

But the technology played second fiddle to the marketing. The launch of Windows 95 was the biggest campaign Microsoft had ever run, the global scale that the company now had meant that it dwarfed even the original Windows announcement twelve years previously.

Microsoft reportedly spent about $300 million on the launch campaign, which included a special thirty minute long 'cyber sitcom' starring Matthew Perry and Jennifer Aniston from *Friends* designed to gently introduce users to the new features Windows 95 introduced. Perhaps more instructional than amusing it did at least show the lengths that Microsoft were prepared to go to in order to make sure Windows 95 appealed to a broader consumer base than the traditional computer market.

In a similar desire to connect with non-geeks, and in honour of the new Windows Start button, they also secured the rights to use the Rolling Stones song 'Start Me Up' as the signature song for the campaign. It was the first time that Mick Jagger and Keith Richards had allowed anyone to use one their songs in an advert, and it didn't come cheap. Reports at the time claimed that the Stones had held out for $12 million for the rights but the Microsoft PR team laughed aloud when the figure was mentioned to them. A figure of $3 million has since been quoted but the people closest to the deal are staying mum about exactly how much it cost.

At the launch event itself, held in Redmond with 2500 guests and 9000 Microsoft staff, comedian Jay Leno appeared on stage with Bill to entertain the attendees.

But, celebrity connections were only a part of the marketing blitz. If you couldn't come to Redmond and somehow avoided the television adverts, Microsoft were prepared to bring Windows 95 to meet you in your home town. Londoners were given a free copy of the Times (containing a large Microsoft spread, of course); in New York the Empire State Building had the Windows logo beamed onto it; and in Toronto the CN Tower had a three hundred foot long Windows 95 banner draped down the side.

If you lived in the West, anywhere that wasn't under a rock, you knew about Windows 95. And it worked, in the six weeks after release seven million copies were sold. Not bad for an operating system.

Bill's other milestone was the completion of his lakeside house.

He had begun work on what would become the family home seven years earlier but in 1995 it was finally finished.

Rather than a single huge mansion, Xanadu 2.0, as Bill named the house, was designed to blend as far as possible into its surroundings.

Sitting on the waterfront of Lake Washington, with 500 feet of lakefront access, the house is invisible from the road thanks to the hill that rises above it, and almost invisible from the lake thanks to the trees that cover the estate. The main building is built into the hillside, so that it appears to emerge from the ground.

Bill went to great lengths to avoid annoying his neighbours during the construction. Rather than have the construction workers drive in and clog up the neighbourhood with their cars, he had them shuttled by the construction company. Each month he notified his neighbours of the work that was planned and, to keep the inevitable dust under control as far as possible, the site was sprayed with water weekly through the construction. And because that could only be so successful he leant out the construction crew to wash cars and help out with projects that the neighbours were carrying out.

Altogether the buildings cover sixty six thousand square feet and there are seven bedrooms, however, the family area only(!) occupies eleven thousand of those square feet and contains four bedrooms. Not bad planning considering work started before he'd even proposed to Melinda, never mind before they'd had their three children.

To get to the guest areas from the road it is necessary to walk down five flights of stairs, totalling eighty four steps, although if you weren't feeling up to it then there's an elevator.

Once you're on the lakeside level there is a reception area that can sit one hundred and fifty people for dinner (or two hundred if they're standing for a cocktail party), a home cinema with twenty seats and a popcorn machine, and an exercise suite that includes a trampoline room with twenty foot high ceilings to allow for those really impressive bounces.

And if the trampoline doesn't give you enough exercise then there is a sixty foot indoor swimming pool separated from an outside pool by a glass wall which doesn't quite go all the way to the bottom, meaning the adventurous can swim underneath it and surface outdoors.

However, as a committed bibliophile, the library may well be Bill's favourite place. It covers two thousand square feet and consists of three interconnected rooms, the middle one of which has a domed roof with an oculus to allow light inside. Around the base of the dome is inscribed one of Bill's favourite quotations, *"He had come a long way to this blue lawn, and his dream must have seemed so close that he could hardly fail to grasp it."* from the Great Gatsby.

It has two secret pivoting bookcases (intriguingly, while one of them has been reported to have a bar hidden behind it, the other remains a mystery!), and holds over ten thousand books including rare manuscripts by Abraham Lincoln, Isaac Newton and of course Leonardo da Vinci's Codex Leicester. The codex is probably the most famous of his book collection. Bill bought it at auction in 1994 for $30.8 million, and has regularly leant it out for display at museums since. Written in Leonardo's mirror writing, it includes the sixteenth century genius' thoughts on fluid dynamics and the interaction of the earth, moon and sun.

Windows 95 and the completion of Xanadu 2.0 with its dream library, were certainly major arrivals for Bill, however they were nothing compared to the arrival in 1996.

***

On 26th April 1996, Melinda gave birth to their first child, a daughter, Jennifer Katharine Gates. By this time Bill had been named the wealthiest man in the world by Forbes for two years running (a spot he would hold until 2007 and again on and off after that), so to keep Melinda and the baby safe from the prying eyes of the press, and potentially other even less savoury characters, Melinda checked into the Overlake Hospital under an assumed name.

They would continue that practice for much of their children's early life. At school, all three children were registered under Melinda's maiden name.

***

Three days before the launch of Windows 95 a five year long on and off investigation into Microsoft by the US government came to an end.

It had begun in 1990 when the Federal Trade Commission became concerned that Microsoft's overwhelming majority of the operating system market (at that time approximately 70% of PCs ran a version of DOS or Windows) made them a monopoly, and that they were abusing that monopoly to gain a foothold in the applications business.

The FTC began an investigation which ran for almost three years and resulted in a 250 page report from staffers recommending action be taken against Microsoft. However, when it came time to vote, the four commissioners were split 2:2. After some further work, a second vote on July 21st 1993 resulted in another deadlock and the FTC dropped the case.

Bill felt that the prolonged FTC investigation had been unfounded and driven largely by rival software companies who couldn't compete in the marketplace and were using the courts as a proxy, in particular his anger was directed at Ray Noorda of Novell. Given that Novell were supplying the FTC not only with documents through their investigation but also staff, it is hard to see Bill's view as anything other than reasonable. Of course that didn't mean that Novell's complaints were inaccurate.

Bill and the Microsoft executive team no doubt breathed a sigh of relief when the FTC decided not to proceed, but it was short-lived.

Exactly one month later, in an unprecedented move, the Department of Justice's Antitrust Division picked up the case that the FTC had dropped and began their own investigation.

The DOJ investigation ran for another eleven months and, after much negotiation between Microsoft and the DOJ, including eventually Attorney General Bingaman and Bill themselves, it finally resulted on the 15th July 1994 in an agreement between the two parties.

Microsoft, while not acknowledging any wrongdoing, agreed to a legal Consent Decree which placed a number of limitations on their licensing arrangements. The agreement included limitations on the lengths of licenses, the terms of non-disclosure agreements that they could insist other parties signed and a number of other issues. The most relevant point for our later story, however, was that the Consent Decree prevented them from making customers who wanted to buy an operating system buy any other product as well. Importantly though it did not prevent Microsoft adding new features to those operating systems.

Once again Bill presumably relaxed, while it was galling to be forced to agree to restrict the company's sales methods when he was confident he had done nothing wrong, at least it was over.

In the normal course of events the DOJ would put the Consent Decree before a judge for what was usually effectively a rubber stamp approval and the decree would take force.

However, the judge assigned to the case, Judge Stanley Sporkin felt that the consent decree was not in the public's interest because it did not go far enough to censure Microsoft's behaviour. He carried out investigations of his own, including reading a notoriously negative biography of Bill and decided that Microsoft's behaviour needed to be punished.

He refused to sign the decree and issued a forty five page opinion explaining that the government had not been firm enough in their remedy.

Microsoft appealed and an appeals panel quickly supported their view that Judge Sporkin had acted beyond his remit in refusing to sign the decree. They also publicly rebuked him for his reliance on the biography of Bill to inform his judgements. He was removed from the case and it was reassigned to another judge.

On August 21st 1995, Judge Thomas Penfield Jackson, who we will meet later with very different views, signed the decree into law in a hearing that lasted less than half an hour.

It was over. Bill was disappointed that Mary wasn't there to see it, she knew the toll it had taken on him over the years and it would have been nice to share the end with her, but at least now he could finally put the whole thing behind him.

He had no way of knowing that this had simply been the prologue to what would become an even bigger case.

***

Melinda folded the top of the New York Times down and fixed Bill with a stare.

"Do you know that people are dying of diarrhoea?"

Bill looked up from the business section.

They were sharing the paper, sitting together in the family breakfast room, overlooking Lake Washington. Jennifer was occupied on her playmat on the floor between them, attacking the dangling toys above her, and Bill and Melinda were enjoying one of the rare moments of quiet that new parents cherish when their children are nearby but happy and not needing attention.

"You mean as a complication, right?" Bill said. "It's not the thing that actually kills them."

"No, it says here 3 million people die of diarrhoea from drinking contaminated water every year."

"Globally?"

"The article is talking about India and Cambodia but I guess the number is a global one."

"Thee million people?" he said, incredulously.

"Three point one. And it says it's mostly kids, Bill."

"Can I?"

287

Discarding the business section, he reached for her paper and she passed it over. He laid it out on the table in front of him and hunched over it, adjusting his glasses.

Melinda pointed at Jennifer who had moved onto the serious business of chewing on a teething ring and drooling all over the place.

"If Jenn gets diarrhoea then we'll just pick something up from the pharmacy. At worst we'll take her to the doctors. There's no way she's dying from it."

"No," Bill said, but Melinda could hear from his tone that he wasn't really listening to her.

She looked back at him and saw that he had started rocking, his attention fixated on the paper. She waited and then a minute later he stopped rocking, stood up and shook his head violently.

"This is crazy!"

"Didn't I say?"

"Half a million kids die of rotavirus every year."

"What's rotavirus?"

"I don't know. How come we've never heard of this before?"

"Well, it's not like we're idiots. There's a good chance if we haven't heard about it lots of people haven't."

"I can't believe this, if this was happening here there'd be uproar."

"We should do something about it Bill."

"Why don't we get Dad to look into it? Maybe there's something the Foundation can do."

Melinda cut out the article and included it in the next box of grant requests that got sent to Bill Sr. with a handwritten note saying, "Dad, maybe we can do something about this."

But Bill, being Bill, didn't leave it there.

Alongside his normal reading material on technology and business he threw himself into learning about disease, how it was spread, the financial impact it had on the world, and the role of vaccination and sanitation in fighting it.

His first stop was the 344 page long 1993 World's Bank, World Development Report.

He read it twice.

C:\PART\CHAPTER> 6.2

"Bill, you need to see this," Neukom said.

"What is it?" Bill said, looking away from his computer monitors.

When he saw the look on Neukom's face he was concerned. Neukom wasn't a man who was easily ruffled but he looked agitated as he handed Bill an envelope addressed to him as Microsoft's senior legal counsel. It was already open.

"William, what's the matter?" Bill repeated.

Bill pulled the thick sheaf of papers from the envelope and just had time to read the top of the cover page as Neukom replied.

20th October 1997
IN THE UNITED STATES DISTRICT COURT
FOR THE DISTRICT OF COLUMBIA

UNITED STATES OF AMERICA,
                    Petitioner,
           v.
MICROSOFT CORPORATION,
                    Respondent.

"It's the DOJ, they're coming after us again," Neukom said.

"What?!"

Neukom started to summarise the twenty one page lawsuit while Bill simultaneously skimmed the legalese, picking out the most relevant clauses.

"They're looking to hold us in civil contempt for failing to comply with the previous consent decree."

"Not failing to comply," Bill said, quoting from the document. "It says, 'knowingly disobeying and resisting'! The bastards. What the hell is wrong with them?"

"They've petitioned the court to fine us $1 million per day that we don't comply."

"And exactly what are we supposed to comply with?" Bill was angrily flicking through the dense document looking for the specific charge, but in his anger he had gone past the section, while he looked for the right part of the document he took a guess. "Are they coming after us about the Apple stuff?"

Microsoft had made a $150 million investment in the computer manufacturer just two months earlier, following Steve Jobs's return to the company. Apple was on the verge of bankruptcy before the investment and Steve had publicly thanked Bill for 'making the world a better place' by saving his company. He had arranged for Bill to appear on a giant screen at the most recent Apple convention to the delight of Jobs but the disgust of most die hard Apple fans who had booed him. They'd been unimpressed but not nearly as unimpressed as the Department of Justice who'd opened an investigation into whether the investment by one tech giant in another was anti-competitive.

"No," said Neukom. "It's about bundling our browser with Windows."

Bill finally gave up looking.

"Where the hell is the actual accusation?!" he said throwing his hands up and just barely holding on to the document.

"Section five, third page."

Bill turned back to page three and looked at the section that Neukom was referring to. Sure enough, there it was:

Microsoft has produced and aggressively marketed several successive versions of Internet Explorer...

In direct violation of the Final Judgment, Microsoft has required OEMs, as part of their license for Microsoft's Windows 95 operating system and as a condition of receiving that license, to license, preinstall, and distribute Microsoft's Internet Explorer 3.0 browser on their PCs that also have Windows 95 installed.

He read it and then threw the whole document down on his desk angrily and bellowed to his secretary.

"I need Steve and Mike in here now! And I'm going to need a meeting with the Board as soon as possible. Get them on a conference call."

He usually kept his door open so his secretary should have heard but because of how sensitive it was, Neukom had closed the door when he came in. A second later Bill tore his eyes off the offending document and looked up to see the door was closed. He stood up so violently that his chair clattered back against the wall and stormed across the office, flung the door open and repeated himself.

***

On December 11th 1997 Federal Judge Thomas Jackson threw out both the fine and the contempt charge, declaring that the DOJ had not provided enough evidence to make it clear that Microsoft had definitely breached a specific part of the original consent decree. However, rather than dismiss the case altogether he requested additional evidence, and in the meantime he ordered Microsoft to stop shipping Windows with a bundled version of Intenet Explorer unless they also provided manufacturers with an option that didn't include the browser.

Bill met with Neukom and Steve Ballmer as soon as they got the news.

"Can he do that? Ask for more information if they didn't give him enough already?" Bill asked Neukom.

"In reality he probably can, but I want to challenge it. The matter before him was whether Microsoft could be held in contempt for violating the 1995 consent decree. I'm going to argue that if he couldn't hold us in contempt then the case should have ended there. Asking for more is going beyond the scope of the petition."

"Do you think that'll fly?" Steve asked.

"Not at first but this is going to be a long battle and we need to kick things off on the right foot. We don't want to roll over straight away."

"Cool. Makes sense to me. What about this thing about giving people an option to get Windows without IE? It's ridiculous, does he know what it would take to untangle them?" Bill said.

"Of course not, he has no idea but he doesn't have to, does he? And legally that bit's actually defensible, if the original consent decree does apply then we have to do something to comply with it and giving manufacturers an option would mean we could still ship the current bundled version. I think he's trying to be balanced."

"Balanced my ass. He's an idiot. You can't rule on something you don't understand." Bill started tapping his pen rapidly on the desk. "I don't see how we can quickly put together a version that pulls out all of the IE code and still works. When do we have to comply by?"

Neukom started to answer but Steve spoke first.

"He didn't actually say it has to work," Steve said.

"What?" Bill said.

"Hang on, I don't like where this is going," Neukom said.

"No, hear me out. Bill, you said we can't quickly get to a version without IE that still works, right?"

"Yeah."

"Well, how easy would it be to just clumsily rip out the browser code and not worry about what else stopped working?"

"Simple enough."

"So, we do that and we have an option to offer the manufacturers. They can have the current version of Windows with IE in or one without that we haven't had time to test and that might not work. It's up to them which one they choose. Nice and legal."

"William?" Bill said.

"It's clearly not the spirit of the thing," Neukom said reluctantly. "But I think Steve's right, it would be *legally* compliant with the order."

Bill hesitated.

"What about if we offer them an old version of Windows from before IE as well?"

"A working version?"

"Absolutely. It isn't up to date and it will be missing recent functionality but it will work."

"That's better then. I can make that argument with a straight face. Three options: current version with the IE browser, current version with IE removed which probably doesn't work, and an old version which works but isn't up to date."

Now it was Steve's turn to get cold feet.

"Are we sure we want to go down this route? I mean I know I said it, but it's kind of slapping them in the face."

"It's your call Bill," Neukom said.

"I'm sick of smiling sweetly while people who have no clue what they're talking about pass judgement on my business. Let's do it."

Four days later Microsoft legally appealed the court order and simultaneously announced to the industry that they had come up with some options to comply until the judge ruled on their appeal.

On the conference call explaining the options Brad Chase, the VP of Internet Marketing was perfectly clear that the options existed merely to satisfy the legal requirement and wasn't expecting anybody to order them. Particularly the second option, which, as he explained at the time, didn't work.

The Justice Department were not amused.

On the day of Microsoft's announcement a Justice spokesperson said baldly, "The conduct announced by Microsoft today doesn't comply with the order."

And just days later they filed a motion asking Judge Jackson to hold Microsoft in contempt which contained language that showed how inflamed passions on both side had become.

The DOJ's motion accused Microsoft of acting cynically and that its,

"naked attempt to defeat the purpose of the Court's Order and to further its litigation strategy is an affront to the Court's authority; the Court accordingly should hold Microsoft in civil contempt and act swiftly to bring it into compliance."

***

Bill put his book down on the arm of the chair a little harder than he'd intended and startled Melinda. He saw a slight frown wrinkle her face. She didn't look annoyed though, more concerned, and even though he knew it was irrational her concern annoyed him more.

He knew that she was worried about him and he knew she was right to be, but he was trying to ignore it. Hence the reading. He just wanted a break from the whole government thing. It was one thing to fight the competition but to have to fight the government as well!

Previously if he'd focussed on something else, say the charity work, however briefly, he'd always slightly resented the fact that it was pulling him away from what he knew he should be focussed on: Microsoft. Over the last week or so though he'd noticed that he was spending more time when he was out of the office reading up on the global disease burden than he was catching up on email.

If he was honest with himself it had been an attempt to distract him from Microsoft. He could never remember doing that before.

Never.

He looked at the book at his side.

But hey, what's wrong with focusing on the world's problems. It's important stuff, isn't it? he thought.

"We need to do more," he said.

"What about?" Melinda asked.

"This," he said, rapping his knuckles on the cover of the book.

He heard his own tone of voice and winced a little. He hadn't meant to snap. Luckily for him Melinda let it go.

She knew his real goal here and she *was* worried about him, however much he tried to brush it off. But maybe focussing on some of the good they could do would kill two birds with one stone. They did have an opportunity to do more. And filling his mind with working out how to do it effectively could help her husband at the same time as helping others.

"Okay, I agree," she said. "So how do we decide where to focus?"

She saw the shift in his eyes as he moved more deeply into the problem.

"Think of it like work. If this was a challenge at Microsoft what would you do?"

"I'd want data."

"Okay, so we get data. Lots of it probably already exists and if not we can commission it. Then what do we do?" he challenged, sounding just like the Bill at Microsoft.

"Start at the top of the list," she said, with a shrug. "We'd never heard of rotavirus before. What else is killing people that we don't know about…"

"Or people like us don't think about…" he interrupted.

"Exactly, or we don't think about, and then we see which of them is under funded and start there."

She checked her watch then stood up and grabbed his hand, pulling him out of the chair.

"Why don't we go to your study and work some of this out now. I bet we've got enough information to make a start, what do you think?"

He pursed his lips and for the first time in a week he looked like his old self.

***

In January Microsoft reached a compromise with Justice department and Judge Jackson in which they agreed to give manufacturers the option to install Windows with the Internet Explorer functionality still present but without the icon on display.

In the background Justice continued to build their case but the action moved away from the courtroom.

Then on March 3rd 1998 Bill, whose testimony in the DOJ's antitrust case would be restricted to a videotaped deposition, was called to Capitol Hill to give evidence to the Senate hearing on Computer Industry Competition.

In theory the hearing was not specifically targeted at Bill or Microsoft, however, all of the three hundred or so people who crowded the gallery and those who read about it or watched it on the news, knew that Bill was the real centre of the senators' attention. In case anybody could have missed it, Bill was joined on the panel by Jim Barksdale and Scott McNealy. Neither could be considered disinterested parties, and they certainly weren't fans of Bill.

Barksdale was the CEO of Netscape, the alleged victim in the Justice department investigation. McNealy was the CEO of SUN Microsystems, who made the Java programming language which allowed software developers to write software that did not have to be tied to any one operating system. McNealy's VP was testifying for the DOJ in the antitrust case, arguing that Microsoft was trying to undermine Java because it was a threat to Windows' dominance.

Bill, in a dark blue suit and blue tie reminiscent of the IBM of old, was seated beside Jim Barksdale so there was no light hearted chat before the session began. Support came in the form of Melinda and Bill Sr. who had come with him to the committee hearing and were sitting directly behind him in reserved chairs.

While the other panelists talked to one another, Bill Sr. leant forward and squeezed his son's shoulder. And then it began.

As more than twenty photographers crammed into the space between the row of tables set out for the panel and the raised dais on which the senators sat, committee Chairman Orrin Hatch called the meeting to order.

"Good morning," he said. "I want to make it clear at the outset that this hearing is not intended to serve as an arena for criticising or attacking any single company. I'm sure there will be some hard questions today, but I think there is a single basic one underlying our inquiry: Is there a danger that monopoly power is being, or could be, used to stifle innovation in the computer industry?"

Senator Hatch gave each of the committee members and panelists an opportunity to make some introductory remarks. Senator Herbert Kohl directed his comments straight to Bill.

"Business is all about creating value and offering consumers better products than your competitors, and all of the companies represented here are certainly hard-nosed competitors who've brought great value to Americans. And no one more than you, Mr. Gates. But, no one, Mr. Gates no matter how powerful or successful they are, is above the law. You have nearly 90 percent of the market for operating systems, clearly a monopoly and probably a legal one. And yet you refuse to concede it. As a businessman I can admire that kind of dominance, but we need to explore whether you and your company have crossed the line or if, on the other hand, this is just the carping of disgruntled rivals."

Bill sat perfectly still throughout with a polite smile painted onto his face.

When Hatch gave him an opportunity to speak Bill reminded the committee and the crowd that Microsoft had started as a small company and hadn't been prevented by IBM who at the time were a dominant force accused of stifling innovation.

He read a prepared speech that was clearly articulated but lacked passion and failed to move the audience. He smiled only when a bell went off to warn him that his allotted five minutes were up. It didn't stop him talking for another two minutes and finishing his point.

Jim Barksdale on the other hand made the room laugh several times while he hammered home the point that Microsoft had a monopoly.

"Can I ask the room a quick question?" he asked at one point. Hatch nodded and Barksdale turned to the room behind him. "How many of you use PCs? Not Macintoshes, PCs. Raise your hands."

Most of the room put their hands up. Bill Sr. and Melinda did not join in.

"Good," he continued. "Now, keep your hand up if you use a PC without a Microsoft operating system."

Barksdale turned back to the senators and looked directly at them, intentionally ignoring every single hand in the room falling.

"Gentlemen, that's a monopoly. That's a lock. 100 percent. I didn't even have to turn around. But there's nothing wrong with being a monopoly, everybody hates monopolies unless they've got one." The room laughed again. "But monopolies have to play by different rules."

Senator Hatch allowed the other panelists time to pass comment and then opened the questioning from the committee.

"Let me begin with you, Mr. Gates. Recognising that there is nothing illegal about being a monopoly, but acknowledging that you have over 90 percent market share, do you seriously dispute the proposition that Microsoft Windows has monopoly power?"

Bill refused to concede.

"I do. Microsoft makes products with a very short lifetime. In the span of the term of a senator, we create a product, it becomes very popular and then it has no demand whatsoever. When we build a product we know that customers will expect more, the only question is, will they replace that product with our next one or someone else's? And everybody in the industry knows it. Even members of this panel will tell you say, outside of this room of course, that their products will replace Windows, how Java will supersede Windows, or how the browser will turn into an operating system and make the operating system worthless. So there is competition."

Later, discussion moved to the browser and Senator Hatch pressed Bill on whether Microsoft's licensing practices put Netscape at a disadvantage.

"I understand that your agreements with ISPs have exclusive licensing provisions. Is that right?"

"Like most companies we do occasionally enter into exclusive licenses, so sometimes, yes."

"And I doubt those exclusive licenses are meaningless in terms of which browsers are shipped."

Bill struggled to contain his irritation.

"Exclusive licenses do not stop end users choosing which browser they use. When we released the first version of our browser, Internet Explorer, it shipped with Windows, like it does today. But at that time it wasn't as good as some of our competitor's products, so almost nobody used it.

"No matter what relationships we had with manufacturers or ISPs, people didn't choose that browser, because it is so easy to pick the browser you want to pick. It was only with version three, when we won the majority of the reviews, that then people started to switch to our browser.

"And if somebody else releases one that people prefer then they will switch to that and we will lose market share again. Somebody who uses these ISPs has the ability in five seconds to switch their browser to whatever they want to. It makes no difference to that process whether we have exclusive licenses with ISPs."

Barksdale got Senator Hatch's attention and, as Bill finished, the committee chairman gestured for him to speak.

"I would say that what Mr. Gates is saying there is just not the way it works," Barksdale said. "The fact is, Microsoft work very hard to get exclusive licenses. Microsoft, because of their operating system dominance, are able to force some people to do things that are not necessarily in their best interest…"

"No, these are not…" Bill started to interrupt and then stopped himself, but Barksdale had stopped speaking and waited, making sure no-one missed the fact that Bill had interrupted him.

"Excuse me, Mr. Gates," he said when Bill had already fallen silent. He looked at Senator Hatch and said, "I let him finish his statement."

"Why don't you finish Mr. Barksdale, and then we'll come back to Mr. Gates," Senator Hatch said.

"If the licenses weren't a problem for Microsoft, they would not have changed 40 licenses the day before this hearing," Barksdale said, then sat back in his chair and rolled his pen between his fingers.

"Mr. Gates?" Hatch prompted.

"Actually, we changed the licenses in Europe a few weeks ago as part of a business review. The licenses are *not exclusive*. I mean, let's be very clear about that."

"They're exclusionary," Barksdale said.

Bill paused and smirked, tilting his head from side to side as though choosing his words very carefully. A second later, suppressing a laugh, he answered.

"They do ask that when a customer is referred, that the person not promote the Netscape browser, and that became controversial. I don't think it's an unusual thing when you refer a customer to someone you ask them not to switch over to the competitive product. That became a focus of attention and so we've gotten rid of that. That's, you know, completely behind us."

***

About fifteen minutes before the end of the four hour and ten minute long hearing, Senator Hatch got frustrated with Bill and the two of them started talking over each other.

"Mr. Gates, you've been somewhat hard to nail down on a very specific question, and I would appreciate just a yes or no if you can. Do you put any limitation on content providers for advertising or promoting Netscape? Yes or no, if you can."

"Every Internet content provider that has a business relationship with Microsoft is free to develop content that uses competitors' platforms and standards," Bill said.

"I'm asking do you put limitations on, meaning Microsoft and I guess when I say Microsoft I mean you too because you're…"

"I don't know what you mean 'me too'?" Bill interrupted.

"Well, Microsoft, let's look at Microsoft..."

But Bill wasn't prepared to let it go.

"No," he said. "What do you mean me too?"

"Well, because you're a powerful and dominant force within Microsoft. There's no question. Look, forget about you."

"I don't put any restrictions on..." Bill said, smirking.

"How about Microsoft?"

"... I've never met with any internet content providers..."

"How about Microsoft? Do they put limitations or restrictions on people from advertising or promoting Netscape?"

Bill froze as Hatch used the word 'people'. There's a difference between people and content providers which Bill was very aware of and which the senators were less conscious of.

"I'm not aware of any limitation that prevents them from doing any content that promotes Netscape..."

"Does Microsoft use any influence of force, or market power, or monopoly power to stop people from advertising or promoting netscape. That's a pretty simple question."

Bill paused for another two seconds, before furrowing his brow and clarifying.

"For the people... I..."

"For the people you're dealing with."

"We've talked about the ISP agreements right?"

"No. We've talked about them, but I'm talking about content providers at this point."

Bill hesitated once more.

"There are many content providers who are on the Microsoft channel guide, who do things to promote Netscape. For example, Disney..."

Bill emphasised his words with a stabbing motion with his pen.

"That's not my question," Hatch said as the two men spoke over each other again.

"I'm saying there's no..." Bill said.

"I'm saying do you put any limitations..."

Bill held his hands apart, palms up towards Senator Hatch and shook his head vigorously.

"I'm giving you an example... I'm giving you a perfect example."

Eventually Senator Leahy, the ranking minority member of the committee stepped in and attempted to defuse the exchange, however, Hatch was not satisfied and Bill knew he had failed to land his point.

***

As soon as the questioning was finished and Senator Hatch had struck his gavel to bring the hearing to a close, Bill Sr. and Melinda joined Bill, and the three of them went to shake hands with the senators.

Despite the occasional lapse into irritation by just about everybody involved, the session itself had been about as cordial as it was possible for these things to be and Bill felt he had acquitted himself reasonably well. However, if Bill's goal had been to defuse the DOJ case he failed, in discussion with reporters after the hearing, Senator Hatch made his position clear.

"Microsoft are now a monopoly, and they will have to learn to live by the rules that govern monopolies."

"Should the Justice department expand their case beyond its current remit to cover some of the topics that were brought up today?" one of the reports asked.

"It looks like they probably should."

C:\PART\CHAPTER> 6.3

In May 1998 the Department of Justice and the twenty state attorneys who had joined the DOJ in the case, formally filed suit against Microsoft under the Sherman Act, the basis of Antitrust law in the US.

Microsoft filed a number of motions to dismiss, delay or limit the case but each was rejected. By mid September, with the trial set for October, Bill was beginning to feel punch drunk.

"Are you awake?" Bill said.

"Mhmm," Melinda said, sleepily.

"Do you know what happened today?"

"No," she mumbled, clinging onto the edge of sleep.

"Microsoft IE passed Netscape in browser market share. More people now use IE than Netscape."

"That's good news."

"I'm not so sure. I don't know whether it would be better to just give up."

That woke her up completely. They had gone to bed half an hour before. Bill had said he'd read for a while but she had been trying to sleep. Jennifer was teething and with Bill at work all day she'd been home alone with the baby as usual. It didn't make for an easy day. She shuffled and adjusted her pillows so that she could sit up.

"What do you mean give up?" she asked. "Surely passing Netscape is a good thing?"

"It would be but with the Justice case hanging over us I just don't know."

"This isn't like you Trey."

"It just seems so personal. It doesn't matter what we do, they're never going to stop. And Jackson. I don't know what I did to that man but every decision he makes goes against us. I still can't believe that he ordered my deposition should be in open court, that's practically unheard of."

"It was overturned."

"Only because we appealed. He rejected our request to dismiss. He rejected the request to limit scope."

"You always expect him to reject the dismissal. And it isn't all going against us. They ruled the injunction didn't apply to Windows 98."

"Another appeal! Really, Jackson hasn't made a single decision in our favour. He's prejudiced against us. Against me. Him and the DOJ, it's like a witch hunt. Maybe if I leave, they'll leave Microsoft alone."

"You couldn't leave Microsoft."

"I could. It's not like we'd starve."

She looked at him and smiled gently.

"That really wasn't what I meant, Trey. You couldn't leave Microsoft, you have to have something to push for, something to achieve." She put her arm around him and pulled him closer. "Come on, this was never going to be a fair trial. We're Goliath. Nobody routes for Goliath. You've got what, two months before your deposition? Go back in tomorrow and work on prep with Neukom's team. Make them sorry they ever picked a fight with Bill Gates."

Bill smiled. Melinda was right. He'd pull himself together and go back in fighting. He really needed to get more sleep, this self pitying crap was not his style at all.

***

The trial started on 19th October 1998 and, including a three month recess from March to June, took eleven months.

The government made two main arguments. First they showed that Microsoft had made Internet Explorer free specifically to put Netscape out of business, and second that Microsoft had intentionally tied sales of IE to Windows in a way that forced manufacturers to favour IE over Netscape. Through the course of the trial they also repeatedly demonstrated Microsoft's threatening behaviour towards competitors and manufacturers, with the goal of establishing that Microsoft was generally anticompetitive. On one occasion when Apple were developing a product that would compete with a Microsoft one, the DOJ presented evidence that Microsoft executives had told Apple to "…knife the baby…"

Microsoft, on the other hand, argued that they didn't charge for their browser because it was just a feature of Windows and couldn't be thought of as a separate product. Perhaps even more importantly they tried to convince the court that Microsoft did not have a monopoly so couldn't possibly be in violation of the Sherman antitrust law that the government was using.

Neither side covered themselves in glory.

The government's first witness was Jim Barksdale of Netscape who elaborated on some of the things he had said on Capitol Hill. Amongst many other things, he testified that once Netscape had refused to split the market with Microsoft (which would have been illegal and which Bill always denied happened), Microsoft had decided to put them out of business.

"I had never been in a meeting in my 33-year business career in which a competitor had so blatantly implied that we should either stop competing with it or the competitor would kill us," he said.

For three days starting on 27th August 1998 Bill was deposed by the DOJ attorney, David Boies. The deposition was videotaped for the record.

Legally the government's case was against Microsoft not Bill personally, however, as Senator Hatch had said during the senate hearings, Bill was inextricably linked with Microsoft. More than most chairmen or CEOs Bill was identified completely in the public's mind, and the government's, with Microsoft and Microsoft with him.

No doubt realising that fact, Bill and his legal team had decided that Boies would be trying to trip Bill up during the deposition and that the best thing for Bill to do would be to avoid giving any ground or volunteering anything other than complete facts. Throughout the deposition he stated that he didn't recall the events Boies asked him about, and argued over the precise definition of Boies' questions, so many times that it descended into parody.

"Depends on what you mean by 'compete'," he said, at one point.

The plan probably wasn't a bad one for many people under deposition, but it backfired on Bill when the government chose to play excerpts of the video in court throughout the trial, despite challenges from Microsoft's lawyers about how relevant they were.

Bill came across as either arrogant and evasive, or incompetent. And nobody was prepared to believe that he was incompetent.

It didn't help Bill that, while he later acknowledged that he could have handled it differently ("Was I rude? Absolutely, I plead rudeness to Boies in the first degree," he would say to an interviewer), at the time he was unable to see that there was anything wrong with his behaviour.

"I answered every question, completely, truthfully through many, many, many long days," he said. "The fact that they're taking snippets out of that and holding them up without having me there because they chose not to call me as a witness, I think, is quite novel."

But Judge Jackson disagreed, openly laughing and shaking his head while the video was played.

"If anything, I think the problem is with your witness, not with the way in which his testimony is being presented." He told Microsoft's lawyers when they challenged the use of the videotape. Adding, "I think it's evident to every spectator that, for whatever reasons, in many respects Mr. Gates has not been particularly responsive."

For those prepared to question the government's intentions it wasn't a complete a home run. Boies was forced to admit when challenged by reporters that the case wasn't about Bill, but claimed that since he was the CEO "what he says matters a lot." He had no answer when the same reporter pressed him as to why, in that case, he hadn't put Bill on the stand.

In the end though Microsoft's lawyers probably thought it was a good thing he hadn't. The tapes played no better in public than they did in the courtroom and although Microsoft's lawyers were probably right to point out that most of it was completely irrelevant to the case, they did set an unhelpful tone which played into the government's presentation of Microsoft as a bully, and presumably had an influence on the perception of Judge Jackson.

After hours of technical evidence from both sides, the lawyers presented their closing arguments to the judge on 21st September 1999.

The government stated that, "Microsoft achieved its anticompetitive objectives by conducting a campaign of predation against Netscape, SUN and others. The evidence leaves no doubt, however, that microsoft's illegal conduct has been bad…very bad for consumers."

And accused Microsoft of having,

"…Coerced, induced, solicited, and forced many people in this industry to do its will: OEM's, Intel, Apple."

Microsoft's lawyers, however, speaking after lunch, called into question both the government's witnesses,

"The government claims to be protecting the interests of consumers but no consumers testified at the trial… The government's witnesses were microsoft's competitors, several of whom actively lobbied the Justice Department to bring this case."

And their conduct of the case itself,

"There were moments during the trial when the government had the rapt attention of the gallery as it questioned aspects of a videotaped demonstration or an e-mail message of marginal relevance. It is telling, however, your honor, how few of those moments made their way into the government's proposed findings. Why? Because the moment for courtroom melodrama has passed. Now is the moment to confront the evidence, and it is clear that the government has failed to present the evidence needed to support its claims, both the claims in the complaint and those they tossed in along the way."

Judge Jackson took a month to consider the arguments and then, on 5th November 1999, he issued his initial findings of fact.

In a judgment that ran to more than two hundred pages, he concluded that Microsoft:

"… enjoys monopoly power in the relevant market.

... engaged in a concerted series of actions designed to protect the applications barrier to entry, and hence its monopoly power, from a variety of middleware threats, including Netscape's Web browser and Sun's implementation of Java. Many of these actions have harmed consumers in ways that are immediate and easily discernible. They have also caused less direct, but nevertheless serious and far-reaching, consumer harm by distorting competition.

... has demonstrated that it will use its prodigious market power and immense profits to harm any firm that insists on pursuing initiatives that could intensify competition against one of Microsoft's core products. Microsoft's past success in hurting such companies and stifling innovation deters investment in technologies and businesses that exhibit the potential to threaten Microsoft. The ultimate result is that some innovations that would truly benefit consumers never occur for the sole reason that they do not coincide with Microsoft's self-interest..."

So the judge essentially found Microsoft guilty on all counts, but it would be seven long months before he ruled on what he intended to do about it.

In the meantime Bill took a radical step that some had said would never happen.

C:\PART\CHAPTER> 6.4

"It is a great pleasure for me to announce that Steve Ballmer, my long term partner in building Microsoft and a great business leader, is being named CEO," Bill said to the cameras on 13th January 2000. "I'm returning to what I love most: focusing on technologies for the future."

The world's press was taken aback. Just two months earlier at Comdex, Bill had told Forbes that "it could be possible" within the next ten years that Steve could take over, but now?

There was immediately speculation that the decision was in response to rumblings coming from the government that they would be asking Judge Jackson to order Microsoft to be broken up, but Bill was quick to squash that.

"This was a personal decision," he insisted. "One I have discussed with Steve and our board of directors for some time. It will allow me to spend almost 100% of my time on new software technologies. It's an exciting evolution for me and a very good transition for the company.

"Although I've been able to spend more time on our technical strategy since naming Steve as president in July 1998, I felt that the opportunities for Microsoft were incredible, yet our structure wasn't optimal to really take advantage of them to the degree that we should."

C:\PART\CHAPTER> 6.5

Finally, after months of wondering what Judge Jackson's order would be, he released his answer on 7th June 2000. And, if Bill had hoped that stepping down as CEO would soften the blow, then Jackson's judgement must have fallen like a hammer.

The judgement ordered that Microsoft should be split into two separate companies exactly as the government had requested, between an operating systems business and an applications business. And it went further, ordering that no individual could hold stock in both companies, effectively meaning that Bill would have to choose which half of his company he kept. He couldn't be a shareholder in both.

Judge Jackson's Memorandum and Order was scathing, highlighting that it was necessary to break the company up, because they couldn't be trusted to fall in line with any order he might issue short of that. And, just like in the trial itself, it is clear that although the legal framing of the order refers to Microsoft, the judge was taking aim squarely at Bill.

"...Microsoft claims, in effect, to have been surprised by the "draconian" and "unprecedented" remedy the plaintiffs recommend. Microsoft's profession of surprise is not credible...

... Microsoft as it is presently organized and led is unwilling to accept the notion that it broke the law or accede to an order amending its conduct...

...Microsoft has proved untrustworthy in the past. In earlier proceedings in which a preliminary injunction was entered, Microsoft's purported compliance with that injunction while it was on appeal was illusory and its explanation disingenuous..."

Six days later Microsoft, to no-one's surprise, appealed the ruling. What was more surprising was that they fought back against Judge Jackson personally.

Neukom's team lodged standard appeal arguments that the court had ruled incorrectly and that the proposed remedy of breaking up the company was unnecessary, but they shocked everyone following the case by also arguing that Judge Jackson had behaved unethically and therefore all of his judgements should be overturned.

***

Another year would pass before the D.C. Circuit Court of Appeal delivered their formal finding but, in February of 2001, Bill and Microsoft had an early indication that it would be at least partly favourable.

Judges on the Court of Appeals spent an hour tearing apart Jackson's conduct.

After Judge Jackson had ruled in the case the news broke that he had granted secret interviews to journalists while the trial was ongoing. In the interviews, which he had forbidden the journalists to publish until he had made his decision public, he described Bill as a "...smart-mouthed young kid who has extraordinary ability and needs a little discipline..." and said that he had "... a Napoleonic concept of himself and his company, an arrogance that derives from power..."

His fellow justices were outraged at something which is clearly forbidden by the judicial code of conduct.

"We don't run off our mouths in a pejorative way... The system would be a shambles if all judges did that," Chief Judge Harry T. Edwards said.

Still, just because they were angry at Judge Jackson allowing a perception of bias to taint the judgement it didn't mean they'd necessarily disagree with his findings or the proposed remedy of splitting Microsoft.

To find out whether that was the case Bill had to wait until June.

***

When the final decision landed on 28th June 2001, Bill was in Steve's office. Neukom came as soon as he received the judgement. He didn't bother explaining why he'd come, or asking if the other two men had time. He just walked into the office and Bill instantly asked.

"What does it say?"

"I'm still looking, it's a hundred and twenty five pages," Neukom said.

"Well, that's why we pay you William, summarise," Steve snapped.

Bill wasn't rocking for once but he did lean forward in the chair, his hands clasped and his elbows pressed into his lap.

Neukom, ever the lawyer, caveated.

"I'll have to read it all to give you a full view... but the key bits are that they won't overturn Jackson's findings of fact completely..."

"Shit," Steve said and looked at Bill angrily but Bill was silent, watching Neukom intently and listening.

"The finding that we monopolised operating systems stands…"

"Double shit! How does this fit with what they were saying February?"

"Steve!" Bill raised his hand to silence his CEO. "Let him speak."

He nodded at Neukom, who continued.

"It's not all bad. They've reversed the charge of monopolising the browser market and the tying charge. If you read through the legalise they rip into Jackson almost as badly as they did in February. They've disqualified him from the case." He changed his voice slightly to show he was quoting, "the District Judge violated each of these ethical precepts by talking about the case with reporters. The violations were deliberate, repeated, egregious, and flagrant… [His] comments were not only improper, but also would lead a reasonable, informed observer to question the District Judge's impartiality."

"Wow!" Steve said.

Neukom turned another couple of pages, skim reading to find more to share.

"What about the split?" Bill asked, feeling like the other two men were missing the most important point.

Neukom nodded slowly, still reading.

"That's where it's best for us. They've thrown it back to the District Court so technically it's not decided yet, but yeah, here…" He put on his quotation voice again, "… 'This court has drastically altered the District Court's conclusions on liability. The District Court… blah-blah… can fashion an appropriate remedy for Microsoft's antitrust violations. In particular, the court should consider which of the decree's conduct restrictions remain viable…"

"That's great," Ballmer said.

"It's about as strong an indication as you'll get that they think splitting the company would be inappropriate."

"Thank God," Bill said, his voice cracking. "I can't believe it."

His arms fell to his side and he sagged in his chair, his eyes tearing up.

"What a fucking couple of years," he said.

"But we won Bill," Steve said, comfortingly. "It's over."

Neukom was less sanguine.

"It's not quite over Steve," he said. But when Bill looked up at him, the tears now rolling down his face from relief, Neukom took pity on him. He'd known his boss for twenty three years and he'd never seen him look so close to defeat. "Not quite, I said, but almost. It'll be easier from here Bill. I promise."

Bill let out a huge sigh, took his glasses off and rubbed his face vigorously. When he was done and the glasses were back on the moment of weakness had passed.

He stood up.

"Steve, sort me a press conference for as soon as possible. We're going to get out ahead of this and position it right. I'm going to go and call Melinda."

***

Bill was on televisions worldwide almost instantly. Bill glossed over the remaining charges of monopolisation and focused on the positive messages for Microsoft. However, he avoided any mention of the judge's conduct and left it to Microsoft's PR people to quietly make sure that none of the reporters missed the severe reprimand Jackson had received.

"The Appeals Court's ruling removes the cloud of breakup from the company, reverses the tying claim and says clearly that we did not attempt to monopolize the browser market," he said to the cameras. "The legal process can be hard on anyone who goes through it, and the last four years have been challenging for all of us here at Microsoft, and for me personally. But with this ruling there is a new framework. It is a good time for all parties to sit down and see what kind of resolution can be worked out."

The government also claimed victory, the new Attorney General John Ashcroft, saying, "This is a significant victory. The department is not, I believe, in a weakened position here."

But in early September, just days before September 11th would pull any remaining attention away from the story, the Department of Justice confirmed that it had dropped its request for Microsoft to be broken up.

There would be other legal challenges over the years, in a company the size of Microsoft that is to be expected, but there would never be the same active threat of the company being broken up.

This time the sigh of relief could last.

C:\PART> 7: THE FOUNDATION

C:\PART\CHAPTER> 7.1

In the early 2000's, a couple of years after the antitrust case concluded, Bill started to consider leaving Microsoft.

"I'm thinking of stepping down," he said to Melinda one evening, as he lowered his briefcase to the floor.

Melinda blinked, it wasn't what she'd expected her workaholic husband to say as soon as he came home. Or ever.

"And good evening to you too," she said.

"Sorry," Bill said, shaking his head and bending over to kiss the top of her head. "How was your day?"

She brushed it away.

"It was fine. Tell me what you're thinking."

Instead of answering directly, he asked her a question.

"What has excited me most over the last couple of years?"

"Fertiliser," she said with a smile.

The Foundation was starting to work in agriculture and, as Bill wanted to be better informed, on their last holiday he'd taken along a book about fertiliser and devoured it. He'd spent almost a full day on the beach talking about nothing else until eventually she had told him it was time to change the topic. It had become a bit of a running joke between them.

"Very funny," he said. "But that's my point. It's been the Foundation. Not Microsoft."

Melinda pulled her feet up underneath her on the sofa and patted the seat beside her.

"Come, sit down. You're serious, aren't you?"

"I really am."

"And you've not just had a bad day?"

"Not at all, today was fine, this has been a while coming. You know how much the antitrust stuff took out of me. Making Steve CEO was supposed to give me a chance to focus on the bits of the job that I loved but it isn't setting me on fire any more. I think the time has come to switch."

"Are you sure it's what you want? You could try taking a sabbatical, like an extended Think Week, not one of the new ones with the company, a real one on your own like you used to do. But longer, a couple of months maybe? Lock yourself away in the guesthouse or go over to the canal."

"No, I don't want to be away from you and the kids. In fact that's part of the appeal. If I left I could spend more time with you and the kids."

By this time Bill and Melinda had three children, filling the family wing they had designed all those years ago.

Their son, Rory, had been born on 23rd May 1999, while the antitrust case was still underway; their youngest, another girl they'd named Phoebe Adele in memory of Gam, was born on 14th September 2002.

"I could carry on at Microsoft forever but it just doesn't feel as urgent for me to be there any more."

"You've climbed that hill," she said, placing her hand on his arm.

He sighed.

"I guess, that's it. It's strange, I didn't think anything would excite me as much as software."

"It's the learning, that's what excites you," she said. "And doing something no-one thinks is possible. It's basically the same thing, it's just another way to change the world."

He looked at his wife and wondered how he had got so lucky. She understood him.

"That's it! That's exactly it!" Momentarily animated, he quieted again and said, "You wouldn't be disappointed? I'm not letting you down?"

Melinda gently pulled his head onto her shoulder and stroked his hair. "Don't be daft."

After a moment enjoying simply being held, he spoke and she felt his voice through her shoulder.

"I'll talk to Dad, it's only fair. He's been running the Foundation and I wouldn't want to step on his toes."

"I bet he'll be thrilled for you both to work together."

***

After setting up the original William H. Gates foundation in 1994 which Bill Sr. had managed, Bill and Melinda had started to get more serious about their giving. Under Bill Sr.'s direction they stepped up the amount they gave with grants targeted mainly at global health, and in 1997 they formed a new foundation, the Gates Library Foundation, and endowed it with $200 million with the goal of getting all US libraries connected to the internet.

Bill was convinced that overpopulation was a key problem to global health and development, and so in the early days much of their giving was focussed on what was euphemistically called 'reproductive health', which in practice meant birth control.

Melinda, who was a practising Catholic, struggled with the idea of taking a public stance at odds with the Vatican. In the end though, comfortable that the decision was the right one for her personally, then it wasn't right to deny other women the same opportunity.

"I didn't wrestle with whether or not I believed in contraceptives," she said. "I use them. My mother used them. My friends use them. It was more taking on an institution you believe in."

However, when Bill started to consume the World Health reports he zeroed in on the fact that all of the countries with high birth rates also suffered from high infant mortality. Wherever infant mortality had been reduced, and birth control options were available of course, the birth rate had naturally fallen. In Bill's programmer's mind the connection clicked.

"...Parents choose to have enough kids to give them a high chance that several will survive to support them as they grow old. As the number of kids who survive to adulthood goes up, parents can achieve this goal without having as many children," he would later write.

And so the focus of their giving changed to reducing mortality, particularly infant mortality.

In 2000 in order to bring all of their charitable work together, they combined both organisations under a single new foundation, the Bill & Melinda Gates Foundation. They gave it an initial endowment of $16 billion but even more significantly Bill and Melinda committed to donate 95% of their wealth to the foundation. To ensure that it did not simply become a storehouse for their wealth for others to operate, they committed that the money would all be spent fifty years after the last one of them died.

Over the first few years of the new millennium, the new foundation's goals gradually evolved into three main arms: Global Health, which funds both basic research in the science of health, and ways to change market forces so that they support poorer countries; Global Development looking at family health, emergency relief, and the actual delivery of vaccines and other medicines; and finally a United States programme that is focussed on education and internet access, and also provides the vehicle for the family's continuing support to the Seattle area.

All of this work was bracketed under a single vision *All Lives Have Equal Value* and Bill was brutally honest about what he saw as the widespread failure across all sectors to think in this way.

"In my view—and there is no diplomatic way to put this: The world is failing billions of people. Rich governments are not fighting some of the world's most deadly diseases because rich countries don't have them. The private sector is not developing vaccines and medicines for these diseases, because developing countries can't buy them. And many developing countries are not doing nearly enough to improve the health of their own people."

***

In December 2005 Time magazine named Bill, Melinda and Bono of U2 as their 'Persons of the Year'.

The magazine said that they had been selected 'for being shrewd about doing good, for rewiring politics and re-engineering justice, for making mercy smarter and hope strategic and then daring the rest of us to follow'.

It was the tenth time that Bill had been featured on the cover since his first appearance in 1984, but it was the first time that it hadn't been connected to the computer industry.

As unlikely as the trio might seem, the three had actually become close enough friends by the mid 2000's that Bono would stay over at the Gates' home when he was in the northwest US.

Bono had previously tried to make contact with Bill and Melinda through Paul Allen (Paul and Bono were actually a much more likely pairing, having been brought together by a shared passion for music), but Bill had rebuffed it.

"You know, Bono is really serious about poverty and the stuff you're working on; you should talk to him," Paul said.

Bill said he 'did not make it a priority' while Bono has joked that it was more a case of "Bono who? You mean Sonny Bono?"

The two men eventually met at the 2001 World Economic Forum which usually took place in Davos but was being held in New York that year following the World Trade Center attacks.

Bill admitted later that he was amazed that Bono actually knew what he was talking about and had a real commitment to making things happen.

"It was phenomenal. Ever since then we've been big partners in crime," Bill said.

It wasn't long before he had introduced the U2 front man to Melinda and the three of them had become friends.

In their article celebrating the three 'Good Samaritans' as it called them, Time said that while sudden disasters grab the headlines other tragedies unfold daily.

'And who is proving most effective in figuring out how to eradicate those calamities? In different ways, it is Bill and Melinda Gates, co-founders of the world's wealthiest charitable foundation, and Bono, the Irish rocker who has made debt reduction sexy,' the magazine wrote, pointing out that Bill and Melinda had, 'spent the year giving more money away faster than anyone ever has.'

"It has been a great year for global health to get more visibility," Bill said, during the photo shoot for the cover. "The more people know about it, the more they want to act."

***

On 15th June 2006, Bill held a press conference to announce that two years later he would step down as Chief Software Architect and no longer have a day to day role at Microsoft.

"I've decided that two years from today, I will reorganize my personal priorities," Bill announced. "I'm not leaving Microsoft today. What's happening now is we're starting the transition plan. I'll be working as hard as I ever have during these next years.

"This was a hard decision for me. I'm very lucky to have two passions that I feel are so important and so challenging. As I prepare for this change, I firmly believe the road ahead for Microsoft is as bright as ever but I believe with great wealth comes great responsibility, the responsibility to give back to society and make sure those resources are given back in the best possible way, to those in need."

In answer to the question of whether he was retiring he said, "It's not a retirement, it's a reordering of my priorities."

The first part was definitely true, the second was a lie. Possibly even to himself. His priority had been the Foundation for a couple of years by the time he made this announcement. All that was happening now was an outward acknowledgement of that fact.

***

Ten days later, in a move that he insisted was a coincidence, Warren Buffett announced that he would be giving 70% of his fortune to the Bill and Melinda Gates Foundation (and a further 15% away to other foundations).

It was undeniably a vote of confidence in his friends. Warren placed only three conditions on the gift, the first was that it only applied while either Bill or Melinda were alive and active in the Foundation. The second was that the Foundation had to retain charitable status and the third was that his money couldn't simply be used to top up the Foundation, it had to be given away each year.

The letter he published at the time said,

Dear Bill and Melinda:

I greatly admire what the Bill & Melinda Gates Foundation ("BMG") is accomplishing and want to materially expand its future capabilities. Accordingly, by this letter, I am irrevocably committing to make annual gifts of Berkshire Hathaway "B" shares throughout my lifetime for the benefit of BMG. The first year's gift will permit an increase in BMG's annual giving of about $1.5 billion. In the future, I expect the value of my annual gifts to trend higher in an irregular but eventually substantial manner.

319

...

Working through the Foundation, both of you have applied truly unusual intelligence, energy and heart to improving the lives of millions of fellow humans who have not been as lucky as the three of us. You have done this without regard to color, gender, religion or geography. I am delighted to add to the resources with which you carry on this work.

Sincerely,

Warren E. Buffett

To mark the occasion, Bill, Melinda and Warren took to the stage of the magnificent New York Public Library on 26th June so that Bill and Melinda could publicly give Warren a gift: a first edition copy of Adam Smith's *Wealth of Nations*.

As Bill shook hands with Warren and gave his friend his rare, two-volume edition of the founding text of modern economic theory, he quoted from another of Smith's works.

"However selfish soever man may be supposed, there are evidently some principles in his nature, which interest him in the fortune of others, and render their happiness necessary to him, though he derives nothing from it except the pleasure of seeing it."

The line is from the opening of Smith's book on morality and Bill felt it applied particularly well to Warren.

"I think Warren will not only be known as the world's greatest investor, but the world's greatest investor for good," he said.

But he did acknowledge the pressure that Warren's gift added.

"It's almost scary making sure we spend it right. If I make a mistake with my own money it just doesn't feel the same as if I make a mistake with Warren's money. This is his life's work."

C:\PART\CHAPTER> 7.2

Malaria was one of the diseases which Bill and Melinda settled on early as ripe for their type of intervention.

Malaria used to be endemic in every region of the world, as recently as 1935 there were one hundred and fifty thousand cases per year in the United States. However, through a combination of pesticide spraying and drugs which were then effective, most rich countries eliminated it in the middle of the twentieth century (the US was declared malaria free in 1951) and it fell from attention.

Unfortunately, the lack of attention did not mean that it had gone away. For those prepared to look even cursorily at global health, malaria was still known to be a global killer, prompting Bill and others to describe the mosquito as the most dangerous animal on the planet.

From Bill's earliest reading he had learnt that malaria killed about one million people worldwide, more than any other disease apart from Aids, and that it was the leading killer of children under the age of five.

"Our children will not die from malaria, thank God," he told an audience. "Since that is true, no child should die. It should never be too expensive or too inconvenient to give those most in need a chance to survive when the well-off already have it."

The drugs which had historically been effective in the developed world were by this time almost useless. Ninety percent of infections in sub-Saharan Africa did not respond to treatment by Chloroquine, the cheapest and most readily available treatment.

Work on new treatments was still going ahead in labs across the world coordinated by groups such as the WHO, but Bill felt that there were two main problems holding back a solution.

The first was the application of scientific attention:

"In the early 1900s, Nobel Prizes were awarded for discoveries about the causes of both tuberculosis and malaria. Yet, more than a hundred years later, we don't have effective vaccines for either one. It's not because the problem is unsolvable; it's because we haven't put our scientific intelligence to this task…"

And the second was the lack of appropriate funding. When, in response to a fifty million dollar grant the foundation gave early on, somebody told him that it would cause a fifty percent increase in the amount of research that goes on in malaria, he was outraged.

"That is the most horrific thing I've ever heard. How can that be true?" he exploded. "Malaria causes more lack of productivity than any other single disease. It happens to kill young children and pregnant mothers quite a bit but the actual loss goes way beyond the deaths that are caused. It is absolutely outrageous how little has been put into research on malaria. We are not doing enough to *deliver* the solutions we do have, and we're not spending enough to *find* the solutions we don't have. As a result, people die every year. This doesn't tell a flattering story about humanity. But the story isn't over. In fact, the story is starting to change."

In short, malaria was a perfect candidate for the Gates Foundation to work on.

In 2001 the foundation had started collaborating with GlaxoSmithKline to ensure that a vaccine that GSK had been working on for thirty years would be finished and leave the lab.

Bill and Melinda visited Africa in September 2003 as part of an effort to draw attention to the way that Aids and malaria were ravaging the continent.

Before spending time with Nelson Mandela in South Africa where they focussed on the Aids epidemic, they stopped in Mozambique to visit the Manhica Health Research Center and met the Prime Minister of Mozambique, Pascoal Mocumbi. Sitting on the rolled grass matting Bill made an announcement.

"It's time to treat Africa's malaria epidemic like the crisis it is. It is unacceptable that 3,000 African children die every day from a largely preventable and treatable disease."

He and Melinda made public the grants that had been made by the Foundation just the day before, $168 million investment into malaria research.

"A lot is riding on the outcome of this research," Bill said. "Malaria is the leading cause of hospitalisation and death for children here in Mozambique, and we're losing ground — the number of infant deaths in eastern and southern Africa has doubled over the past two decades."

The money was the largest donation that anyone had given up to that time to fight the disease. And just under sixty percent of it was aimed at research into vaccines, which Bill thought of as medical miracles.

"In the same way that during my Microsoft career I talked about the magic of software, I now spend my time talking about the magic of vaccines. They are the most effective and cost-effective health tool ever invented. I like to say vaccines are a miracle. Just a few doses of vaccine can protect a child from debilitating and deadly diseases for a lifetime. And most vaccines are extremely inexpensive."

By 2007 the vaccine work was well underway. Several candidates had been ruled out but the more promising GSK vaccine would be released into Phase 3 trials in 2009.

Now Bill, never one to place all his eggs in one basket, was looking to come up with novel solutions to reduce or eradicate malaria altogether.

And he knew just the man to turn to.

***

Bill had met Nathan Myhrvold in 1986 when he had bought Nathan's company Dynamical Systems Research and brought it under Microsoft.

Nathan was a genius in precisely the sort of way that was bound to appeal to Bill.

He started college at 14, earned a masters in mathematics from UCLA, then moved to Princeton where he got a masters in mathematical economics and a PhD in applied mathematics, before studying as a postdoctoral fellow at Cambridge under Stephen Hawking. But he had a mind which wasn't satisfied with merely being an expert on one field.

He left Cambridge to set up his first company to produce an IBM compatible operating system and for fun he wrote a five volume 'cookbook' on the science and art of baking bread, and articles on the aerodynamic properties of dinosaur tails which were published in peer reviewed scientific journals.

At Microsoft he worked on a number of projects including Windows and ended up as Chief Technology Officer, basically a role that meant he acted as Bill's chief futurist, responsible for forecasting technological advances. In 1995 he had helped co-author Bill's book *The Road Ahead*. Although Bill's was the only name that appeared on the cover he made no secret of the fact that Nathan was a co-author (there was a third co-author as well, Peter Rinearson, who Bill was equally open about).

Nathan left Microsoft in 1999 and set up a venture capital firm called Intellectual Ventures focussed on cutting edge technology, but he and Bill remained close. So Bill came to Nathan with a challenge. Use the brainpower at Intellectual Ventures to think up innovative ways to help combat malaria.

Now he had come to the Intellectual Ventures headquarters in Bellevue to see what the self proclaimed geeks had come up with.

Nathan, sandy haired with a close cut beard and a t-shirt that read *'SCIENCE: Ruining everything since 1543'* stretched over his portly frame, led Bill through the building. He had talked rapidly as they walked, a stream of words coming out at a hundred miles an hour, describing the projects Intellectual Ventures had on the go but never mentioning the real reason Bill was here.

Bill waited patiently, he knew Nathan wanted the excitement of a grand reveal and he knew that if Nathan had nothing he wouldn't have wasted Bill's time. Whatever Intellectual Ventures had come up with Bill was sure it would be worth the wait.

Finally they reached the lab and Nathan hesitated on the threshold.

"Ready?" he said dramatically.

"Just about," Bill replied and rolled his eyes good naturedly.

Nathan flung open the door and showed the way in with a flourish of his arm.

Bill scanned the room quickly.

On one side of the lab was a desk holding a Rube Goldberg-like contraption cobbled together out of five flashlights, a zoom lens that looked like it had just been ripped off a camera, and a series of mirrors and lenses that reminded Bill of a laser, although he assumed it wasn't. Cables snaked from the whole affair to a Dell laptop. The flashlights and lens were pointing towards the opposite wall where a sheet covered something cube shaped.

Bill pointed at the covered cube and Nathan's eyes twinkled.

"Wait here," he said, then scurried across the room and pulled back the cover on the box to reveal a ten gallon fish tank.

"Mosquitoes?" Bill asked, straining to see the twenty or so flying insects trapped inside.

"Yes, or TIE Fighters as I think of them," Nathan said, referring to the spaceships used by the Empire in Star Wars.

Bill raised an eyebrow but Nathan just waved his hand dismissively.

"You'll see why in a minute," he said and chuckled.

He bustled over to the other side of the room and adjusted something on the machine, powering it up.

"Oh, you'll need these!" he said slipping a pair of goggles on and handing Bill the same. "Now if you're ready, watch the box. We used an idea that Lowell came up with in the eighties."

Lowell was Lowell Wood, an astrophysicist and previous proponent of the Reagan era Strategic Defense Initiative that had been dubbed the Star Wars programme.

"Okay, I'll play along" Bill said, following Nathan's finger. "What am I looking for?"

"Just keep watching carefully."

Nathan hit a key on the laptop, the flashlights came on and illuminated the mosquitoes casting shadows on the reflective screen behind the tank.

After a second the laptop played a Star Wars laser sound effect half a dozen times and Bill saw some of the mosquitoes drop to the floor of the box. He laughed.

"So it *is* a laser. That is so neat. But really, sound effects?!"

"It amuses the team. Hence TIE Fighters."

"I got it. I'm more of a Star Trek man myself, but I got it." He gestured to the box, "Can I?"

"Let me just shut this off. There, go ahead."

Bill took his goggles off and approached the box so he could look inside. Sure enough about half of the mosquitoes were lying on the floor, most of them were dead but two were walking around, though Bill would have said they were doing the mosquito equivalent of stumbling. When he looked closer he could see that they had lost their wings.

"It didn't get them all?" he said, pointing to some of the insects still on the side of the tank.

"It detects them in flight," Nathan said, as he crossed the room to join Bill. "I assume the ones it didn't get weren't flying. We'll try it again in a minute and you can make sure they're all airborne."

Bill nodded, with the exception of the two stumbling ones on the floor, the others that were still alive were all perched on the side, so Nathan's explanation made sense.

"Cool," he said. "So talk to me. How does it work?"

"It's pretty simple in theory. The camera identifies a mosquito in flight and the laser shoots it down. Most of the work has been trying to get it reliable and working out exactly how much energy we need to hit them to kill or disable them."

"How long do you need to hit them?"

Nathan frowned. "We hold the beam on them for 25 milliseconds to finish them off but if you mean how long between shots, then we have about 100 milliseconds to target them, identify it's something we want to kill then take the shot."

"What about other insects though? We can't afford to exterminate pollinators. Half of the world already thinks I'm the devil, I don't really want to give them a good reason."

"It will only target mosquitoes." Nathan looked at him. "How do you think it does it?"

Bill looked thoughtful.

"Shape of the shadow?" he ventured.

"Nope," Nathan shook his head and looked delighted that his old boss hadn't immediately grasped it. "The shadow is just to enlarge the image for the targeting. The identification works by the frequency of their wingbeat."

"You're joking. That's unique?"

Bill had thrown himself into a deep study of malaria and the mosquito as a result, and was surprised to learn such a fundamental new fact.

Nathan nodded excitedly.

"All insects that we've looked at are distinct. In fact in the mosquito even the males and females have distinct frequencies."

"I had no idea. Cool."

"I know. If you wanted to then we could set it to only kill the females. Thanks to Moore's law we've made computing cheap enough that we can weigh the life of an individual insect!" Although Nathan hadn't dived as deep as Bill on mosquito physiology, he knew that only the female mosquitos sucked blood and therefore they were the only ones that could transmit malaria.

Bill crossed to the machine and bent over to examine it closely. He was silent for a moment and Nathan knew him well enough to leave him be.

Here it comes, he thought and then resisted a smile as, after a couple of beats, Bill started rocking.

"Cost?" Bill said, breaking the silence but still moving.

Nathan had been expecting the question and, knowing the challenge, the team had intentionally kept all of the parts off-the-shelf.

"This is all consumer grade stuff, so the cost is going to be manageable. I think we could get it under $50 when we're at production scale. Even the prototype cost under two hundred dollars. If you don't count the time on the supercomputer or the staff salaries, of course," he said, winking at one the technicians who was standing quietly to the side and letting her boss have his time in the spotlight.

"Consumer grade, cool. I'm guessing the laser is from a CD player?" Bill kept his eyes on the machine while Nathan answered.

"Blu-ray."

"Hm. How is it targeted?" he said quietly, half thinking to himself. He couldn't think of any consumer product that would have a directed laser. "Wait!" he said as Nathan started to answer. "Laser printer, right?"

Nathan smiled.

"Yeah, that's it. Specifically we repurposed the mirror galvanometer."

"What about power?"

"Definitely a limitation. But there are plenty of people working on that anyway, I'm assuming someone will sort it."

Bill nodded curtly. It would need to be solved but Nathan was right, there's a limit to what needed solving in one day.

Nathan suddenly realised that he had leant forward so much that his heels had actually left the ground. He shook his head and marvelled at what Bill could still do to him. As befitted a grown man with the number of degrees he had, he usually felt like a fairly self-contained guy. He was comfortable with the value he brought and didn't need a lot of outward validation, but all the time spent at Microsoft had conditioned him to want Bill's approval.

He was pretty confident that a working prototype of a Strategic-Defense-Initiative-inspired, fully automatic, laser-powered, mosquito-killer couldn't earn him a 'stupidest fucking idea I've ever heard', but long habit made him steel himself.

He also knew that one of the worst things you could do with Bill was ask for feedback. But he had to know.

He gave in and asked.

"So, what do you think?" he asked eventually.

Bill straightened up and pushed his glasses back up his nose where they'd slid down when he bent over to look at the machine.

The two seconds he waited for Bill to reply gave Nathan just long enough to feel like an idiot for asking.

"Nathan, it's really cool. You've done a great job."

***

Back at the foundation offices that afternoon, Bill knocked on the door connecting his and Melinda's offices. They had access to one another's calendars so he knew she had nobody with her, but it was a habit. He didn't actually wait for her to answer before walking in, and he started talking even before he was through the door.

"You're not going to believe what Nathan just showed me!" he said.

Melinda lifted her left hand and gestured for Bill to wait while she continued typing with the other. After a second she looked up and smiled at him.

"Sorry, I just had to send that. I forgot you were seeing Nathan, this was his grand reveal wasn't it?"

"Yeah, there's no way you're going to guess what it is."

"Lasers?"

"Get out! You didn't guess that!"

She laughed.

"No. He sent over specs to us both after you left."

"It's super cool, you have to see it."

"I bet. Tell me about it."

He did and she listened patiently, only interrupting once to ask the obvious question about power, but when he had finished she fixed him with a firm look.

"You know I think it's right to look at this sort of thing, but we need to do something today. The vaccine development, Nathan's laser, gene editing. They are all great things but none of them are ready."

He tilted his head and his eyebrows drew together as he thought. A second later he nodded.

"Agreed."

"We need to make sure we don't lose sight of the basics. Bed nets with proper insecticides, indoor spraying. Stuff that's already here. Less than five percent of children in Africa sleep under a net. That's madness."

"You know we have a compliance problem with the nets. When we first bring them out people use them well but you're dealing with humans, over time they stop bothering. And even when people do use them properly, eventually they fall apart. We really need to look at that durability issue."

"All of that's true but they exist today, and when they're used they make a huge difference. We just need to work on the messaging, make sure that it is reinforced regularly. And in a way that speaks to the people. Local community messaging that kind of thing."

The division between their styles was obvious when they worked together like this. The foundation was made up of about eight hundred people by this time and the work certainly didn't all fall to Bill and Melinda, but brainstorming together like this on the problems helped them keep current and sharp. And neither of them were the type to write a cheque and leave the details to someone else.

"Not all biting is indoor," he said. "If it's outdoor then the nets won't help."

"There are still low tech solutions. We can use sugar bait traps."

"We can't put every solution in everywhere."

"No?" she said, raising an eyebrow even though she knew it was true.

"Well, it wouldn't be efficient. We need to know what's most effective where."

"Data again," Melinda said, with more excitement than most people would use the word.

"Exactly." He strode over to the whiteboard on Melinda's wall and picked up a pen. "We need…"

"A model."

"Exactly," he said again and looked into the distance for a second, then started scribbling a mindmap furiously, thinking aloud as he did so. "We'll need population numbers, human and mosquito; cases…"

"Population mobility. Human population I mean. Last time I was in Kenya no-one could work out why malaria kept coming back to this village until the observers on the ground saw that the villagers were working in a forest which was sheltering the mosquitoes."

Bill added 'mobility - work - home' to the whiteboard which was gradually getting covered with random words, bubbles and arrows.

"Genetic info on the parasites and the mosquitoes," he muttered.

Finally he stopped and stepped back to take in the board.

"That's just a start," he said.

"Oh! Weather," Melinda said.

Bill leant back in and wrote 'weather / climate' up on the board, then turned away from it.

"Just a start as I say but let's get someone to work it up properly."

"And in the meantime…"

"We'll step up the nets," he completed her sentence and she nodded. Then he smiled. "It's cool though isn't it, a mosquito laser?"

"Super cool!" she said and laughed again.

C:\PART\CHAPTER> 7.3

The invitation went to a cross section of 'financial and philanthropic leaders'. Billionaires basically.

It pointed to the recent global financial crisis that had thrown the world into recession, and asked the invitees to come and share their thoughts on how philanthropy might help some of the problems that the recession was bringing to the fore.

The letter was precisely the sort of fairly vague invite that these people might receive any number of times each day. It would probably have been put straight in the trash by an assistant, except for the signatures at the bottom:

David Rockefeller, Bill Gates and Warren Buffett.

Even for the people who received the invitation these were names that it would be difficult to ignore.

Fourteen of the invitees agreed to come and, on 5th May 2009 at 3pm, they arrived in secret at the President's House at Rockefeller University in New York. The university's then president, Nobel prize winning Sir Paul Nurse, was out of town but David Rockefeller, who was ninety five and had served on the university's board for seventy years by that point, asked if they could use it and Sir Paul agreed.

It's probably difficult to turn down the man whose grandfather founded your university.

The President's House was the perfect location for such a private gathering of the ultra-wealthy. One of the very few free standing private residences on Manhattan, it is elegant and modern without being ostentatious, and it sits on the University's secluded tree filled campus behind fences and guarded entrances.

Most of the attendees would be known to the public some, like Oprah Winfrey, at a glance, others by name if not by face. One or two of them, despite their great wealth, were largely unknown outside of their own circles. All of them, however, were billionaires and were known to have been active in philanthropy.

***

In the years since Warren had made his momentous decision to gift his fortune to the Gates Foundation, Bill, Melinda and he had decided to try to do something to encourage other billionaires to engage more in philanthropy.

Was it necessary? Well, according to some back of envelope calculations in Fortune, in the year 2009 US taxpayers with enough property to warrant paying estate taxes (i.e. more than three and a half million dollars) had made charitable bequests of only 12% of their combined assets. Of course, that includes many who made no donations to charity at all and some who donated the bulk of their fortune, and it doesn't account for giving during their lifetime (Fortune did a separate calculation on that and got to the equally uninspiring figure of 11%). Nonetheless clearly the majority of billionaires were not working to the same model that Warren, Bill and Melinda had landed on.

So the three of them had decided that they would go on the offensive and try to recruit others to take the same approach. It would obviously be a tough ask so they had decided to start with this crowd of already committed philanthropists and quietly test their ideas.

They had asked David Rockefeller, as the most long established philanthropist they knew, to host the dinner, so on the day he welcomed everybody and explained the format and goal.

The meeting would last for six hours and there'd be dinner, of course, but before they got to the food each of the attendees would spend about fifteen minutes describing the ideas and goals behind their philanthropy, what they thought the future of the global economy looked like, and whether there was something that this group could do differently to encourage others to give.

Warren laid out the thinking behind his donation to the Gates Foundation.

"I cannot think of anything that's more counter to the idea of meritocracy than dynastic wealth. My kids have had all kinds of advantages, let alone being given billions of claims cheques on other people. The idea of passing those from generation to generation so that your descendants can command resources just because they came from the womb fly in the face of a meritocratic society."

The guests' existing philanthropy and other interests covered a wide range of topics, so the meeting necessarily did the same. They discussed education; cultural donations to museums and art galleries; global health; overpopulation; aligning public policy and government action more generally with global issues; US health efforts.

When it was Bill's turn he explained the reason for his focus on global health instead of staying in the technology space.

"Many people would have expected most of my giving could be in the area of 'let's give everyone personal computers, let's make sure they all have a lot of software', and there is a portion of my foundation that's involved in that, including getting computers into various libraries and making sure that teacher training programs are very strong. But over 60% of what we do is in world health. And that's because I think it's far more basic. In fact whenever the computer industry has a panel about the digital divide and I'm on the panel, I always think: OK, you want to send computers to Africa, what about food, and electricity? Those computers aren't going to be that valuable, if you don't do those things. It's a little bit like being a troublemaker, they want to sit on the panel and talk about how the computers will solve all the world's problems. They're amazing in what they can do, but they have to be put into perspective alongside human values."

After the talks had wrapped up and the guests had moved in to eat, the conversation drifted onto specific ways to promote more giving. And while they were happy if that took the form of bequests in wills, Warren and the Gateses really wanted people to act before then.

Warren summed it up.

"If you wait until you're making a final will in your nineties, the chance of your brainpower and willpower being better than they are today is nil," he said.

When that first dinner was finished the group went their separate ways, convinced that while the goal of increasing philanthropy was a good one it would take significant work to make it happen. And while Bill, Melinda and Warren, and indeed everyone present, were happy to encourage others to give, there wasn't an obvious concrete way to do it.

***

The meeting was supposed to have been secret, however, news of the dinner broke on 18th May and it was reported across the world. Inevitably some people were threatened by the gathering of wealthy individuals, even if it was ostensibly about how to give that wealth away. They saw the establishment of a group of wealthy and powerful individuals and families, particularly one that met in secret, as sinister.

But Melinda, Bill and Warren did not let it stop them, a number of other quiet dinners were held over the next few months to further test their thoughts with other groups and win people over to the cause of giving.

As they did so, the idea had crystallised and they had settled on what they felt was the simplest way to encourage action, the Giving Pledge.

The Pledge was not an organization itself, and it didn't require the people signing up to contribute to a single pool.

Instead, to try to get the greatest take up possible, it left signatories free to pursue their philanthropy independently and give in any way they wanted, to any charitable cause they wanted.

The idea was simply to get the rich to make a public moral commitment, nothing contractual or legally binding, to give away at least 50% of their wealth.

Scepticism, even cynicism, from people who didn't have enough money to be invited to the Pledge was perhaps inevitable, but there were plenty of questions at the dinners themselves and in the realms of the ultra-rich that the founders approached outside as well.

Some of them were relatively easy for Bill to knock down, like whether he was personally focussed on the wrong things:

"Why not be the guy who cures cancer instead?" someone asked Bill.

"The motto of the foundation is that every life has equal value," he said. "There are more people dying of malaria than any specific cancer. When you die of malaria aged three it's different from being in your seventies, when you might die of a heart attack or you might die of cancer. And the world is putting massive amounts into cancer, so my wealth would have a meaningless impact on that."

Or when the idea of giving internationally was challenged because you can't be sure it's going to reach the people who need it.

"What about Robert Mugabe's henchmen skimming off millions in Zimbabwe?"

"Well, no one gives aid to Zimbabwe through the Mugabe government. We go in on a direct basis. When we buy vaccines we are super-smart about what we pay. We get price reductions. We can track how many kids get the vaccines. It's not like you're going to go to Mugabe's mansion and you'd find polio vaccines in the basement and he's going... 'Mua-ha-ha-ha! I took it ALL!'," Bill said, giving free rein to his withering sense of humour, with an impression of Dr Evil from the Austin Powers movies.

But ultimately those sort of questions were easy because he wasn't really trying to persuade these people to put money in the same places he was. Maybe it would be nice but just giving it away was the starting point. What was harder to overcome were the objections to the whole idea, and some of them came from surprising sources.

Robert Wilson, a hedge-fund executive who was already a committed philanthropist famous for giving away more than $600 million, was unimpressed with allowing the donors to set up foundations.

And despite exchanging a number of emails Bill was unable to convince him.

From: Robert W. Wilson

Sent: Wednesday, June 16, 2010 12:16 PM
To: Bill Gates
Subject: Re: Giving Pledge discussion

Mr. Gates, I decided more than ten years ago to try to give away 70% of my net worth and have already given away one-half billion dollars. (I've never been a Forbes 400) So I really don't have to take the pledge.

Your "Giving Pledge" has a loophole that renders it practically worthless, namely permitting pledgees to simply name charities in their wills. I have found that most billionaires or near billionaires hate giving large sums of money away while alive and instead set up family-controlled foundations to do it for them after death. And these foundations become, more often than not, bureaucracy-ridden sluggards. These rich are delighted to toss off a few million a year in order to remain socially acceptable. But that's it.

I'm going to stay far away from your effort. But thanks for thinking of me.
Cordially
_____

From: Bill Gates
To: Robert W. Wilson
Sent: Saturday, June 19, 2010 1:23 AM
Subject: RE: Giving Pledge discussion

What you are doing is fantastic. You are giving a high percentage and doing it in a very efficient way to causes you have thought deeply about.

The key benefit of your getting involved in the pledge would be having people learn more from your example both in your pledge letter and your participation in the yearly events. We believe the more people we get involved the stronger the effort will be and the more people who will join.

…

You are also right that some people set up foundations without a strong focus or leadership and with high overhead.

…

So it is fine for you to stay out but I want you to know that we agree with your views on philanthropy and we would benefit from your joining in. If you are willing to talk further about this I would love to chat on the phone sometime.
_____

From: Robert W. Wilson
To: Bill Gates

Sent: Saturday, June 19, 2010 4:15 PM
Subject: Re: Giving Pledge discussion

Mr. Gates, thanks much for your email. But as my previous email indicated, I wouldn't have much fun or add much value to this group. You, being a liberal, think you can change people more than I think.

…

I'd greatly appreciate just leaving it at that. Cordially

And Wilson was far from alone but Bill, Melinda and Warren went ahead with the formal announcement of the Pledge, and as Bill reminded the billionaires who weren't yet convinced, "No one has ever said to me, 'We gave more than we should have'."

The three of them made the announcement on June 16th 2010 in an article in Fortune written by Warren's friend Carol Loomis, the editor of his annual letter to Berkshire Hathaway shareholders (as well as the author of his biography).

And to get the message out further they followed up with an interview with CBS's Charlie Rose.

"Incremental wealth, adding to the wealth they have now, has no real utility to them but that wealth has incredible utility to other people," Warren said of billionaires.

While he reiterated his view that inherited wealth was bad for society, Melinda focused on the impact on the kids of billionaires themselves.

"If you're a billionaire," she said. "Do your children need more than 50 per cent of it? I don't think so. Our three children understand that when they grow up they will get something, but that they have to find their own way in society. When I left college and I was working and making ends meet, that was hugely empowering. If you have access to huge levels of worth when you are young but you haven't worked to earn the money, you don't appreciate what it means."

"This is about building on a wonderful tradition of philanthropy that will ultimately help the world become a much better place," Bill said.

Six months before launching the Giving Pledge he had put his money where his mouth was by committing another $10 billion to what he termed the 'decade of the vaccine'.

By the end of 2010 fifty seven billionaires had made the pledge, including Bill's old friend Paul Allen who, while he had never found it difficult to spend more money on toys than Bill had (including the original Captain Kirk's chair from Star Trek!), was already a significant philanthropist as well.

Just the previous year Allen had been diagnosed with cancer for a second time. Although unrelated to the Hodgkin's Lymphoma that had prompted him to leave Microsoft in the early eighties, it was another bout with life threatening illness that meant more chemotherapy. Bill had visited Paul several times while he recovered from the medicine which can take such a toll on the body, but by the time the Giving Pledge was announced Paul's treatment was finished, the cancer had been beaten back and he was hopeful that it was in remission.

But if Bill assumed that this latest alignment of their minds might lead he and Paul to get closer he was mistaken.

***

In 2011, the year after the Giving Pledge, Paul released his autobiography, *Idea Man*, in which he told the story of the early Microsoft days from his point of view. And it was fairly scathing about Bill.

Paul framed himself as the one with all of the ideas and Bill as the business man who executed on them. And his view of their share split, and the way that Bill and Steve Ballmer had treated him during his first illness, cast Bill in a particularly bad light. But worse than what he'd written in the book itself, were some of the interviews Paul gave as part of the book's launch. Or perhaps the way that the reporters wrote them up, since many of the worst comments weren't actually quotes. The Times in London for example wrote that Bill was, "a scheming and self-interested leader". It wasn't a phrase that Paul had used but he maintained that what he'd written was accurate.

"I don't think the book is bitter at all," he said, when one reporter suggested that he could be accused of bitterness. "I think it's a direct telling of what happened, and tries to give you a real feel of the personalities involved. I just felt it was important to tell my side of the story in as accurate a way as we could."

And he tried to minimise the revelations of the arguments they'd had at Microsoft, "After a few years all that passes. Bill and I have always been friends, even through the ups and downs, and there have been some. Those events were in 1982, there's been a lot of water under the bridge since then."

But it was clear that he was aware of the potential fire he was lighting.

"We haven't had the chance to discuss the details of the book yet," he said. "I think Bill was a bit surprised by some of the elements in it, and he'll want to have a very intense discussion about that. That's the way Bill is."

Whether or not that intense discussion ever came in private, in public at least Bill tried to rise above it.

"While my recollection of many of these events may differ from Paul's, I value his friendship and the important contributions he made to the world of technology and at Microsoft," he said in a statement put out when reporters asked him for comments.

It was possible they'd have got past Paul's own book but in 2014 another book came out which damaged their relationship even further.

Walter Isaacson's *Innovators* was about the founders of the computer age and contained a chapter on software which focussed on Apple and Microsoft, or, as Paul saw it on Bill. Isaacson had interviewed Bill for the book and the first edition gave an account of Microsoft which Paul thought gave undue credit to Bill and relegated him to the sidelines. He was livid and complained to Isaacson who released a second edition the following year in which Paul's version of events was given more of an airing, but it also included quotations from emails Paul had sent Isaacson which showed where his head was really at.

"I was the one with the ideas that propelled Microsoft in the 1970's through the early 1980's," he wrote.

Bill and Paul didn't speak for some time after that.

C:\PART\CHAPTER> 7.4

On February 4th 2014 Bill stepped down as chairman of the Microsoft board.

The previous August Steve Ballmer had announced that he would retire from the role of CEO as soon as a replacement could be found, after a six month process that search was complete. Bill and the rest of the board appointed Satya Nadella as CEO.

Satya was an internal Microsoft candidate, who had worked for the company since 1992 and been Vice President of the cloud computing division since 2011.

As part of the transition out of the role of chairman Bill remained a director and took the title Founder and Technology Advisor. According to Microsoft's press release Bill would,

'devote more time to the company, supporting Nadella in shaping technology and product direction.'

John Thompson, an independent member of the board who had led the search for Steve's replacement, succeeded Bill as chairman.

C:\PART\CHAPTER> 7.5

"If you gave me only one wish for the next fifty years… This is the wish I would pick. This is the one with the greatest impact," Bill told the TED crowd in Long Beach, California.

A vaccine? The eradication of polio? Neither, Bill was imagining the invention of a technology that would provide the world's energy needs at half the current cost, and more importantly, zero carbon dioxide emissions.

In November 2015 Bill attended the COP21 Paris Climate Conference where he announced the formation of the Breakthrough Energy Coalition, a group of business leaders who would invest in companies trying to make that imagined technology a reality.

Clean energy technology had a bad history for venture capitalists. A study at MIT estimated that of the approximately $25 billion invested between 2006 and 2011 over half of it was lost. As a result energy investment was hard to come by in the mid 2010's. Bill released a paper explaining the goals of, and need for, Breakthrough Energy and in it he suggested that investment in energy by both the industry and government was below 1% (against revenue in the case of the companies themselves, and of 'sector spend' for the US government).

"In the United States, consumers spend more on gasoline in a week than the government spends on clean-energy research in a year," he wrote in his paper.

And drawing on his reading of Vaclav Smil, one of his favourite authors, Bill pointed out that the adoption of new energy solutions usually took decades. Another thing that would keep it out of the sights of traditional venture capitalists who usually looked for returns within a decade at most.

Breakthrough Energy was his answer to both of these problems.

"A key part of the solution is to attract investors who can afford to be patient," he said. "And whose goal is as much to accelerate innovation as it is to turn a profit. I am joining with a number of other investors who are fortunate enough to be in this position."

Joining Bill in the new coalition which would soon launch an initial $1 billion investment fund, were twenty eight serious investors including famous names such as Mukesh Ambani, Sir Richard Branson, Jeff Bezos and Jack Ma.

"It has never been more pressing to find clean energy innovations that can change the world. We have an opportunity to build a new economy, and business is poised to help make it happen," Branson said.

"The renewable technologies we have today, like wind and solar, have made a lot of progress and could be one path to a zero-carbon energy future," Bill said. "But given the scale of the challenge, we need to be exploring many different paths, and that means we also need to invent new approaches."

***

One of the more surprising targets of Breakthrough Energy was agriculture.

In fact agriculture cut across several of Bill's obsessions and the different organisations he used to drive them forward.

In the mid twentieth century much of the world had benefited from what was known as the Green Revolution. A combination of new crop varieties and chemical fertilisers led to significantly increased agricultural yields and helped support the growing population. It was one of the lesser known success stories underpinning the strides made in public health over much of the globe in the twentieth century, earning the man most responsible, Norman Borlaug, a Nobel prize in 1970.

For a variety of reasons (some political, some environmental) the Green Revolution was not effectively applied to Africa, so already impoverished African farmers tend to get yields that are significantly lower than their American counterparts. And significant means exactly that, the same area in the US in 2018 produced four times as much maize as the average in Africa, and sadly that is not cherry picking the data, the figures for rice and potato yields are more than three and a half times higher in the US. In fact, of eleven key crop yields only two are higher in Africa than the US, cocoa beans and cassava, and that's only because they're not grown in the States at all.

And due to the impact of climate change being disproportionally borne by tropical areas this will only get worse.

As a result the Gates Foundation had programmes aimed at increasing the productivity and income of small farmers, improving the nutritional quality of the food they produced, and empowering the large number of women who worked in agriculture.

While the foundation's goal was to put in place in-country support systems, in 2019 they spent approximately $392 million (or 8% of the overall spend for the year) on these programmes with a view to helping farmers adapt to the impact of climate change.

However, it would be possible to deliver these programmes and simultaneously make the world a worse place because the Green Revolution, for all of its miraculous nature, is terrible for the environment.

Agriculture done the 'modern' way accounts for 24% of the planet's carbon emissions each year, only one percent less than electricity generation. Helping African and South Asian countries achieve the same level of production using existing methods could quite possibly be disastrous for the planet.

"I wish agricultural innovation got as much attention as the impact on climate change from electricity, because its success is just as critical to stopping climate change," Bill said. "But at the end of the day, people need to eat. That's why the goal with agriculture is not to reduce the amount created, but to reduce emissions per product."

And that is where Breakthrough Energy came in. Amongst the more obvious funding for new methods of generating energy or new types of energy storage, Bill used Breakthrough Energy to fund agricultural innovations that would keep yields high but move towards the goal of a net-zero carbon economy.

Innovations from companies like Pivot Bio.

***

Pivot Bio is a biotech company founded by two UC San Francisco PhD students, Karsten Temme and Alvin Tamsir.

When they met Alvin was working on developing programmable genetic components to make biological computers while Karsten, who had studied previously at the University of Iowa, was already working on the idea of nitrogen fixation which would become central to Pivot Bio.

To understand what Pivot Bio does it's necessary to take a small detour into the world of nitrogen fixation (fear not, it will be brief and extremely high level).

Nitrogen is absolutely essential to plant growth.

Unfortunately most plants cannot take Nitrogen from the air and instead need to extract it from the soil. When they do that the soil is depleted and the next year's plants cannot grow as effectively. Eventually the soil is completely exhausted and it isn't possible to grow crops in it at all. Farmers have known this for centuries. Before the Green Revolution most of them solved the problem by rotating crops. In one year they would grow the food crop they wanted (wheat, maize, etc.), the following year they would plant one of the few crops that could capture Nitrogen from the air (legumes like peas), and in the third year they would let the field rest, or 'lie fallow'. It worked, but it fairly obviously reduces the productivity of the land dramatically.

Fertiliser changed all that.

Fertiliser is basically just an external shot of nitrogen, by adding it to fields farmers can continue to grow crops year after year. It was an essential part of the Green Revolution, so much so that it has been estimated that fertiliser is needed to produce about half of the world's food.

No fertiliser, no nitrogen. No nitrogen, no food.

However, fertiliser has downsides. Most fertiliser doesn't actually get to the plants, it runs off from fields or evaporates as volatile gases. The gas contributes significantly to the carbon emission figure we saw earlier (through nitrous oxide which is 200 to 300 times more powerful in greenhouse terms than carbon dioxide) and the run off pollutes waterways causing dead zones in which almost no life can survive.

So, fertiliser: necessary to feed us, not good for the planet.

That was the problem that Pivot Bio sought to address. In 2011 Karsten and Alvin completed their doctorates and left UCSF to form Pivot Bio with a grant of $100,000 from the Bill & Melinda Gates Foundation.

Building on the work that Karsten had been exploring since his time in Iowa, Pivot Bio replaces the need for fertiliser by using a microbe that has been genetically engineered to allow food crops to capture nitrogen from the air in a similar way to the legumes that traditional farmers had rotated into their fields.

Karsten's early work had involved transgenic genetic engineering, basically artificially moving genes from one organism to another, but it soon became clear that the regulatory and public opinion hurdles were too large to reasonably overcome in the short term. Pivot Bio therefore shifted focus to what they called 'guided microbial remodeling' which uses genetic material that is already in the microbe, sometimes deleting sequences, sometimes rearranging elements in the genome so that the microbe makes more of one of its genes.

"We viewed the DNA of microbes as computer programs that encode instructions," Karsten said.

And by rewriting those instructions they made a microbe that would be better at fixing nitrogen from the air, better at transferring it to the roots of maize (their first target crop), and better at sticking to those roots so it doesn't get washed away.

After the Gates Foundation's initial grant got them started, Bill's Breakthrough Energy fund invested millions in Pivot Bio's Series A, B and C funding rounds, enabling them to reach the market.

Backing from people like Bill, willing to take risks on long term bets and comfortable with the intersection of technology and activist investing, helps galvanise companies like Pivot Bio which, if the market has an answer to environmental problems, have to be part of it.

By 2018 their first product had left the lab and was on farms across the US.

None of this is work that Bill himself has done of course. If Pivot Bio succeeds in replacing significant amounts of fertiliser use then the credit should go to Karsten and Alvin and their team, but it is the perfect example of the sort of investment which may never have seen the light of day without Bill's passion for agricultural improvement.

C:\PART\CHAPTER> 7.6

On October 1st 2018 Paul announced on his blog that the non-Hodgkin's lymphoma which he thought he had beaten nine years earlier, had returned.

Under the title 'Tackling a New, Personal Challenge' the announcement was short but positive.

> "I learned recently that the non-Hodgkin's lymphoma that I was treated for in 2009 has returned. My team of doctors has begun treatment of the disease and I plan on fighting this aggressively.
>
> A lot has happened in medicine since I overcame this disease in 2009. My doctors are optimistic that I will see good results from the latest therapies, as am I.
>
> I will continue to stay involved with Vulcan, the Allen Institutes, the Seahawks and Trail Blazers, as I have in the past. I have confidence in the leadership teams to manage their ongoing operations during my treatment.
>
> I am very grateful for the support I've received from my family and friends. And I've appreciated the support of everyone on the teams and in the broader community in the past, and count on that support now as I fight this challenge.
>
> Go Seahawks! Go Blazers!"

On 15th, just two weeks after posting that message, Paul Allen died of septic shock due to his cancer.

Bill was heartbroken.

It would have been bad enough to lose his oldest friend but it was made worse by the years they had lost after they fell out.

By the time of his death they had taken the first tentative steps towards repairing their relationship, Bill even spoke about them travelling together now that his children were older and he could spend more time away from home. But it came too late.

Asked for quotes by media all over the world, Bill highlighted Paul's impact on Microsoft and his later work in philanthropy.

"Personal computing would not have existed without him," he said. "But Paul wasn't content with starting one company. He channelled his intellect and compassion into a second act focused on improving people's lives and strengthening communities in Seattle and around the world."

But his most poignant comments were personal.

"As the first person I ever partnered with, Paul set a standard that few other people could meet. He was one of the most thoughtful, brilliant, and curious people I've ever met. He deserved so much more time than he got… although no one can say his wasn't a life well-lived."

When thinking about the relationship between Bill and Paul though, the most fitting epitaph may be the final sentence of Paul's Giving Pledge:

'When smart people work together with vision and determination, there is little we can't accomplish.'

It could have been written about his and Bill's partnership.

And their fifty-year friendship.

C:\PART\CHAPTER> 7.7

Paul's optimistic outlook was one of the things that he and Bill had always shared. In the early years of the foundation he and Melinda had given it a label, impatient optimism.

For Bill that optimism was wedded to a relentless drive to do more, regardless of how much he had already achieved. Maybe it wasn't always pretty but it did push him to get results.

Although it was far too early to see much progress from any of Bill's investments in the battle against climate change, by 2019 some of the gains that were coming from their work in public health were already measurable.

As Bill put it, "The country with the worst health outcomes today is better off than the best country a century ago. The world has seen remarkable drops in childhood mortality and amazing increases in life expectancy."

But even measured over a shorter timescale there were dramatic improvements.

"In 1990, the age group with the highest mortality rate was, by far, kids under five. 12 million children died that year. By 2017, under 5 deaths had been cut in half."

Thanks in large part to a coordinated effort to distribute low tech solutions such as bed nets, the number of people who died of malaria each year had also been more than halved from 985,000 at the turn of the new millennium to 405,000 in 2018.

But even the bed nets were helped by the kind of R&D that the foundation specialised in, the most modern nets were treated with a combination of insecticides that increased their effectiveness substantially. And the foundation had been instrumental in supporting modelling work to help determine where the nets should be deployed, and where it would be most effective to use other solutions such as insecticide spraying.

Of course malaria was only one of the many diseases that the foundation was funding work on. Efforts to immunise children against a variety of diseases that had long been under control in the richer world were also making progress. Gavi, the vaccine alliance that Bill and Melinda helped set up in 2000 and for which the foundation remained one of the main donors, helped drive through programmes that resulted in more than 760 million children being vaccinated between 2000 and 2019 and prevented an estimated 13 million deaths.

Gavi now vaccinates almost half of the world's children and has brought down the price of vaccines for those children significantly. In the countries which Gavi supports it costs roughly $28 to carry out the eleven vaccinations that the World Health Organisation recommends. The same vaccines cost $1100 at market prices in the US.

In short, while there was much work still to be done (after all, there are *still* 6 million childhood deaths under the age of 5 each year) it was possible to see that a huge amount was being accomplished through the programmes and organisations that Bill and Melinda had set up.

Of course not everybody was a fan, and the more visible the foundation became, the louder the criticisms that followed it.

***

When he heard the news, Bill was sitting alone at his desk in his Kirkland office. Books covered the wall behind him, while in front of him were his three computer monitors. The one on the left showed his inbox, the middle one the email that had jolted him out of his planned day, and the one on the right had a browser with the news open from a link he had just clicked in his email.

He wasn't looking at any of them. He was staring vacantly past the monitors towards a wall containing a huge display of the periodic table. Six inch square display cases were arranged in the shape of the periodic table and inside each case was a sample of the element (or in some cases something representing them, including an Intel Gold processor for gold). He had been thrilled when he had found the company who designed them and given them ideas about what to include. And when they installed it he'd been genuinely proud to own it.

But now, despite staring straight at it, he wasn't looking at that either. It barely registered. His mind was six and a half thousand miles away in a remote village outside Chaman in western Pakistan, near the border with Afghanistan.

On 25th April 2019 two men on a motorbike rode up to a group of vaccinators in Pakistan and opened fire, killing one of them and critically wounding another.

Since hearing the news he had been trying to decide whether to ring Warren.

He needed someone to test him. Normally Melinda was more than capable of the job, finding the holes in his thinking, inspiring him when he needed it and keeping him grounded when necessary, but he knew what she would say about this, after all they'd had similar news before. He wanted to check his reaction against someone else. And there was only one other person he could turn to now.

He hit the speed dial on his desk phone and a moment later Warren answered.

"Bill," he said with an audible smile. "I wasn't expecting a call from you today."

The two of them spoke weekly but this wasn't their usual time.

"No, I just wanted to talk something through, if you've got time?"

"Of course, what is it?"

"Have you seen the news from Pakistan?"

Warren laughed.

"What do you think?" The investor was very careful about the news he digested.

"No, okay, fair point. I have though and I wanted to talk to you about it. A woman has been killed while on a polio vaccination drive in Chaman."

"Do you know what prompted it?"

"A nationwide push started in Pakistan on Tuesday and according to the reports this vaccinator and her colleagues were just on routine calls."

"Hm, terrible," Warren said, with compassion.

"Two days ago," Bill continued. "On the first day of the drive, two policemen who were protecting another group of vaccinators were killed."

"Are we doing something wrong?"

Bill couldn't bring himself to smile, but he appreciated Warren's use of the word 'we'. Warren had made it clear when he made his donations that he was effectively outsourcing his philanthropy to Bill. He'd said at the time that philanthropists, "...should seek out talent to distribute their money, just as they sought out talent to acquire it." and he'd been true to his word since.

"There's people who say that we don't understand the cultures we're going into," Bill said. "That we approach it wrong because we're imperialists."

"And maybe they're right... about doing it wrong I mean, not the imperialist bit... but before you beat yourself up, it's worth noting that the people moaning tend not to be doing much themselves. You and Melinda are out there pushing for these things."

Warren took a breath but Bill could tell he wasn't finished so he waited. After a moment he spoke again.

"Is the message on vaccines not getting out there? Or is it not clear? Why would they kill the vaccinators?"

"I think it is clear, but in some parts of the country it's maybe not as loud as the 'vaccines are a western plot to sterilise our children and spy on us' message."

"Ah."

"Yeah."

Both men knew that the vaccination programmes struggled with the legacy of the CIA's capture of Osama Bin Laden. In 2011 the CIA had found Bin Laden by running a fake hepatitis vaccination campaign in Abottabad to get DNA samples that proved his family were in the area and, while they had got what they wanted, they had seriously undermined the credibility of legitimate vaccination programmes.

"Well, it's horrible and I don't mean to sound insensitive but why are you ringing? You don't normally ring me when there are problems."

"I want to know that you think I'm still doing the right thing." He could have added 'with your money' but he wanted Warren's advice as a friend, not as a trustee of the foundation.

"You mean to carry on, of course?"

Bill hesitated.

"I know that's the right thing. And it's what we've done every time before, but eventually even I start to question myself. I want to know what *you* think."

"I think I trust you."

"Thank you, I mean that. But right now I want you to challenge me, turn that brain of yours on the problem."

"Okay. I hope you're sitting comfortably Bill because here comes the tough love bit." Warren said, and Bill noted that his voice had taken on the tone it usually did in Berkshire Hathaway board meetings. Not the shareholder meetings which had become such a fun event that they'd been compared to Woodstock for investors and where Warren played to the crowd as the genial old uncle. This was the Warren who chaired the board of a $500 billion company. The hard-nosed business man who had got to the top through his penetrating ability to see risks and opportunities that others didn't. "You don't need permission from me. You know the answer. You and the vaccinators are building something, these people are just tearing it down. They're terrorists. Murderers. You can't let them dictate your actions. Giving up something you believe is right is cowardice."

Bill shuffled in his chair slightly. He knew that but he needed more.

"I know, and if it was just this one time then as terrible as it is, it wouldn't faze me. But they're not alone are they? The people over here aren't shooting vaccinators but I'm still seen as some sort of demon. Listen to this," he said and cleared his throat before reading a comment he'd found from a respected academic and AIDS activist.

"Depending on what side of bed Gates gets out of in the morning, it can shift the terrain of global health. It's not a democracy. It's not even a constitutional monarchy. It's about what Bill and Melinda want…" he read. "That's written by a professor at Yale."

"Well, he's right. It isn't a democracy. So what?" Warren said.

That brought Bill up short.

"I suppose the argument is that Melinda and I, and you for that matter, shouldn't…"

"But mostly you!" Warren interrupted and chuckled.

Bill smiled for the first time since he'd heard about the killing in Pakistan.

"Yes, mostly me," he agreed. "That we shouldn't get to decide where the money gets spent."

"Not decide how we spend our own money." Warren said slowly as though trying out the idea. "Well, okay let's put that aside. So you're supposed to do what, set up a big panel and give everyone a vote on how it's spent? Who's everyone? Everyone in the world? Everyone in America? Just the people moaning about how you do it now? Or maybe you should just give it to the government?"

"I think that last one is the idea."

"Ah, so then the government will give everyone a vote on how it's spent."

Another smile tugged at the corner of Bill's mouth. It was obvious where Warren was leading him but he played along.

"Well, the argument is that government spending is already democratic because they've been voted in."

"By Americans. Or some Americans. So you're saying if we let 'some Americans' decide where the money gets spent that will satisfy your critics. Great, let's do that."

"I think it's safe to assume it won't satisfy them all," Bill said.

"Yes, I think that's a safe assumption."

Bill paused. He'd got the shot in the arm he needed but he and Warren had never really worked through criticisms of the foundation together and now that they'd started the discussion he was interested in getting the older man's take on some of the main complaints that were levelled at him.

"Okay then, what about the argument that we're too close to big business. Or even that we're just doing it to make money ourselves."

"Ha! It's not a very efficient way to make money is it? So let's ignore that. Too close to business? Maybe, what do you think?"

"I think the non-profit sector has always had lots of good intentions but it wasn't really delivering results was it? Apart from occasional high profile interventions like Band Aid and that kind of thing they just kept doing the same thing. They did lots of good on the ground but they weren't making a dent in the problems."

"That's not an answer. Are you… are we… too close to business?" Warren said, having divined the game they were playing.

"Not *too* close, no. We're bringing skills from a different world to bear on global problems and that's helping us make more of an impact."

"Not just skills, though, products sometimes," Warren challenged. "Who makes the vaccines we distribute?"

"Okay, that's true. In that respect yes, almost all of our solutions involve business in some way. I've not met a government who are developing vaccines themselves, or building toilets or breeding new types of seeds. We fund the people who stand a chance of delivering and that's usually business. I don't think that makes us too close."

"No, quite. Next!"

"They say that we should divest the trust's money from any investments that don't align with the foundation's goals. That some of the money is invested in companies that are directly making the world worse in areas we're trying to help with the foundation."

Now Warren paused. He had made it a condition when he became a trustee of the foundation that the investing and spending would be two separate things and he would have nothing to do with the investments. He thought it could lead to a conflict of interest since he was still actively running Berkshire Hathaway.

"You know I don't want to get too close to investment side of things but they're right to say that sometimes activist-investment can work."

"Not on the sort of scale we're talking about," Bill said. "It's not like we'd starve an oil company of capital by pulling our investment. I don't know the mechanism of action where divestment stops emissions going up every year. I'm just too damn numeric."

"But divestment can send a message, like it did in South Africa."

That gave Bill a moment's thought. He didn't believe Warren actually bought the argument to divest but when his mom had been a regent at University of Washington she had led the movement to divest from the apartheid regime in South Africa.

"Hm... I'm not saying I'm convinced but maybe in some cases... I think I'll speak to Melinda, maybe there are some more positions we could take," he said thoughtfully, before changing topics. "The other main criticism is that we're too single issue centred. That our focus on vaccines and eradicating diseases isn't as good as investing in general health systems in the countries we want to help."

This time Warren provided an answer himself.

"Do the people levelling this criticism have any idea what it would take to run a country wide healthcare system? However big the foundation is it would be out of money in less than a year."

"True," Bill replied. "For me though it's more the point that if you eradicate something that's a drain on a health system then it's gone for good. There isn't a health system in the world now that needs to worry about spending money to manage smallpox, because we got rid of it. If we can do the same with some of these other big diseases then we can leave the healthcare systems in a stronger position."

"That sounds like sound thinking to me."

"What about Bregman's objection at Davos, that philanthropy is just a tax dodge?" Bill said, but his heart wasn't really in it any more.

He knew that however it looked from the outside, the tax dodge argument didn't really apply to his situation. He wasn't dodging anything material, the system just wasn't set up to tax large capital holdings. That's why he'd suggested new ways of taxing the rich.

"Plenty true for lots of people. Not at all true for you. You've been arguing you should pay more tax for years. We both have," Warren said, impatiently.

"Yeah, and then I was pilloried on social media because I disagree with Senator Warren's way of doing it," Bill said with a sigh.

It occurred to Warren that Bill had spent too long dwelling on the criticisms and was at risk of slipping back into the dark mood he'd been in when he first rang. He didn't like seeing, or hearing, his friend that way and decided the time had come to bring the discussion to a close.

"Listen Bill, do you want me to tell you it's okay to stop? Because it isn't. Simple questions, yes or no. You set yourself a goal that you believed in. Have you achieved it yet?"

"No."

"And do you still think they're the right goals?"

"Yes."

"Did you start the whole thing to become popular?"

"Pah," Bill snorted. "No."

"Then the rest doesn't matter. It's bullshit, Bill. I mean it. When it boils down to it, most of them don't have a problem with philanthropy, they have a problem with wealth. And maybe they're right to have a problem with it. Maybe the system shouldn't be this way at all. Maybe there shouldn't be billionaires. But it's a consequence of capitalism and I'm not hearing any suggestions of other ideas that result in as much good to society on the whole. And now that you've got it you're doing your best to do good with it. And the Giving Pledge is trying to break the passing on of mega-wealth. What more can you do? If you can think of something else, then do it. If not, then be satisfied with what you're doing."

"You're right."

"You know I am. Trust me, if you weren't aware of how lucky you were to end up in your position then I'd give you a kick up the ass. But you know you're lucky. And I'm damn lucky to have you doing good in the world with my money. Now, are you done whining?"

Bill laughed.

"I'm done."

"Good. Then get back to work young man."

***

Criticism was not a new phenomenon for Bill. He had spent years being vilified by portions of the computer industry and even been cast as the devil more than once on the internet, but most of the people saying those things had believed he was evil because he was a capitalist, or because they thought Apple had a better aesthetic than PCs. If they'd been really pressed, none of them would have actually believed he was trying to kill them.

In 2020 that would change.

C:\PART\CHAPTER> 7.8

In early December 2019 cases of a new 'viral pneumonia' started to emerge in Wuhan in central China. The World Health Organisation (WHO) became aware on 31st December and, having contacted the Chinese authorities for more details, the WHO published the first information on the outbreak on January 5th.

The outbreak notification highlighted how little was known about the virus at this stage, other than that 44 cases had required hospitalisation.

"There is limited information to determine the overall risk of this reported cluster of pneumonia…"

On 11th January the first death from the virus was reported in Wuhan and on 30th January the WHO declared that the virus was a Public Health Emergency of International Concern, the first step before declaring a pandemic.

By the end of January 2020 there were nearly 8000 cases, the vast majority (just under 99%) of which were in mainland China, and 170 people had died from the disease. It had also become clear by this point that the virus was now spreading around the world; the WHO's declaration of a global emergency reported that there were 98 cases in 18 countries outside China.

The declaration also drew the world's attention to the impact that a pandemic would have on developing countries.

"We don't know what sort of damage this virus could do if it were to spread in a country with a weaker health system. We must act now to help countries prepare for that possibility," the Director-General said.

Five days later, the Bill & Melinda Gates Foundation committed up to $100 million to the fight against the disease: twenty million dollars to bolster public health systems in Africa and South Asia to better protect their citizens from COVID-19; another twenty million to help develop better detection methods and treatments; while the majority, sixty million dollars, was ring-fenced for vaccine development.

"By helping countries in Africa and South Asia get ready now, we can save lives and also slow the global circulation of the virus," Bill said.

On the 28th February, with the death toll at 2,923 and more than 83,000 cases across the world, 4,400 of them outside China, Bill voiced his concern that the disease could become an uncontrolled pandemic.

"In the past week, COVID-19 has started behaving a lot like the once-in-a-century pathogen we've been worried about. I hope it's not that bad, but we should assume it will be until we know otherwise."

The WHO officially declared the COVID-19 outbreak a pandemic on 11th March.

120,927 people were infected, 40,000 of them in countries other than China.

***

Two days after the WHO announcement that COVID-19 was a pandemic, Bill made his own announcement on a completely unrelated topic.

"I have made the decision to step down from both of the public boards on which I serve – Microsoft and Berkshire Hathaway – to dedicate more time to philanthropic priorities including global health and development, education, and my increasing engagement in tackling climate change.

...

Serving on the Berkshire board has been one of the greatest honors of my career. Warren and I were the best of friends long before I joined and will be long after.

...

With respect to Microsoft, stepping down from the board in no way means stepping away from the company. Microsoft will always be an important part of my life's work and I will continue to be engaged with Satya and the technical leadership to help shape the vision and achieve the company's ambitious goals. I feel more optimistic than ever about the progress the company is making and how it can continue to benefit the world."

The world had its eyes on other things of course, but for Bill this marked the end of an era. He and Paul had founded Microsoft forty five years earlier and he had worked in the company ever since.

Although both his statement and Microsoft's press release made it clear that Bill would remain a technical advisor to Satya Nadella and the leadership team, in truth his time and attention were now focussed on the work of the foundation and in the short term would be increasingly swallowed up by the pandemic.

For the first time in his adult life, Bill would have no real connection to Microsoft or the computer industry.

Of course, distancing himself from the boards of the company he loved and his closest friend did give him more freedom to speak out and, while he had always attempted to avoid party politics, as the year progressed he would become more outspoken about what he saw as outright mistakes in the political realm.

And with the growing pandemic there was no shortage of targets.

***

On March 24th, when it was apparent that there would not be a quick end to the pandemic, the Tokyo Olympics which were due to take place in July were postponed until 2021. Three days after that the US reported the highest number of COVID-19 cases in the world.

Bill's low opinion of Donald Trump had never been exactly a secret but he had always resisted any comments in public that could be seen as overtly critical. However, from the end of March he began making open statements which contradicted the president's positions.

When Trump said at a press briefing, "America will again, and soon, be open for business. Very soon…We're not going to let the cure be worse than the problem."

Bill was clearly unimpressed.

"…Bringing the economy back … that's more of a reversible thing than bringing people back to life," he said, the day afterwards in an interview with TED. "There really is no middle ground, and it's very tough to say to people, 'Hey, keep going to restaurants, go buy new houses, ignore that pile of bodies over in the corner. We want you to keep spending because there's maybe a politician who thinks GDP growth is all that counts.' It's very irresponsible for somebody to suggest that we can have the best of both worlds."

And on 1st April he wrote an op-ed for the Wall Street Journal. He was careful never to mention Trump by name but the article was unequivocally critical of every step which had been taken by the president so far.

"There's no question the United States missed the opportunity to get ahead of the novel coronavirus," Bill wrote.

"We need a consistent nationwide approach to shutting down… Some states and counties haven't shut down completely. This is a recipe for disaster. Because people can travel freely across state lines, so can the virus. The country's leaders need to be clear: Shutdown anywhere means shutdown everywhere…

"The same goes for masks and ventilators. Forcing 50 governors to compete for lifesaving equipment, and hospitals to pay exorbitant prices for it, only makes matters worse…

"Finally, we need a data-based approach to developing treatments and a vaccine… Scientists are working full speed on both; in the meantime, leaders can help by not stoking rumors or panic buying. Long before the drug hydroxychloroquine was approved as an emergency treatment for COVID-19, people started hoarding it, making it hard to find for lupus patients who need it to survive."

His last comment was a reaction to President Trump's endorsement of the existing malaria drug hydroxychloroquine as a treatment for COVID-19, a claim that was later completely refuted by Dr. Anthony Fauci, director of the National Institute of Allergy and Infectious Diseases and head of Trump's own Coronavirus Task Force.

***

Two weeks later Trump, who had previously praised the Chinese authorities and the WHO, accused the WHO of being too close to China and stopped its US funding.

"Today I'm instructing my administration to halt funding of the World Health Organization while a review is conducted to assess the World Health Organization's role in severely mismanaging and covering up the spread of the coronavirus. Everybody knows what's going on there.

"American taxpayers provide between $400 million and $500 million per year to the WHO. In contrast, China contributes roughly $40 million a year and even less. As the organization's leading sponsor, the United States has a duty to insist on full accountability.

"One of the most dangerous and costly decisions from the WHO was its disastrous decision to oppose travel restrictions from China and other nations. They were very much opposed to what we did. Fortunately, I was not convinced and suspended travel from China, saving untold numbers of lives. Thousands and thousands of people would have died.

"Had other nations likewise suspended travel from China, countless more lives would have been saved. Instead, look at the rest of the world," he said, apparently unaware that the data now showed that the United States had become the country with the highest death toll two days earlier. "Look at parts of Europe. Other nations and regions, who followed WHO guidelines and kept their borders open to China, accelerated the pandemic all around the world. Many countries said, 'We're going to listen to the WHO,' and they have problems the likes of which they cannot believe. Nobody can believe."

Bill, no doubt irritated by the administration ignoring the science, took to Twitter, Trump's favourite medium of communication, and tweeted:

"Halting funding for the World Health Organization during a world health crisis is as dangerous as it sounds. Their work is slowing the spread of COVID-19 and if that work is stopped no other organization can replace them. The world needs @WHO now more than ever."

On the same day, he and Melinda added another $150 million to the commitment they had made in February, meaning the foundation had now pledged $250 million to address the pandemic.

***

Between the increased visibility he was getting from the pandemic and his public statements contradicting Trump, Bill gained the attention of people he'd probably have been happier off without.

According to the New York Times, by mid April 2020 Bill was the favourite subject of alternative theories connected to coronavirus. He was accused of creating the virus to reduce the population, profiteering from it, or using it in some way to control people. Conspiracy theories are nothing new, of course, but what was interesting about these pandemic related theories was the number of usually opposed groups that overlapped when it came to Bill.

Alex Jones whose website, Infowars, is noted for far-right conspiracy theories, told his followers that, "All the big old money is behind Gates, he's the robber barons, the Nazis, all these dead people... The antichrist isn't here yet, but this guy's holding his place for him..."

And that vaccines, "... have been proven to lower immunity in most cases, to be filled with cancer viruses and other pathogens, and to be a scourge from the technocrats, from the eugenicists in the last 60 to 70 years."

Jones didn't cite the sources of this 'proof', but his comments fit into an existing anti-vaccine movement which had an appeal to a broader cross section of society with some more respectable members, including for example Robert F Kennedy Jr.

Kennedy had been a respected environmentalist lawyer before becoming a prominent anti-vaccination proponent in the early 2000's. During the pandemic Kennedy used his Instagram and Twitter feeds to regularly denounce the vaccination movement. Bill was often the target of his posts including one in which he posted a picture of Bill with flames behind him holding a syringe and grinning. The picture was street art from Australia, but Kennedy's accompanying text made his own position clear:

"Rupert Murdoch's News and Vaccine empire have aligned with Bill Gates's international health agency cartel to make Australia the proving grounds for their "Great Reset" the global devolution from democracy to medical fascism."

Michael Lancashire

He also accused Bill of being 'in a position to potentially reap considerable financial gains from the COVID-19 pandemic' due to the foundation's investments in companies that make vaccine candidates.

Whilst it was couched in terms that were grossly unfair and implied much more than was true, the foundation was invested in several vaccine companies, and it would be foolish to assume Bill's personal wealth wasn't exposed to some of the same companies. But what really drove comments like these and provided a receptive ground for them to take root in, were the large growth in billionaires' fortunes seen through the pandemic.

Since a larger portion of most billionaire's wealth is tied up in the stockmarket than the average person, and the stock market fluctuated dramatically through the early part of the pandemic it was true that Bill (and other billionaires) made significant gains.

In August 2020 the Independent reported that Bill's wealth had risen by $7 billion to $120 billion. Jeff Bezos of Amazon had seen his wealth grow by *ten times* that figure to $190 billion.

Although anyone familiar with the structure of Bill and Melinda's foundation, or who accepted the giving pledge they had helped set up, would know that any increase in Bill's fortune would be given away through the foundation, these numbers must have been galling to the people across the world who had been put out of work by the pandemic and the lockdowns. And it won't have helped when news broke in April of a $43 million, six bedroom, holiday home in Del Mar that Bill and Melinda bought in late March.

Robert Reich, a previous US labour secretary, spoke for many people when he pointed out that American capitalism was 'off the rails'.

"Jeff Bezos could give every Amazon employee $105,000 and still be as rich as he was before the pandemic. If that doesn't convince you we need a wealth tax, I'm not sure what will," he tweeted.

The more conspiratorially minded took these facts and ran with them. Next to an image of billionaires, including Bill, with the heading 'The oligarchs who are cashing in on the quarantine' Kennedy posted:

"Led by Bill Gates Silicon Valley applauded from the sidelines as medical charlatans fanned pandemic panic, confined the world population under house arrest, and shattered the global economy… The Tech Barons used lockdown to accelerate construction of their 5G network of satellites, antennae, biometric facial recognition, and "track and trace" infrastructure that they will use to compel obedience, suppress dissent, and to manage the rage when Americans finally wake up to the fact that they have stolen our democracy, our civil rights, our country, and way of life while we huddled in orchestrated fear from a flu-like illness."

362

While it would be easy to write some of these comments off as the harmless opinions of conspiracy nuts, more worryingly it appeared that a surprisingly large number of people of all political stripes were convinced. A Yougov poll in the US in late May showed that 44% of republicans, 19% of democrats and 24% of independents said that they believed that 'Bill Gates wants to use mass COVID-19 vaccination campaign to implant microchips to track people'.

"It is troubling that there is so much craziness," Bill said to the BBC. "When we develop the vaccine we will want 80 percent of the population to take it and if they have heard it is a plot and we don't have people willing to take the vaccine that will let the disease continue to kill people.

"I'm kind of surprised some of it is focused on me. We are just giving money away, we write the cheque… and yes we do think about let's protect children against disease but it is nothing to do with chips and that type of stuff. You almost have to laugh sometimes."

But it was apparent he wasn't really laughing.

***

"I need to get out there and refute some of the worst of the nonsense," Bill said.

It was a Friday night and they had just finished watching a movie in the cinema room, a family tradition they'd started when the kids were younger.

Melinda knew what nonsense he meant instantly, and it struck her as a terrible idea.

"Are you sure that's a good idea? Do you think you could convince anyone who's listening to it?"

"I've got to try. Did you see that study I sent you, the one from University College London?" he asked. Melinda shook her head. "Fifteen percent of people they questioned believed that vaccines didn't work. Twenty two percent said they were unlikely to get a COVID-19 vaccine when one was available. And that's the UK, I daren't think what it would be like here!"

"What was the sample size?" Melinda asked.

"Seventy thousand."

"Oh." She had obviously been hoping to calm him by discrediting the research but that wasn't going to work.

"Exactly. It's dangerous for people to believe the crap these people are putting out."

Melinda sighed.

"You know I agree, but this isn't an argument you can win rationally, Trey. You prove one load of rubbish wrong and they just move on to another."

"But if we can show them there's nothing to it…" Bill started but she cut him off.

"You can't. You can't prove a negative and besides there's usually just enough truth in them that they're always able to say 'Ah, but look at what they were hiding'. It's pointless." Melinda frowned, she had tried not to let this stuff annoy her but now that she'd opened up all of her frustration was pouring out. "First we're releasing the virus to kill people, then we're releasing the virus to make money off a vaccine, then we're releasing a vaccine so we can insert microchips and track everyone. Has anyone even bothered to explain why we'd *want* to track everyone?"

"Hm," he said but he didn't sound convinced so Melinda pushed on.

"Look at the microchip thing. Someone puts out a ridiculous claim and points to a paper they know most people won't bother to read as proof," she made air quotes around the word with her fingers. "Then when someone does read it and points out that it's nothing to do with microchips it's a quantum dot medical record, they're like 'Ha! Yes, so he wants to tattoo us all, I knew it! He's the devil.'."

"The mark of the beast," Bill said, unable to help himself smirking. Although the numbers weren't large there were now people on social media who went further than Alex Jones had and claimed he actually was the antichrist. Including apparently, though Bill hadn't read the original source, the official hierarchy of the Moldovan Orthodox Church.

Oddly, the combination of the more outlandish claims and Melinda's passion had made him see her point. Melinda caught him smiling at her and shook her head, her shoulders falling as she breathed out heavily.

"I'm sorry," she said. "I'm just so annoyed."

"Don't be, it's usually your job to calm *me* down." He put his arm around her and pulled her into a hug. "And hey, I know how you feel, I wanted to make the argument myself remember?"

"It's pointless," she repeated quietly.

Bill pushed her gently away from him so that he could look her in the face and smiled.

"I know. You've made your position pretty clear, and you're right. So we ignore it."

"We ignore it. We need to focus on getting the message out about fair distribution for the vaccine when it comes. That's more important than what a bunch of people who are always going to hate us think."

"Agreed."

***

On June 4th Bill opened the online Global Vaccine Summit, an international meeting to secure more funding for Gavi from donor countries. Obviously, given the pandemic, which by that time had killed 384,137 people and infected nearly 6.46 million people, the summit had an unusual impact on the people who attended.

"We are meeting at a unique time in history. Never have more people been more aware of the importance of vaccines," Bill said. "As we race to develop a COVID-19 vaccine, we must also renew our commitment to delivering every lifesaving vaccine there is to every child on earth..."

"Gavi will have to stay focused on its core work while learning how to address COVID-19. It can't let one task slip while it concentrates on the other, because lives, and children's futures, are at stake in both cases..."

"Our foundation is proud to have been a member of the Gavi alliance from the beginning. It's the largest investment we make – and easily one of the best. We need Gavi now more than ever. Today, we are pledging $1.6 billion dollars to help Gavi continue its work over the next five years."

Bill and Melinda also used the opportunity to pledge another $100 million to the international effort on COVID-19 over and above their commitment to Gavi, bringing the amount they had promised to fight the new pandemic so far to $350 million.

"When COVID-19 vaccines are ready, this funding and global coordination will ensure that people all over the world will be able to access them."

Bill stepped up his public appearances through 2020, in many interviews over the last couple of years Melinda and he had agreed that it would be better to position her to do more of the talking. But now that they felt the discussions required a pushier style he took the lead again. He had mellowed somewhat since the Microsoft days but he was still more comfortable taking an argumentative stance than Melinda was.

The plan for his heightened presence on television was to advocate for poorer countries to have equal access to any treatments or vaccines that were developed. However, on occasion he couldn't help addressing what he still saw as the failings in leadership, for example in an interview with CBS's Norah O'Donnell he openly contradicted Trump's comments about how well the US was doing.

"The president said, just this weekend, that the US has the lowest mortality rate in the world. Is that factually correct?" O'Donnell asked.

Bill didn't hesitate.

"Not at all. Not even close. I mean by almost every measure, the US is one of the worst... I think we can change that but it's an ugly picture." He shrugged.

"Why are we one of the worst?"

"We opened up. We actually had criteria for opening up that said you had to have cases declining," he said miming a downwards slope. "And we opened up with cases increasing." He laughed in despair.

As he got more exercised he adjusted his glasses, and gestured wildly and he began shifting in his seat.

Despite the occasional lapse into criticising the leadership though, Bill kept his message for the most part on the need to ensure that vaccines were shared fairly.

By the end of September he was forecasting that a vaccine was likely to be ready in early 2021, and he and Melinda were highlighting what they had started to call the 'vaccine gap'.

"Ideally, there would be global agreement about who should get the vaccine first, but given how many competing interests there are, this is unlikely to happen. The governments that provide the funding, the countries where the trials are run, and the places where the pandemic is the worst will all make a case that they should get priority."

"It is increasingly clear that the world's response to this pandemic will not be effective unless it is also equitable," Melinda said.

"There is no such thing as a national solution to a global crisis. All countries must work together to end the pandemic and begin rebuilding economies."

But that wasn't what was happening, the richer countries were securing deals with pharmaceutical companies, securing doses of the various vaccines for their populations. And unfortunately it was coming at the expense of poorer countries. According to an analysis Bill had carried out high-income countries had reserved more than two and a half times more doses of vaccine than they needed to vaccinate their populations.

"But what about low- and lower-middle income nations of the world, everywhere from South Sudan to Nicaragua to Myanmar?" he asked. "These nations are home to nearly half of all human beings, and they don't have the purchasing power to make big deals with pharmaceutical companies. As things stand now, these countries will be able to cover, at most, 14 percent of their people."

To start to address that problem, on 29th September the foundation signed contracts with sixteen pharmaceutical companies to cooperate on vaccine production, sharing facilities and research, and providing the means to scale up production as quickly as possible. And through Gavi, ceiling prices had been agreed on some of the vaccine candidates, meaning that if those vaccines were successful then they could be distributed to poorer countries as well as richer ones.

And Bill, ever the optimist, even hoped that there was a way to turn the pandemic into a positive thing.

"In eliminating COVID-19, we can also build the system that will help reduce the damage of the next pandemic," he wrote. "One thing I've learned studying the history of pandemics is that they create a surprising dynamic when it comes to self-interest and altruism: Pandemics are rare cases where a country's instinct to help itself is tightly aligned with its instinct to help others. The self-interested thing and the altruistic thing—making sure poor nations have access to vaccines—are one and the same."

.

C:\PART\CHAPTER> 7.9

So, Bill Gates: Hero or Villain?

Well, he's intelligent and fiercely competitive. He built Microsoft through a combination of undoubted technical and business genius, and an almost inhuman desire to win at everything he does, whether it was playing bridge with Gam as a child or Warren as an adult; writing computer programs in fewer bytes than Paul; being thought of as the super-smart-est by his employees; or crushing anything that looked even remotely like competition at Microsoft (though let's not kid ourselves that many, if any, of the businessmen he beat wouldn't have done the same to him given half a chance).

That competitive drive and innate intelligence have landed him at the top of two totally separate fields.

First, Bill was a key part of changing the world through the home computer revolution. Continuing his combative 'winner takes all' approach after Microsoft became a dominant force definitely earned him the label 'villain' at the time, but subsequent events in the internet and mobile phone spaces have proved that the core of his competition argument was broadly correct. Microsoft couldn't stay on top simply by locking other companies out of the market, witness Google.

Maybe it's naive to say, but as someone who grew up through it, that first wave of home computing definitely seemed to be a more democratising force than the current surveillance capitalism model that the technology industry has moved into. And Bill played a pivotal role in it, however, it's probably true to say that if he hadn't then somebody else would have filled the same function, there were many other candidates.

I don't believe that's quite so obvious about his work with the Foundation.

Some relevant facts here:

- Africa was declared free of wild polio on 25th August 2020, after Nigeria went four years without a case. While there are still several countries with low numbers of vaccine derived strains, wild polio is now endemic in only two countries.

- By September 2020, two hundred and eleven billionaires had committed to give away at least half of their wealth by signing up to the Giving Pledge that Bill, Melinda and Warren had set up.
- Malaria deaths, which were approximately 985,000 in the year 2000, when the foundation became more active, and Bill and Melinda helped set up Gavi, more than halved to 405,000 in 2018.
- And the rotavirus that first got Bill and Melinda's attention? Well, as Melinda recently wrote in an article about Ruth Bishop, the Australian scientist who discovered rotavirus in 1973, "In 2000, six years before the first safe vaccine was available, 528,000 children died of rotavirus. By 2016, that number fell to 128,500."
- Bill and Melinda's longer term bets on climate change, new nuclear power plant designs, energy storage, fertiliser replacements, and plant based meats may or may not come off, but they are precisely the sort of thing that taxpayer money would not be spent on, but all of us are going to depend on for a healthy future.

Of course, these things are not all down to Bill alone. They're not all down to him and Melinda. They're not even, in fact, down solely to the Gates Foundation. None of them could be. The Giving Pledges represent the decisions of hundreds of individuals, and the foundation's work on reducing the disease burden and alleviating suffering in the developing world takes thousands of people to make a difference.

But it is hard to imagine that any of it would have happened without Bill and Melinda's efforts.

There was nothing new about these diseases when the Gateses first became involved. And the idea that rich people should give back a large portion of what they'd amassed over their life was hardly revolutionary either. What marked these things out was the fact that Bill and Melinda Gates, who were lucky enough to have made a huge pile of money, decided that they were worth paying attention to.

If, in his second act, his competitive nature is directed towards eradicating diseases that have a disproportionate impact on the poor, or helping address some of the worst impacts of climate change, then maybe the word 'hero' wouldn't be completely ridiculous.

Ultimately both labels are inappropriate, of course, and the contradictions obvious in his nature are more interesting than any black or white version.

There's so much good in the worst of us,
and so much bad in the best of us,
that it ill behoves any of us,
to find fault with the rest of us.

And if Gates' drive to win helps make the smallest dent in the things he and Melinda have directed their foundation to work on, then we'll all be the better for it.

AUTHOR'S NOTE

Thanks for reading, now it's over to you: tell people what you thought.
I hope you enjoyed *Bill Gates: Hero or Villain?,* if you did can I ask you to do
me a quick favour? Tell other people what you think of it by leaving a review
and talking to your friends.

Reviews help other readers find the book and they help me too. It needn't be
any more than a sentence. **So leave a review somewhere** (anywhere will do)
as soon as you get five minutes. Don't wait or life will get in the way, and
then think how terribly guilty you'll feel when you remember!

And when you've left a sentence or two, tell a friend about it. Books spread
best by word of mouth.

And if you want to keep in touch…
If you have any comments then feel free to drop me an email at
contactus@sannox.org.uk I love hearing from readers and read all of my
email myself (and try to reply to it as far as possible).

Michael Lancashire
2020

INDEX

ABOUT THE AUTHOR

Michael Lancashire lives with his wife, three kids, and an ever changing assortment of chickens, mammals and reptiles. They split their time between the English Midlands and a Scottish island that's remaining unnamed for now.

His other books include:

Fiction:
The Architect series, heist thrillers for adults featuring a criminal mastermind:
The Voynich Deception
Kernel Panic
The Keycode: An Architect Short Story
The Fourth Target
Almost Out
Trapped

He has also written a British political thriller:
Heritage: A short story

And a novel for children:
Jack Hawke in Killer Game

Non-fiction:
Severn Valley Railway: An Illustrated History

Made in the USA
Columbia, SC
23 January 2024